*A*dventure Guide

Barbados

4th Edition

Keith L. Whiting

HUNTER

HUNTER PUBLISHING, INC.
130 Campus Drive
Edison, NJ 08818-7816
☎ 732-225-1900 / 800-255-0343 / fax 732-417-1744
www.hunterpublishing.com
E-mail comments@hunterpublishing.com

IN CANADA:
Ulysses Travel Publications
4176 Saint-Denis, Montréal, Québec
Canada H2W 2M5
☎ 514-843-9882 ext. 2232 / fax 514-843-9448

IN THE UNITED KINGDOM:

Windsor Books International
5, Castle End Park, Castle End Rd, Ruscombe
Berkshire, RG10 9XQ England
☎ 01189-346-367 / fax 01189-346-368

ISBN 978-1-58843-638-2

© 2007 Hunter Publishing, Inc.

This guide focuses on recreational activities. As all such activities contain elements of risk, the publisher, author, affiliated individuals and companies disclaim any responsibility for any injury, harm, or illness that may occur to anyone through, or by use of, the information in this book. Every effort was made to insure the accuracy of information in this book, but the publisher and author do not assume, and hereby disclaim, any liability for loss or damage caused by errors, omissions, misleading information or potential travel problems caused by this guide, even if such errors or omissions result from negligence, accident or any other cause.

Cover photo: *Barbados at Sunset* (Bill Bachman/Alamy).

Most photographs by the author, unless otherwise identified. Special thanks to Rodney Nelson for his images.

Index by Jan Mucciarone
Maps by Toni Wheeler
Printed in China

3 2 1

Contents

Barbados

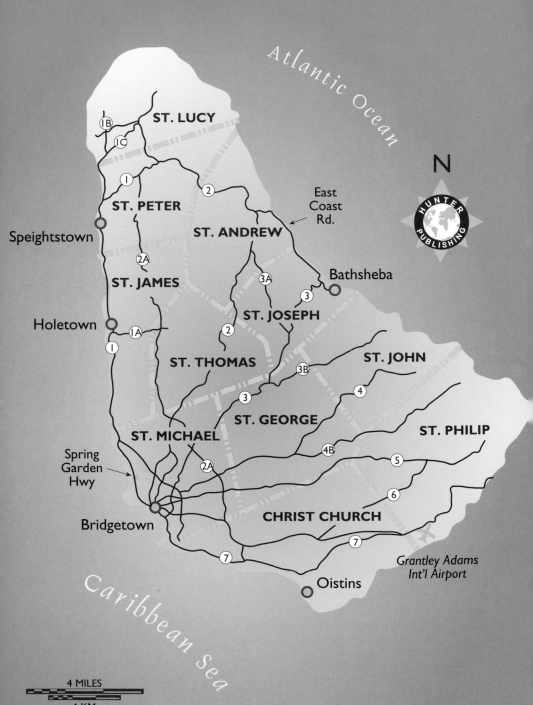

Atlantic Ocean

ST. LUCY

1B
1C
1

ST. PETER

2

East Coast Rd.

ST. ANDREW

Speightstown

2A

ST. JAMES

3A

Bathsheba

3

Holetown

1A

2

ST. JOSEPH

1

ST. THOMAS

3B

ST. JOHN

4

ST. GEORGE

3

Spring Garden Hwy

ST. MICHAEL

2A

4B

ST. PHILIP

5

6

Bridgetown

CHRIST CHURCH

7

7

Grantley Adams Int'l Airport

Oistins

N

Caribbean Sea

4 MILES
4 KM

Introduction

Tek time en' laziness.
(By taking your time, you can achieve a lot.)

Barbados can honestly claim to be the island that has everything under the sun. The most easterly of the Caribbean islands, its 166 square miles of forests, cliffs, fishing villages, wildlife, nightlife, and beaches are pounded by the relentless power of the Atlantic on the east, brushed by the Caribbean on the west and caressed everywhere by the sun.

If your idea of a holiday is lying on the sand with a piña colada by your side, Barbados has numerous white sand beaches, and is home to some of the best rum anywhere. But, if you have a taste for adventure, you can strap on a scuba tank, head out into the ocean, and discover miles of coral reefs teeming with an incredible array of sea life and shipwrecks. If you prefer to be on the water as opposed to under it, Barbados has some of the best sailing in the Caribbean, with southeasterly trade winds to carry you across the water. And if sailing is a little too sedate, there's always jet skiing, parasailing, sport fishing and surfing.

Unlike many other islands, Barbados is more than just sea and sand. Rent a car or bike, hire a taxi, or take a local bus and discover a land rich in history, culture, an abundance of wildlife, and natural beauty – from the rugged beauty of the north to lush fields and forests in the center and sugar cane fields in the south. There are five-star resorts on the west coast and historic plantation and chattel houses spread throughout the island, not to mention world-class golf courses. You can hike through a silent forest or speed along trails on an ATV. This small island is constantly changing and constantly surprising. And, if you get lost? Pull out your map and, before you know it, someone is sure to stop and give you directions!

Another day in Paradise

One of the greatest pleasures of a visit to Barbados is meeting the people, whether staying at a luxury hotel or a local guest house. Almost everyone you pass will wish you a good morning, good afternoon, or good evening. The grinding poverty seen on so many other islands does not exist in Barbados. The population is well educated, and, if you engage them in conversation, they will happily tell you about their history, their future, and the best places to visit in the present.

I have been visiting Barbados for more than 20 years and still find something new every time I visit. There is an abundance of restaurants, an enormous range of accommodations, and I still haven't seen all the beaches. Of all the islands in the Caribbean, Barbados is the most developed and certainly one of the safest. The only downside is the amount of development that has taken place over the last few years. Fortunately, this has been mainly on the west coast, leaving the rest of the island, particularly the east and north, tranquil and mostly untouched.

Whether you visit Barbados for the enormous range of sporting activities, the numerous cultural events, to discover the nature and ecological life of the island, or just to relax on the beach, it really does have everything under the sun.

Natural Areas

1. Charles Fort
2. St. Anne's Fort
3. Barbados Museum
4. Barbados Gallery of Art
5. Tyrol Cottage Heritage Village (Tyrol Cot)
6. Bussa Roundabout (Emancipation Monument)
7. Portvale Sugar Factory & Sir Frank Hutson Museum
8. Arbib Nature & Heritage Trail Kiosk
9. Barbados Wildlife Reserve
10. Grenade Hall Forest & Signal Station
11. Farley Hill National Park
12. St. Nicholas Abbey
13. Morgan Lewis Sugar Mill
14. Flower Forest
15. Welchman Hall Forest Reserve
16. Harrison's Cave
17. Orchid World
18. Gun Hill Signal Station
19. Francia Plantation House
20. Sunbury Plantation
21. Heritage Park & Foursquare Rum Distillery
22. Sam Lord's Castle
23. Codrington College
24. Andromeda Botanic Gardens
25. Animal Flower Cave
26. The Spout
27. Barclay's Park
28. Chalky Mount Village Potteries
29. Pico Teneriffe

N

HUNTER PUBLISHING

ST. LUCY
ST. PETER
ST. ANDREW
ST. JAMES
ST. JOSEPH
ST. THOMAS
ST. JOHN
ST. GEORGE
ST. PHILIP
ST. MICHAEL
CHRIST CHURCH

Speightstown
Holetown
Bathsheba
Bridgetown
Needham's Point & Lighthouse
Oistins

4 MILES
4 KILOMETERS

About Barbados

Geography

Welches Beach

Located 270 miles (434 km) northeast of Venezuela, and part of the Lesser Antilles, Barbados' closest island neighbors are Trinidad and Tobago to the south, Grenada to the southwest, and St. Lucia to the west. It is the easternmost of the Caribbean islands, with a total land area of 166 sq miles (430 sq km) and 60 miles (97 km) of coastline. Some 21 miles (34 km) long and 14 miles (23 km) at its widest point, it is a mostly flat, tropical island, rising to a maximum height of 1,100 ft (336 m) at Mount Hillaby, in the Scotland District.

Surrounded by miles of magnificent white sand beaches, protected by coral reefs and brushed by the constant breeze of the trade winds, Barbados is a swimmer's paradise. The west coast beaches are calm and lapped by the Caribbean. The south coast has small to medium waves that are great for windsurfing and boogie boarding, while the southeast coast has big waves and is only suitable for strong swimmers. Pounded by the Atlantic Ocean the east coast has dangerous undercurrents, and most beaches are NOT safe for swimming. The north coast is rocky and inaccessible to swimmers.

Because of its location, tropical storms and hurricanes common to other Caribbean islands generally miss Barbados. With a rainy season running from June to October, the average time between direct hurricane hits is 26.6 years.

Facing page: Animal Flower Cave

As a coral island, Barbados is home to a vast array of caves and underground lakes, which provide some of the purest drinking water in the world. The island is also home to rainforests, marshes and mangrove swamps, along with pastures and sugarcane fields. It has a diverse and interesting landscape, making it a fascinating place to explore.

Barbados is divided into 11 parishes – Christ Church, St. Andrew, St. George, St. James, St. John, St. Joseph, St. Lucy, St. Michael, St. Peter, St. Philip, and St. Thomas. Bridgetown, in St. Michael, is the capital city. Other major towns include Holetown in the parish of St. James, Oistins in Christ Church, and Speightstown in St. Peter.

History

The Barbados Mulatto Girl, a 1764 painting by Agostino Brunias

The first inhabitants of Barbados arrived from South America around 350 AD, followed by the Arawaks about 450 years later. A third wave of migrants, the Caribs, arrived in the 13th century. The Spanish arrived in the early 16th century, captured the Caribs and used them as slave labor.

As early as 1511, the island was referred to as Isla de los Barbados (island of the bearded ones) in an official Spanish document. The word "bearded" refers to the long hanging roots of the bearded fig tree (ficus citrifolia) which is indigenous to the island.

When the English arrived in the 1620s landing on the west coast at an area now known as Holetown they found the island uninhabited. Assuming control of the island, they began importing slaves to work the plantations. Twenty years later, during the English Civil War, the Royalists, fearing they might rebel against their owners, executed hundreds of the slaves.

From the arrival of the first British settlers in 1627 until independence in 1966, Barbados was under uninterrupted British control. It always enjoyed a large measure of local autonomy, however, and its House of Assembly first began meeting in 1639.

In the 1650s, numerous Scots and Irish were shipped to the island, both as indentured servants and as slaves. The implementation of slave codes in 1661, 1676, 1682, and 1688, led to several unsuccessful slave rebellions. The increasingly repressive legal system increased the gap between the treatment of white indentured servants and black slaves. Black slaves became much more attractive to the plantation owners and many poor whites immigrated to neighboring islands.

The slave trade ended in 1804, but slavery continued, leading to the largest slave rebellion in the island's history in 1816. Over 1,000 people died in the fight, 144 slaves were executed, and 123 deported. Eighteen years later, in 1834, slavery was finally abolished in the British Empire.

The economy remained heavily dependent on sugar, rum, and molasses production through most of the 20th century. Plantation owners and British merchants continued to dominate the island both politically and economically. More than 70% of the population was excluded from the democratic process, and it wasn't until the 1930s that a movement for political rights, under the leadership of Sir Grantley Adams, got underway. Finally, in 1942, women received the right to vote and income qualifications were lowered, allowing the majority of Bajans to participate in elections. By 1949, the plantation owners and merchants finally lost control of the government, and in 1958, Sir Grantley Adams became Premier of Barbados.

In the following years, under the leadership of Errol Walton Barrow, reforms continued including free education for all Barbadians, and a school meals system.

On November 30, 1966, Barbados finally became an independent state within the Commonwealth of Nations, with Errol Barrow its first Prime Minister.

In the 1990s, tourism and manufacturing finally surpassed the sugar industry in economic importance. Additionally, the island is a major offshore financial center.

Government

Barbados is a parliamentary democracy operating under English common law. The bicameral Parliament consists of the Senate (a 21-member body appointed by the Governor General) and the House of Assembly (30 seats, elected by direct popular vote to serve five-year terms).

Represented by the Governor General, the chief of state is Queen Elizabeth II. Executive authority is vested in the Prime Minister and Cabinet, which is collectively responsible to the Parliament. The Prime Minister is appointed by the Governor General as the member of the House of Assembly best able to command the support of the majority of the members. The

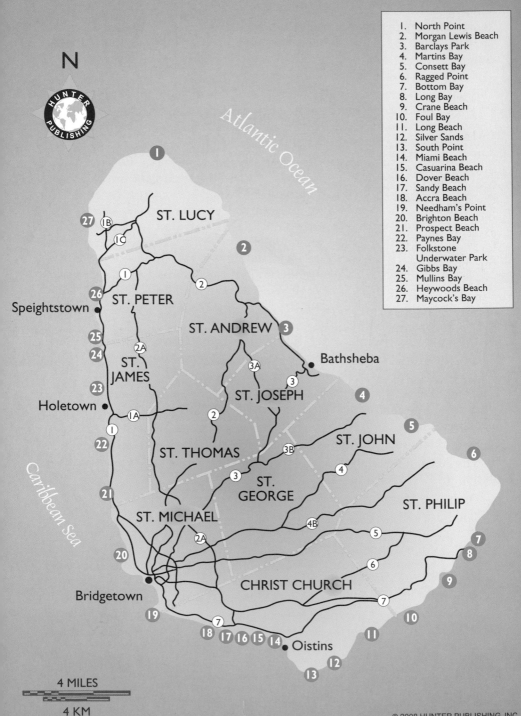

Scenic Beaches

N

1. North Point
2. Morgan Lewis Beach
3. Barclays Park
4. Martins Bay
5. Consett Bay
6. Ragged Point
7. Bottom Bay
8. Long Bay
9. Crane Beach
10. Foul Bay
11. Long Beach
12. Silver Sands
13. South Point
14. Miami Beach
15. Casuarina Beach
16. Dover Beach
17. Sandy Beach
18. Accra Beach
19. Needham's Point
20. Brighton Beach
21. Prospect Beach
22. Paynes Bay
23. Folkstone
    Underwater Park
24. Gibbs Bay
25. Mullins Bay
26. Heywoods Beach
27. Maycock's Bay

Atlantic Ocean

Caribbean Sea

ST. LUCY

ST. PETER

Speightstown

ST. ANDREW

Bathsheba

ST. JAMES

Holetown

ST. JOSEPH

ST. THOMAS

ST. JOHN

ST. GEORGE

ST. PHILIP

ST. MICHAEL

Bridgetown

CHRIST CHURCH

Oistins

4 MILES

4 KM

© 2008 HUNTER PUBLISHING, INC

Prime Minister selects the cabinet from his party members in the legislature.

There are three national parties: The Barbados Labour Party or BLP; The Democratic Labour Party or DLP; and The People's Empowerment Party or PEP

Suffrage is universal for any citizen 18 years of age or older.

Flora & Fauna

Palms, casuarinas, mahogany, and almond trees are all found on the island, but no large forest areas exist, most of the level ground having been turned over to sugarcane. The wide variety of flowers and shrubs includes wild roses, carnations, lilies, and several cacti. Natural

Flamingoes at Graeme Hall Nature Sanctuary

wildlife is restricted to hares, monkeys, mongooses, tree frogs, and various species of birds, including finches, blackbirds, and moustache birds.

Some of the best places to see plants, birds and other wildlife are:

- The Animal Flower Cave
- The Barbados Wildlife Reserve
- Orchid World
- The Flower Forest
- Welchman's Hall Gully & Forest Reserve
- Ocean Park
- Graeme Hall Nature Sanctuary

Getting There

By Plane

 Barbados has a large international airport with dozens of flights arriving from the UK, Europe, Canada and the United States.

Grantley Adams International Airport is on the island's southern coast, 16 km (10 mi) southeast of Bridgetown.

FLYING TIMES TO BARBADOS	
New York	4 hrs 20 min
San Juan	1 hr 30 min
Miami	3 hrs 40 min
Montreal	5 hrs
Toronto	5 hrs
London	8 hrs
Brussels	9 hrs
Caracas	2 hrs 30 min
Frankfurt	9 hrs

Airlines

USA . . . . Air Jamaica, American Airlines, US Airways, Delta
Canada . . . . Air Canada, BWIA
UK . . British Airways, Excel Airways, Virgin Atlantic, BMI, First Choice
Frankfurt . . . . Condor
Amsterdam . . . . Martinair
Several airlines – including LIAT, BWIA and Caribbean Star – offer flights from Barbados to other Caribbean destinations.

By Boat

 Many cruise ships dock in Bridgetown. Recently expanded, the Bridgetown deep-water harbor can now accommodate even the largest cruise ships. Private moorings are also available around the island.

☞ **Note:** Stiff penalties prohibit the dropping of anchors on coral reefs.

Before You Go: A valid passport is required and must not expire less than three months after your trip ends. Visas are not required for travelers from North America, Canada and Europe. Check with the local consulate for other countries.

People & Culture

The official name for residents of Barbados is Barbadians, but residents generally refer to themselves as Bajan.

Bajans are friendly, but somewhat reserved, probably reflecting the strong influence of the English. This influence is stronger in Barbados than on other former British colonies, and extends to the national sport of cricket. Bajans are cricket fans in the truest sense of the word – fanatics!

The school system, also based on the English model, mandates that every child has to attend school and wear a school uniform.

The British influence, combined with the African roots of most residents, creates a rich culture that is both down-to-earth and welcoming.

Barbados school girls

Population

Barbados has a population of close to 270,000. Approximately 90% are of African descent, many directly descended from slaves brought to the island to work the plantations. The other 10% includes Europeans, Chinese, and Indians.

Language

The country's official language is English, but many locals speak a dialect known as Bajan. Essentially, Bajan is a combination of English and West African. This mixture produces a unique vocabulary and speech pattern.

Religion

Most Bajans are Anglican (67%), but over 100 religions are practiced on the island.

Festivals

No matter what time of year you visit Barbados there is a good chance a festival will be going on.

Barbados Jazz Festival . . . . January
The year begins with The Barbados Jazz Festival. An international selection of jazz and rhythm & blues artists descends on Barbados to perform at sites throughout the island. Stars as diverse as Ray Charles, Roberta Flack, Nancy Wilson, Patti LaBelle and Al Jarreau have all brought their unique sounds and rhythms to this annual celebration of music under the sun and stars.

The highlight of the festival is two days of open-air concerts at the spectacular Farley Hill National Park. Jazz fans, both locals and visitors, bring coolers of drinks and food and enjoy hot jazz, sitting in the cool shade of the trees on the hillside. Green monkeys often stop by to listen to a few tunes before heading off to their feeding grounds.

Holetown Festival . . . . February
The Holetown Festival celebrates the arrival of the first settlers in 1627. Holetown was the site of their first landing and now hosts a weeklong celebration. Medieval songs waft from churches while fairgrounds pulse to the sounds of contemporary music. Folksongs, dancing, sports, games and general revelry fill the streets, while the markets and food stalls tempt your taste buds with the smells and flavors of Bajan cooking.

Holders Season . . . . March
Spring brings with it the annual Holders Season. This month-long festival, founded in 1993, is held on the grounds of the 18th-century Holders Plantation House. Presenting opera, classical music, jazz, Latin, and Caribbean music, as well as poetry, and drama. New and emerging artists perform alongside world-renowned performers such as Luciano Pavarotti and the London Symphony Orchestra. And, if your tastes run to some-

Holetown Festival
(BarbadosTourism Authority)

thing a little more contemporary, there are always crossover artists. The Holders Season is acclaimed as one of the premier international festivals in the Caribbean.

Oistins Fish Festival . . . . Easter
Fish boning demonstrations combine with boat and crab racing, while steel bands provide the musical background for dancing at this annual tribute to the island's fishing industry.

Congaline Carnival. . . . . April
The name says it all! Late April sees the streets filled with calypso bands and dancers in the "World's Greatest Street Party." Daily entertainment, exhibitions, crafts and food all lead up to the Congaline Street Parade, an all-day event featuring music, dancing, and partying that goes on till late in the night.

Celtic Festival . . . . May
Held during the last two weeks of the month, this festival features traditional Welsh Gymanfa Ganu community hymn singing, traditional Scottish music, Welsh clog dancing, Appalachian music and dancing, Highland Games on the beach, a rugby tournament at the Garrison Savannah, and workshops at local schools, halls, and churches.

Gospelfest. . . . . May
Also in late May, gospel singers and groups from around the world arrive on the island to take part in one of the greatest festivals of its kind – Gospelfest. The island comes alive with some of the most exciting, soul-stirring music, in the world. From solo singers to massive choirs, from new voices to established stars, no matter what your spiritual beliefs, Gospelfest will send a shiver down your back and put a song in your heart.

Crop Over Festival . . . . July - August
Celebrating the final harvest of the sugar cane, Crop Over begins early in the season and culminates in August when the crop is over. "Calypso tents" throb to the sounds of musicians competing for the Calypso Monarch award. Bajan delicacies fill The Bridgetown Market Street Fair, while celebrations and festivities take over the whole island. The crowning of the King and Queen of the crop is the regal highlight, while on "Kadooment Day" costumed bands fill the streets by day and fireworks fill the skies by night.

Crop Over

NIFCA
November
November 30 is Independence Day in Barbados and the National Independence Festival of Creative Arts takes place throughout the month.

Bajans of all ages display their talents in music, performing and visual arts, poetry, and writing, with final exhibitions and performances taking place on the last day of the month as the island celebrates its Independence.

Along with these major festivals, there are a number of smaller festivals and events taking place throughout the year, so, whenever you come, there is almost certainly going to be something for you to join in and celebrate.

Kadooment

Accommodations

 For such a small island, the choices are enormous. Choose a local guesthouse from as little as $40 per night or a world-class luxury resort for $10,000 per week or more.

 Listings in this book with one star (★) are highly recommended. Those earning two stars (★★) are considered exceptional. A few attractions, resorts and restaurants rate three stars (★★★), which means they should not be missed.

Eating & Drinking

You can find everything, from some of the world's finest restaurants overlooking the ocean, offering gourmet meals, to roadside vendors selling local dishes and hot dogs. The water is the cleanest in the world and you can safely eat the food and drink the water straight from the tap. Although not an inexpensive island, there are lots of places where you can eat well without spending a lot of money.

No visit to Barbados is complete without a visit to a rum shop. These locally owned and operated bars can be found throughout the island, and offer a great opportunity to meet the locals while enjoying a local beer or glass of rum. You can also enjoy sandwiches, known as cutters, or a hot meal, all at a price far below what you would pay at the tourist destinations.

20 Things You Must Do in Barbados

This guidebook covers pretty much everything you need to know about the island and its attractions. By reading it you can decide exactly what you want to see and do before you go. I would personally recommend the following, as things you should not miss.

- Spend a day on Crane Beach and have lunch at L'Azure in the hotel at the top of the cliffs.
- Swim with the turtles.
- Have a drink at the bar, check out the art on the walls then have dinner at Tides restaurant (ask for a table upstairs overlooking the ocean).
- Go to a Polo match.
- Visit a rum shop.
- Play golf at the Royal Westmoreland or Sandy Lane (if you can't get in there play at the Barbados Golf Club).
- Visit St. Lawrence Gap at night and stop for drinks or dinner at one of the bars or restaurants.
- Have breakfast at the Bean N' Bagel.
- Visit the Graeme Hall Nature Sanctuary (go early in the day or late in the afternoon).
- Visit Bathsheba and have lunch at the New Edgewater Hotel.
- Have lunch at Naniki.
- Scuba, snorkel, fish, sail, ski, or swim in the ocean.
- Visit the parish churches.
- Go to the Oistins fish fry on Friday night.
- Rent a mini-moke and explore the island without a map.
- Dance under the stars (at one of the many clubs or on an evening cruise).
- Take a Land & Sea Safari.
- Visit the Wildlife Reserve.
- Meet the locals.
- Float face up in the Caribbean and realize how perfect everything is.

Travel Information

Buying Property

After a few days in this tropical paradise, many visitors' thoughts turn to the idea of staying here permanently. Although covering an area of only 166 square miles (430 sq km), Barbados is home to some of the most magnificent properties found anywhere. From a 17th-century plantation house to brand new luxury villas and condominiums Barbados has something for everyone. There is a broad range of properties available, from timeshares starting at about $12,500 to luxury villas costing millions. Barbados is a safe place to buy since it is relatively unaffected by hurricanes; they usually pass well to the north.

The island is recognized by the United Nations as having the highest quality of life anywhere in the developing world. A stable US dollar-based currency, social and political stability, a low crime rate, a growing economy, world-class telecommunications, a well educated and skilled labor force, an excellent health care system, a good road network, dependable public utilities and great weather all year round make it a favorite destination for everyone from budget travelers to rock stars and royalty.

Buying real estate in Barbados is not difficult, but there are factors you need to be aware of. There are no restrictions on non-Barbadians owning property, but there are certain formalities that have to be followed, including getting permission from the central bank. Financing is not generally available to non-Barbadians so you will be required to bring the full amount of the purchase price with you. You must register the amount you are bringing in with the Central Bank so you can repatriate the funds if you decide to sell your property later.

Title conveyance must pass, and deeds and certified survey plans must be registered. Purchasers require a registered Barbadian to search the register and establish title to the property prior to completion of the sale and it is essential that you use a reputable real estate agent and lawyer to handle these transactions.

Sellers pay a transfer tax of 7.5% on any value over $125,000 BDS plus a sales commission of 5%. Legal fees for both the seller and the purchaser are usually about 1.5%-2%. Once an agreement is signed and a 10% deposit is paid, the deal must proceed or the deposit is forfeited.

Facing page: Green monkey in Barbados Wildlife Reserve

Owners pay an annual property tax based on the value of the property:
On the first $125,000BDS = 0%
The next $350,000BDS = 0.10%
The next $500,000BDS = 0.65%
Thereafter 0.75%

As with real estate everywhere, the three most important factors are location, location, and location, which means properties on the west coast are usually the most expensive, the south coast is next and the east coast and inland properties come last.

If you don't plan to spend all year in your villa, rentals can provide a good return and cover your regular maintenance and management costs. Prices have risen steadily over the years and you can expect a reasonable capital gain if you sell later.

There are always new developments being built and, depending on your tastes, you can find a home close to a beach, a golf course, a tennis facility, a marina, a polo field or just about anything else you can imagine.

If you are interested in purchasing, there are a number of well established local and international real estate agencies that can provide information about available properties and purchase requirements.

Altman Real Estate,
☎ 246 432 0840, realestate@aaaltman.com

Bajan Services
☎ 246 422 2618, villas@bajanservices.com

Hamptons International
☎ 246 422 5550, barbados@hamptons-int.com

Realtors Limited
☎ 246 432 6930, realtors@sunbeach.net

Rex Realty
☎ 246 420 6906, homesales-rentals@caribsurf.com

Climate

 Barbados has a tropical climate, cooled by sea breezes. Average annual rainfall varies from 3.3 inches (1,000 mm) on the coast to 7.6 inches (2,300 mm) on the central ridge, with the lowest precipitation in February and March, and the highest from June to November. Water temperature in Barbados averages 78°F (25°C) year-round.

Crime

Serious crime is unusual in Barbados, but visitors should take sensible precautions. Do not leave your valuables unattended or in your car. Stay in well-lit familiar areas at night and always lock your hotel room door.

Dress

Swimsuits should only be worn on the beach, the swimming pool or when sunbathing.

In the evening, restaurants are casual but elegant. Shorts are acceptable except in very exclusive restaurants; if in doubt phone ahead.

Any style of camouflage gear is illegal in Barbados.

Drugs

Drugs are illegal and penalties are severe, up to 20 years in jail even for softer drugs like marijuana.

Electricity

115/230V 50Hz.

Emergencies Numbers

Police – ☎ 211

Ambulance – ☎ 511

Fire – ☎ 311

Hospital – ☎ 246 436 6450

FMH Emergency Centre – ☎ 246 228 6120

Immigration & Customs

Passports

Everyone who enters Barbados, including all North American citizens (Americans and Canadians), must have a valid passport and return ticket.

Cruise Ship Passengers

Cruise ship passengers who are "in-transit" and stay less than 24 hours are not required to carry a valid passport.

However, if you are beginning and ending your trip in Barbados or are "in-transit" to take a flight at the Grantley Adams International Airport, you are required to possess a valid passport.

Duration of Visit

Visitors to Barbados must provide proof of adequate means of support for the duration of their stay if requested by an immigration officer at the port of entry. They must also be in possession of a valid return ticket.

Extension of Stay

Visitors wishing to extend their stay should apply to:

The Chief Immigration Officer
Immigration Department
Careenage House,
The Wharf
Bridgetown,
Barbados
☎ 246 426-1011

Immunization

For travelers who come from areas infected with yellow fever, a vaccination certificate is required for travelers over one year of age.

For all others, no immunization is required, but a good insect repellent will help protect you from mosquitoes, sand flies and other insects.

Marriage & Honeymoons

Many couples choose Barbados as the location for their marriage and/or honeymoon. There are only minimal legal requirements to get married in Barbados, and there are no minimum residence requirements. The only mandatory requirement is to obtain a marriage license at the Ministry of Home Affairs in Bridgetown. You need a valid passport or an original or certified copy of your birth certificate and identification card.

If either party was previously married, you will need a certified copy of the marriage and death certificate (if your spouse is deceased). Alternatively, an original Decree Absolute or certified copy of the Final Judgment (NOT the decree Nisi) must be presented if you are divorced.

Documents not in English must be accompanied with an English translation certified by an authorized Notary Public (NOT a justice of the peace). A letter from the marriage officer who has agreed to perform the ceremony is also required.

If you are under 16, you cannot get married in Barbados. People between the ages of 16 and 18 must have the consent of both parents, who must be present at the time of application.

There are many great locations for weddings in Barbados. You can get married on a boat, in a church, in a plantation house, by sea cliffs, or on a beach.

Wedding Planners

Professional wedding planners can make all the arrangements, even before you arrive on the island or you can select a wedding package at a local hotel. Professional services like flower shops, caterers and bakeries are all readily available.

The following is a list of experienced wedding planners in Barbados.

Pangroove Entertainment Inc.
#3 Keswick Center
Hastings, Christ Church
☎ 246 435 9264 or 246 428 1368, fax 246 420-4483, info@pangroove.com

Lisa St Hutchinson, Cupid's Way Corp.
#154 Atlantic Shores, Christ Church
☎ 246 420 4832, cupid@barbadosweddings.com

Sunbury Plantation House
St Philip
☎ 246 423-6270, fax 246 423-5863, sunbury@caribsurf.com

Destination Management Services, Inc.
#9, Golf View Terrace, Rockley, Christ Church
☎ 246 429-6016, 246 429-6024, dmsi@sunbeach.net

The Indar Weir Travel Centre
Lower Bay Street, Bridgetown, St Michael
☎ 246 228-7748, 246 228-7755, info@caribbeanvacationsonline.com

Concierge Gold Services
Porters, St James
☎ 246 269 4867, fax 246 434-0969, contactus@conciergebarbados.com

Weddings By Malissa,
☎ 246 437-9330, weddingsbymalissa@hotmail.com

Island Weddings Inc.
☎ 246 424-7181, fax 246 424-6209, (from the US, 1-800 945-3289

St James Travel & Tours Ltd.
GH House, Trents, St James
☎ 246 432-0774, 246 432-2832, stjames@stjamesgroup.com

Weddings in Barbados
26 Warners Gardens, Christ Church
☎ 246 437 2023, 246 437 2023, mwood@sunbeach.net

Tropical Weddings
☎ 246 430 1077, fax 246 228 9869, info@tropicalweddingbarbados.com,
www.tropicalweddingsbarbados.com

Medical

 Barbados is a safe place to visit, with no severe tropical diseases. Make sure your polio and tetanus shots are up-to-date. There is no malaria, but very occasionally, after very heavy rains, there is an outbreak of dengue fever, which is a mosquito-borne disease. Take normal precautions against mosquito bites, and make sure to use insect repellent.

Local pharmacies can fill prescriptions, following consultation with a local physician.

Hospitals

Medical facilities in Barbados are among the best in the Caribbean. There are eight polyclinics throughout the island and two hospitals. The general hospital is **Queen Elizabeth Hospital** in Bridgetown, which has a 24-hour Accident & Emergency department.

There is a private facility at the **Bay View Hospital** in St Michael, which does not have an Accident & Emergency Dept. However, the **FMH Emergency Medical Clinic** is in St Michael. The **Sandy Crest Medical Centre** can be reached at ☎ 246 419 4911.

Money

The Barbados dollar is tied to the US dollar at a rate of $1US =$1.98 BDS (Barbados dollars).

US dollars are accepted everywhere and most stores and restaurants accept major credit cards and travelers checks.

Most prices in this guide are quoted in US dollars.

Banking

Banks are open from 8:30 am to 3 pm Monday-Thursday and 8 am to 5 pm on Friday.

Credit Cards

Most hotels, restaurants and shops accept major credit cards. Traveler's checks in US, UK and Canadian funds can also be used at many outlets. There are numerous Banks in Barbados and most have ABMs that accept credit cards and Interac. The following cards are readily accepted:

- American Express
- Carte Blanche
- Diners Club
- EnRoute
- Eurocard
- MasterCard
- Barclaycard
- Visa

Taxes & Gratuities

15% VAT is included in quoted prices at stores and restaurants. A 7.5% VAT and 10% service charge will be added to your hotel bill.

Gratuities are normally 10%-15%.

There is a departure tax of $55 BDS ($27.50 US) payable in cash (no credit cards) at the airport when leaving.

Pets

An import permit must be obtained before entry. Dogs and cats my be imported by permit directly from the UK, the Republic of Ireland, Jamaica, St Kitts/Nevis, Antigua, St Lucia, and St Vincent. Cats and dogs coming from any other country must undergo six months quarantine in Great Britain, after which time an import permit will be issued.

Photography

 Barbados is full of beautiful vistas and interesting sites so pack a camera and, if it's not digital, take plenty of film. There are a number of **Photo Finish One-Hour Labs** throughout the island, where you can buy film and get your photos developed. There are also a number of duty free shops where you can buy a camera, if you forget to pack your own.

Shopping

 Stores are normally open from 8:30 am to 4:30 pm, or 9 am to 5 pm Monday to Friday, and 8:30 am to 1 or 2 pm on Saturday. Most stores are closed on Sunday.

Barbados' retailers offer high quality, good value, and good service. The island is the tax-free haven of the Eastern Caribbean and one of the best shopping destinations in the entire region. When shopping in Barbados, you can be sure that you are buying genuine, high quality products. The tax-free system and competitive pricing guarantee good prices, which can often be 30% to 50% below those in Europe and North America. Sales staff are accustomed to dealing with international buyers, the shops are well appointed and air-conditioned and the sales assistants are helpful and friendly.

Tax-free purchases, with the exception of alcohol and tobacco, can be taken with you at the time of purchase. All tax-free stores offer free delivery service to the airport or harbor.

Barbados has a wide variety of stores, ranging from small privately owned craft stores to large multi-national duty-free retailers, casual open-air markets to elegant air-conditioned plazas. Jewelry, watches, crystal, cameras, audio and video equipment, and fine fragrances are available at up to 50% off the cost of similar items in the US and Europe. When making a duty-free purchase you must present your passport or travel documents, then, either take your purchase with you, or have it delivered directly to the airport, for pick-up on your way out of the country. Visitors to the island can also shop tax-free by mail order for up to one year after their visit.

Harrison's and **Cave Shepherd** are the two biggest department stores, with locations throughout the island. Harrison's has nine locations, including Broad Street, Hastings Plaza, the airport and various hotels. Cave Shepherd has locations in Bridgetown, DaCostas Mall, Sunset Crest, the Bridgetown Cruise Ship Terminal, and the airport.

Duty-free jewelry and gemstones are also available at **Columbian Emeralds**, **Columbian Jewel**, **The Royal Shop**, **Correia's Jewellery**, **Jewellers Warehouse**, **Diamonds International**, and **Little Switzerland**.

Columbian Emeralds has locations in Bridgetown, the airport, and the Bridgetown Cruise Ship Terminal. They provide a full guarantee on all their products, plus free 90-day insurance for damage, loss or theft, and certified appraisals on jewelry and gemstones.

The **Royal Shop** is the place for watches, manufacturers include Rolex, Omega, Cartier, etc. they also stock a selection of fine jewelry, silver and gemstones.

Correira's Jewellery specializes in loose diamonds, gemstones, and gold jewelry. Every stone comes with an appraisal certificate from one of the certified gemologists on staff.

Jewellers Warehouse is a unique store with a traditional atmosphere and friendly service. All purchases are guaranteed and certified.

For fashion and accessories, **Colours of De Caribbean** is located in Bridgetown, while **Gatsby**, with nine boutiques along the west coast and in Bridgetown, is the place to go for designer clothing, shoes, swimwear, jewelry and accessories.

If you're looking for something unique, island artisans sell fine arts and collectibles at craft fairs held throughout the year and at **Daphne's Sea Shell Studio**, **Earthworks Pottery**, **Fairfield Pottery and Gallery**, **Iron Gardens**, and **Pelican Village**.

Many hotels are also home to small stores carrying a wide array of local crafts and designer fashions, and many villages and towns have stores carrying unique island crafts, as well as cigars, liquor, and collectibles.

Shopping in Barbados is not limited to Bridgetown. Several smaller towns like Holetown in St James and Speightstown in St Peter feature craft shops and gift shops. Several shopping malls and plazas are also located outside of Bridgetown. Chattel Village shopping areas are becoming increasingly popular in Barbados. They feature shops in traditional chattel house style and sell souvenirs, gift items, clothing and local arts and crafts. You can find these chattel villages at Holetown, St James and St Lawrence Gap, Christ Church.

Supermarkets

If you are staying in an apartment, a villa or a hotel with kitchen facilities, you may choose to do some cooking yourself. There are a number of local supermarkets, mini-marts, and markets. Some of the more popular ones are:

- **Big B Supermarket** in Worthing
- **Julie 'N Supermarket** in Worthing
- **Jordan's Supermarket** in Payne's Bay
- **Super Centre** in Holetown
- **Esso AutoMart** in Payne's Bay

Sunburn

 The sun is hottest between 10 am and 3 pm so a strong sunscreen is imperative during these hours. However, the sun is still strong outside these hours and you can still get burned if you don't take precautions. Overcast days and windy days, particularly on the east coast, can be deceiving so it is advisable to wear a good sunscreen at all times.

Telephone & Internet

 To place a call to anywhere in North America or Canada, simply dial 1 plus the area code and number.

For calls to the UK, dial 011 44, the area code minus the 0, then the number.

There are payphones in all major towns, communities, and tourist areas. You can either use coins or obtain a Cable & Wireless calling card from any authorized agent or retail outlet.

If you are traveling from the US or Canada, you can use your own mobile phone. Travelers from Europe can rent mobile phones. Digicel is a good local supplier.

There are Internet cafés throughout the island, offering high-speed Internet access. Many hotels provide high-speed and wireless access in-room or in business centers.

Time

 Barbados time is GMT minus four hours in winter and minus five hours in summer. It is one hour ahead of EST in the fall/winter, and the same as EST during the summer.

Tours

There are a wide variety of guided tours available including coach, minivan, ATVs, limousine, taxi, and helicopter.

Helicopter Rides

Bajan Helicopters offer flights for up to five people in air-conditioned jet helicopters. ☎ 246 431 0069, fax 246 431 0086, helicopters@sunbeach.net, www.bajanhelicopters.com

Tour Operators

Facilitators Unlimited arranges tours on land, under, on, or above the water, plus unique tours of the night skies. ☎ 246 434 1111, fax 246 434 1112, facilitators@sunbeach.net.

Material Things located in Worthing, offers discounts on a wide range of land and sea tours. ☎ 246 435 9009, www.vipbarbados.com.

Adventure 4X4 Tours and Island Safari provides off-road tours in Land Rovers and Patrol Safaris. They travel through 10 of the 11 parishes of Barbados, visiting areas not normally seen by visitors, particularly along the north and east coasts. Tours begin at 8:30 am and include a number of scenic stops where rum, and fruit punch is offered. Lunch is provided at a local restaurant and the tour drops you back at your hotel at about 3:30 pm. Adventure 4X4 Tours, ☎ 246 429 3687 or 246 418 3687. Island Safari, ☎ 246 429 5337.

 Note - The tours spend considerable time traveling off-road, along bumpy tracks and unmarked trails. They are not suitable for anyone with back or heart problems, and at five hours, young children will probably get bored and tired. Women who are pregnant should not participate in these tours.

Starline Taxi Services offers customized tours in their fleet of air-conditioned vehicles. ☎ 246 421 2015, starlinetaxiservices@hotmail.com.

Transportation

Buses

 Traveling by bus is one of the best ways of seeing the island and meeting the locals. Although buses are often crowded and chaotic, the drivers are helpful and the routes scenic. There are three different bus systems, all running seven days a week, and the cost is only $1.50 BDS per trip. The smaller buses from the two privately owned systems "ZR's" (pronounced Zed Rs) and "minibuses" can give change; the larger blue buses from the government-operated Barbados Transport Board system cannot.

Most buses depart from Bridgetown in the south or Speightstown in the north. Competition for riders is intense, and the 'ZR' bus conductors often engage in spirited discussions with other drivers and conductors while escorting you to their vehicle.

Shuttles & Taxis

Some hotels provide visitors with shuttles to points of interest on the island or, for a more customized approach, there are numerous taxis available for hire, although they can become expensive.

 One of the best taxi drivers on the island is Emerson Clarke. His car is always immaculately clean, he knows the island and, it seems, just about everyone on it. He was twice voted Taxi Driver of the Year.

Emerson Clarke
☎ cell 246 230 1986, 246 228 6192

Rental Cars

A third option is to rent a car for the day or week. There are several locally owned and operated vehicle rental agencies renting everything from Mokes to Mercedes.

If you drive yourself, be aware that driving is on the left, the roads are generally quite narrow with sharp turns, steep inclines and, although paved, they are often quite bumpy. Many roads do not have sidewalks, so you will also be sharing them with pedestrians.

Courtesy Rent-A-Car
☎ 246 431 4160, fax 246 429 6387, reservations@courtesyrentacar.com

Direct Car Rentals
☎ 246 420 6372, fax 246 420 6383, directrentals@barbadoscars.com

Executive Rentals
☎ 246 228 1993, fax 246 228 3736, reservations@executive-rentalsbarbados.com

Fat Jack Rentals
☎ 246 420 6502

1st Choice Car Rental
☎ 246 434 2277

National Car Rental
☎ 246 422 0603, fax 246 422 1966, reservations@carhire.tv, www.carhire.tv

Premier Car Rentals
☎ 246 425 5200

Coconut Car Rentals
☎ 246 437 0297, fax 246 228 9820, coconut@caribsurf.com

Mopeds & Bikes

Mopeds and bikes can also be rented to explore sites that aren't easily reached by cars.

Drivers License

You can obtain a Barbados drivers license for $10 BDS by bringing a valid national or international license to a police station or authorized car-rental company.

Water

The water in Barbados is naturally filtered through the island coral and is some of the purest water in the world. It is safe to drink directly from the tap.

When to Go

 With a consistent average temperature of 80-87°F, (27-30°C) Barbados is beautiful any time. The rainy season runs from June to November (although the Bajans refer to it as liquid sunshine).

Land of Adventure

For such a small island, Barbados has an enormous range of clubs, sports and activities available for visitors of every age and skill level. From bird watching to jet skiing, from scuba diving to karate, from archery to just lying on a beach and sunbathing, you'll find something in Barbados.

Bird Watching

Barbados is home to a wide range of rare and unusual birds, making it a great vacation spot for birders. Some of the rare birds spotted in Barbados include the masked booby, the grey heron, the Pacific golden plover, the Eurasian whimbrel, the Alpine swift, and the giant cowbird. There are a total of 144 species in 34 families, and five of the 58 Caribbean species can be found here.

Graeme Hall Nature Sanctuary is the last remaining stand of mangrove swamp in Barbados.

Alpine swift (Jonathan Hornung)

On an early morning trip you can spot numerous herons and egrets, including the elusive purple heron.

At **Coles House**, an area of marsh and ponds, near Ragged Point, the western-reef heron has been spotted.

To the east is **Cape Verde**, where you can sometimes see both the little and snowy egrets.

Purple heron (Marcus Antonius Braun)

Wildlife

Hawksbill turtle (B. Navez)

There are lots of opportunities to see wildlife in Barbados. Along with the famous green monkey, you can also see mongoose, eight species of bat, the European hare, red-footed tortoise, three species of lizards, whistling frogs and toads.

The island is home to many turtles, including the leatherback and hawksbill. In some areas, the turtles are relatively tame and you can enjoy the unique experience of swimming with them as they feed among the coral.

Good places to see a variety of wildlife are the **Graeme Hall Nature Sanctuary**, **The Barbados Wildlife Preserve**, and **Ocean Park**.

Barbados Sea Turtle Project

The Barbados Sea Turtle Project (BSTP), started in 1987 to promote the conservation of sea turtles in Barbados, is a joint activity of the Department of Biological and Chemical Sciences at the University of the West Indies, Cave Hill Campus and the Fisheries Division of the Government of Barbados. The BSTP works with the public, and people living and working near the beach, to monitor nesting and hatching activity during the turtle season (April-December).

Marine Reserve

The conservation area extends from the Colony Club in the south to Sandy Lane in the north, and is the primary observation ground of reef life for the nearby Belairs Institute. The museum, which at the time of writing is undergoing renovation, charges a nominal entrance fee. The museum contains artifacts from the sea, including antique bottles, samples of coral, shells and whalebones. There is also a mini-aquarium and play park.

 Note: When I visited, the museum and the beach were somewhat disappointing, but if the renovation and expansion plans are put into place, it has the potential to be a much more interesting attraction, particularly for children.

Boating & Sailing

 There are a number of companies providing yachts and catamarans for charter. Scheduled cruises or customized tours are available. You can charter large catamarans and yachts for guided sailing tours

Whether you're looking for a quiet sail along the coast, an exciting water sports adventure, or a romantic

Ocean Adventures

sunset cruise, warm weather, calm seas and gentle southeasterly trade winds combine to provide perfect conditions for your cruise.

If you arrive in Barbados by yacht, Port St Charles on the north-west coast provides shelter to yachts up to 130 feet. Haul-out and repair facilities are available in Bridgetown for yachts up to 40 tons.

The **Barbados Yacht Club** offers sailing, recreation and dining facilities. Visiting sailors are welcome and receive seven days complimentary membership.

Tiami Catamaran Cruises offer lunch cruises, sunset cruises, snorkel with the turtles, and private charters, ☎ 246 430 0900.

Small Cats specializes in personalized cruises. Their 30-ft vessels carry a maximum of 12 people. They offer three-hour and five-hour cruises, as well as private charters. ☎ 246 421 6419 or 246 231 1585, smallcats@ sunbeach.net.

El Tigre Cruises has three-hour and five-hour cruises in a 60-ft catamaran. Available for private charter. ☎ 246 417 7245 or 246 231 1585, fax 246 421 7582, eltigre@sunbeach.net.

MV Harbour Master is a custom-built 100-ft-long, 40-ft-wide, four-deck floating entertainment center. It offers five-hour lunch cruises with entertainment and stops for swimming and snorkeling. They also offer starlight dinner cruises, with live entertainment and dancing. ☎ 246 430 0900, tallships@sunbeach.net.

Cool Runnings has custom-built catamarans providing personalized service, and a limited number of passengers. Private charters available. ☎ 246 436 0911, coolrunnings@caribsurf.com.

Silver Moon catamaran

Heat Wave Sailing Cruise has dinner cruises, three-hour sunset/snorkel cruises and a Wet 'n' Wild Watersports package, as well as private charters. ☎ 246 429 9283, hwscb@caribsurf.com.

Rubaiyat Catamaran Cruises offers Lunch and sunset cruises aboard a 50-ft catamaran, ☎ 246 436 6921, rubaiyat@hotmail.com.

Good Times Barbados. ☎ 246 422 1900, info@goodtimes-barbados.com.

Just Breezing Water Sports. Two-hour cruises on a 32-ft glass bottom boat. ☎ 246 432 7645, fax 246 432 7062, contactus@justbreezingwatersports.com.

Silver Moon Luxury Catamarans has two catamarans, one holding up to 12 passengers the other accommodating up to 40. ☎ 246 438 2088, fax 246 438 3650, ceanadventure@sunbeach.net, www.oceanadventures.bb.

Golf

 Home to four PGA standard golf courses, Barbados is a great golf destination. On the west coast, Sandy Lane has two Tom Fazio-designed courses, The Country Club, and The Green Monkey. The Royal Westmoreland is a Robert Trent-Jones Jr.-designed course.

On the south coast is the links-style, 6,705-yard, par 72, Barbados Golf Club, and the 9-hole Club Rockley, both open to the public.

There are plans in place for building several more courses.

Barbados Golf Club is a 6,805-yard par-72 championship golf course in St

Ninth hole at Barbados Golf Club

Michael. ☎ 246 428 8463, teetime@barbadosgolfclub.com, www. barbadosgolfclub.com.

Rockley Golf Club is a nine-hole (18 with alternative tees) par-70, 5,620-yard course in St Michael. ☎ 246 435 7873, info@rockleygolfclub. com.

Sandy Lane Golf Club has two 18-hole courses, the Country Club and the Green Monkey, designed by Tom Fazio, and a nine-hole course, the Old Nine. ☎ 246 444 2500.

The Royal Westmoreland, a members-only 18-hole course, is considered one of the world's most exciting courses. Guests at Glitter Bay and the Royal Pavilion, through a special arrangement, may use the course.

The Royal Westmoreland. ☎ 246 422 4653, fax 246 419 7205.

Almond Beach Village is an easy nine-hole par-three course for hotel guests. ☎ 246 422 4900.

Hiking

 The **Barbados National Trust** organizes Sunday walks at 6 am and 3:30 pm. The hikes are listed in the newspaper, or you can obtain a schedule for $2.50 from the National Trust. ☎ 246 426 2421, fax 246 429 9055, www.barbados.org/hike.htm.

Join **Hike Barbados** for hiking tours through cane fields, gullies, tropical forests and coastal communities. Explore the unique geological and social structure of Barbados, and observe the delicate balance of the unique heritage and environment.

Hikes are free but donations are welcome toward the work of the Barbados National Trust (preserving our built and natural environment) and Treading Lightly (problem solving for sustainability).

Morning hikes start at 6 am, afternoon hikes (Stop 'n' Stare only) start at 3:30 pm, and Moonlight Walks are at 5:30 pm (bring a flashlight!).

Walk Descriptions

"Stop 'n' Stare" are walks of five to six miles, "Here 'n' There" are eight-10 miles, and "Grin 'n' Bear" are 12-14 miles. All are group walks.

Wear loose clothing, comfortable hiking boots/sports shoes, sunscreen, a hat, and sunglasses. Bring your camera and a bottle of water. Refreshments are offered for sale after the hikes.

Peach & Quiet, a small oceanfront property on four acres of tropical gardens at the southern tip of Barbados, offers weeklong hiking packages. There is a restaurant serving breakfast and candlelit dinners, a freshwater swimming pool, bar with lunchtime snacks, and the island's only sea rock pool. Don a snorkeling mask and swim in an ocean aquarium, surrounded by multi-colored fish! ☎ 246 428 5682, fax 246 428 2467, res. peachandquiet@caribsurf.com.

Monday: Arrival/free day.

Tuesday: Afternoon walk following the former railway line from Bathsheba to Bath. Non-walkers option: Bathsheba and Andromeda Gardens.

Welchman Hall Gully

Wednesday: Highland Hike. From the lush Canefield Plantation of St Thomas, climb to Barbados' highest point, Mount Hillaby.

Thursday: A full day visiting the Flower Forest, Welchman Hall Gully, Harrison's Cave, plus a scenic east coast drive. Including all entrance fees. Non-walkers option – as above but transport provided between sights.

Friday: Early morning walk following the deserted South East Coast from Salt Cave Cove with its ancient Arawak settlements, past Gerald Bull's so called Iraqi super gun to the spectacular Long Beach and Chancery Lane swamp (nesting area for pelicans, blue herons and the magnificent frigate birds).

In the afternoon a private charter with a small group, or exclusive-use catamaran, cruise along the west coast and stop at different areas where there are great snorkeling opportunities.

Saturday: Coves and Castles. Afternoon walk from Bottom Bay past the ruins of Harrismith Great House, Ginger Bay, Sharks Hole and Crane Beach.

Sunday: Early morning walk of Bridgetown, with guide, exploring the historical sights. Or National Trust afternoon walk (area varies each week).

Bicycling

Race bicycling and mountain biking are very popular sports in Barbados, and the island has a number of excellent bike routes and tracks.

Whether cycling along the east coast with the Atlantic Ocean's wave crashing to the shore, climbing up steep hills, riding down roads framed by lush, tropical vegetation, or just cruising through the scenic countryside, Barbados is a cycler's dream.

You can rent a bicycle at several locations across the island, including the Cruise Ship Terminal.

Guided Tours

Highland Adventure Centre offers a spectacular 12-km/7.2-mile mountain bike tour that travels through the heart of Barbados, with a stop at a local rum shop! ☎ 246 431 8928, fax 246 438 8070.

Horseback Riding

 Highland Adventure Centre. Exploring Barbados on horseback provides a unique way of discovering the island. Riding centers offer a variety of trail rides and rides along the beach for riders at every level of experience.

The Highland Adventure Centre has a 1½-hour scenic horseback tour through the countryside of Barbados, providing views of old plantation houses, quaint villages, and three different coastlines. ☎ 246 431 8928, fax 246 438 8070.

Beach riding (Barbados Tourism Authority)

Just Breezing Watersports. Ride through country trails and secluded beaches, visit the Atlantic Ocean on the east coast, then cross over and snorkel with green sea turtles in the Caribbean Sea on the west coast. ☎ 246 432 7645, fax 246 432 7062, contactus@justbreezingwatersports.com.

Jahworks Stud & Riding Stables, located in the Scotland District National Park and overlooking the spectacular east coast, specializes in mountain and beach trails, lessons, horsemanship, dressage and show jumping. They also have a unique therapy program for "differently abled" persons. ☎ 246 422 9905.

Polo

Polo is known as the Game of Kings, but in Barbados, you don't need to be royalty to play. The officers of the British West India Regiment first introduced the game to the island in the 1800's. The **Barbados Polo Club** (☎ 246 437 5410) was established in 1884 and has been in almost continuous operation ever since. There are four polo clubs on the island, where you are welcome to visit and watch a game. At Waterhall you can take lessons, so the next time you are entertaining

Polo (Barbados Tourism Authority)

royalty you can casually suggest a quick game before tea! The regulation field is 300 yards (100 m) long and 160 yards (53 m) wide, so you will need a fairly large backyard.

If you really want to get a feel for the game, try a Polo Day Package at Waterhall. With 108 stables, over 100 trained horses, a full-size polo field, a clubhouse, a grandstand, and two professional polo instructors, this is the place to learn. You start the day with a morning coffee and instructional video, followed by a lesson on a wooden horse, (even kings have to start somewhere). After a break for lunch, it's time for a lesson on a real horse. Don't worry, the horses are well trained and won't laugh. Your lesson is recorded on video for analysis, then, to end the day you get to play a chukka (there are six chukkas in a polo match, each one lasting seven minutes).

Polo tails (Barbados Tourism Authority)

After completing the chukka, you may find that you have a somewhat more regal bearing as you stroll inside for refreshments. After two or three glasses of refreshment, however, your regal bearing may disappear, and it will be time to head back to your hotel for a well-deserved rest.

If playing is a little too much, the polo season in Barbados runs from October to May and, besides local matches, the island often hosts international teams. Visitors are always welcome, the matches are always exciting, the bar is always open and a barbecue dinner is served. If you've never seen a game before, it's definitely worth a visit. You'll be amazed by the speed of the horses, the skill of the players and will be enthralled by the game.

Sport Fishing

 Fishing is a way of life in Barbados. The waters around the island are home to a wide variety of fish and numerous boats are available for charter, half- or full-day.

Most fishing charters provide tackle and bait, drinks, refreshments and transportation to and from your hotel. Barbados has big open-water fish, including blue marlin, white marlin, billfish, sailfish, kingfish, dorado, barracuda, bonita, and yellowfin tuna.

Barbados fishing boat
(Barbados Tourism Authority)

Barracuda (Clark Anderson / Aquaimages)

Crews are happy to assist in making sure both beginners and experienced anglers have a good time. Some charters will arrange to cook what you catch, or advise you on cooking arrangements at your hotel or a nearby restaurant.

April sees the **Sagicor/ Mount Gay Rum International Tournament**. This annual event attracts anglers from the Caribbean, Europe, North and South America, and Canada.

Between February and April the Barbados Game Fishing Association (BGFA) holds their annual **Deep Sea Fishing Tournament**, consisting of five one-day events. In late November and early December, the **Wahoo Tournament**, consisting of three one-day events, takes place.

For a completely different experience, you can try

Yellowfin tuna (Adamahill)

Bajan fishing 'in the raw.' Ask to go out with one of the local fishing boats at Oistins, Bridgetown or Tent Bay. Fishermen are often grateful for another pair of hands. Make sure you establish exactly what is expected. Although it may well be an exhilarating experience, pulling lobster pots and fishing nets can be extremely difficult and tough work and you can't come back to shore whenever you've had enough!

 Barbados Game Fishing Association, www. barbadosgamefishing.com.

Honey Bea 111 offers half-day (four hours) and full-day tours (eight hours). ☎ 246 428 5344, fax 246 420 7483, honeybea111@hotmail. com.

Fishing Charters Barbados Inc. has 36-ft, 42-ft, and 45-ft boats, offering four-hour, six-hour, and eight-hour charters. ☎ 246 429 2326, 246 234 1688, fax 246 228 5117, burkes@caribsurf.com.

Cannon Charters. ☎ 246 424 6107, fax 246 421 7582, cannon@ sunbeach.net, www.fishingbarbados.com.

Parasailing

Soaring into the sky, strapped into a parachute towed behind a speedboat, is an experience like no other. Head over to the **Falcon at the Boatyard**, on the outskirts of Bridgetown. Harness into your parachute, sail into the sky, and get a bird's eye view of the Barbados coastline beneath you.

For the really adventurous, you can join the high flyers club and soar all the way up to 800 ft! ☎ 246 419 0579, 246 230 4507, 246 230 9549, lourdes@ caribnet.net.

Parasailing (Barbados Tourism Authority)

Surfing

Barbados has the Caribbean's most consistent surf conditions, with steady swells all year round, and a water temperature that never drops below 77°F/25°C, which makes Barbados a popular surf destination.

In winter, the north and west coasts pick up plenty of swell and the constant trade winds ensure that the east coast breaks consistently.

On the east coast, at the town of Bathsheba, is the **Soup Bowl**. Recognized worldwide in the surfing community, it is home to many international competitions

On the south coast is **South Point**, also home to surfing competitions. It features a powerful and clean wave.

Barbados surfer

Surf Barbados offers surf lessons for everyone from beginner to expert. ☎ 246 256 3906, www. surferbarbados.com.

Windsurfing

Windsurfing (Club Mistral)

November to July are the best months for windsurfing in Barbados. The south coast, with consistent wind and sea conditions and steady trade winds of 15 to 35 knots is the most popular area for windsurfers. Silver Rock Beach is the venue for the **Barbados Waterman Festival**, held every February. Between Maxwell and Hastings, there are ideal conditions for beginner and intermediate windsurfers. Along this coast, there are a wide range of accommodations, restaurants, and bars. The best place to learn windsurfing is **Sandy Beach**, also known as Carib Beach. It has a shallow lagoon, calm water, and is protected by an offshore coral reef, providing perfect conditions for the novice windsurfer.

Club Mistral. ☎ 246 428 7277, fax 246 420 8291, company@club-mistral. com.

Kayaking

Exploring Barbados by kayak provides a fascinating look at the sea life and colorful reefs that surround the island.

The west coast is ideal for heading out on calm waters. For a more exciting adventure journey head to the south coast, where you can rent kayaking gear from many of the water sports shops there or at Dover Beach.

At Ocean Adventures, you can take a guided tour and learn interesting facts about the island as you make rest stops along the way. A highlight of the tour is the chance to mingle with and feed the sea turtles! The tours are perfect for people of all ages and skill levels.

Kayaks can also be rented at the Boatyard.

Ocean Adventures. ☎ 246 438 2088, fax 246 438 3650, oceanadventure@sunbeach.net.

The Boatyard. ☎ 246 436 2622.

Snorkeling & Diving

Ecodive Barbados

The waters around Barbados are perfect for snorkeling and scuba diving, with visibility from 80 to 98 ft (23 to 33 m) most of the year.

Barbados' barrier reefs are between half a mile and two miles off shore, and many rise to within 60 ft (20 m) of the surface. Closer in are fringe and patching reefs, which range from 40 to 60 ft (13-20 m) in depth. Visibility is good and there are plenty of corals, sponges, and sea life, including stingrays, barracuda, seahorses and turtles.

There are more than two dozen dive sites between the western and southern coasts of Barbados and the calm waters along the west coast are perfect for snorkeling. The north and east coasts have very strong currents and diving is extremely limited.

The sunken freighter **Pamir** lies off the coast of Six Men's Bay. It is 165 ft (53 m) long, and its hull remains intact. Divers can look through the freighter's portholes and view the fish and aquatic animals that call it home. Another sunken ship off the west coast is the **Stavronikita**, a 365-

ft (120-m) Greek freighter which was purposely sunk in 1978 (off Fitts Village), and sits at a depth of 137 ft (44 m).

Just off the southwestern shore of Barbados is **Carlisle Bay**, a natural harbor that has been turned into a marine park. When exploring the sea floor, you can find empty bottles that have accumulated from the generations of sailors that tossed them overboard. You can also see cannonballs, cannons, anchors, and a few shipwrecks at 25 to 60 ft (nine-20 m), all close enough to visit in one dive. Barbados' newest shipwreck, the **Bajan Queen**, was sunk in 2002 and is another popular dive destination.

There is a recompression chamber at St Ann's Fort, on the outskirts of Bridgetown.

 Snuba: For those unable or unwilling to scuba dive there is Snuba, a cross between snorkeling and scuba diving. The diver is attached to an air cable run from a tank located on an overhead dive boat. (See *Holidaying with Children.*)

Ocean Adventures. ☎ 246 436 2088.

Dive Barbados offers diving instruction for all levels, reef and shipwreck dives, as well as underwater camera rentals. ☎ 246 422 3133.

Hightide Watersports is a west coast dive shop with equipment rental and PADI instruction. ☎ 246 432 0931, fax 246 432 6628, hightide@sunbeach.net.

The Dive Shop Ltd. is the oldest, best-known dive shop on Barbados. They have three dives daily, plus special dives for beginners and scuba diving certification. ☎ 246 426 9947.

Reefers & Wreckers. The northern-most dive shop offers access to unspoiled northern reefs. ☎ 246 262 6677, 246 422

West Side Scuba

5450, scubadiving@caribsurf.com, www.scubadiving.bb.

West Side Scuba Centre has two dive boats, air-conditioned classrooms, on-site swimming pool and complete certification courses including night diving. ☎ 246 432 2558, peterg@sunbeach.net, www.westsidescuba.com.

DivePro Barbados is a 5 Star PADI facility with a fully equipped Pro 42 custom dive boat and air-conditioned classrooms. ☎ 246 420 3337, info@diveprobarbados.com, www.diveprobarbados.com.

Eco Dive Barbados is an environmentally friendly dive company, dedicated to providing each client with a personalized diving experience. They specialize in semi-private and small group dives. ☎ 246 243-5816, dive@ecodivebarbados.com.

Barbados Blue has PADI certified instructors. Two of them are marine biologists. ☎ 246 434 5764, barbadosblue@caribsurf.com.

Shooting

Set in 70 acres of rural St Philip, the **Kendal Sporting Clays** country club offers indoor and outdoor pistol shooting ranges, archery, clay shooting, and paintball. Lessons are available for all skill levels and include all equipment. They also have a number of other activities, including, table tennis, swimming, darts, pool, etc. ☎ 264 437 5306/5594, fax 246 437 5598, kendalsports@sunbeach.net, www.go-kendal.com. The **Flying Rabbit Restaurant** serves lunch between 11 am and 3:45 pm.

Tennis

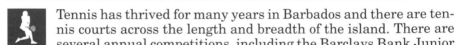 Tennis has thrived for many years in Barbados and there are tennis courts across the length and breadth of the island. There are several annual competitions, including the Barclays Bank Junior Championships, the National Tennis Centre Barbados Futures event, and the BMW Challenge.

On the west coast, the David and John Lloyd Tennis Village at Sugar Hill has four well lit Omni courts. The Sandy Lane hotel has nine hard courts. There are two courts at the Royal Westmoreland.

In the south, there are courts at the Barbados Hilton, Club Rockley and the Casuarina Hotel. The National Tennis Centre has its home at the Sir Garfield Sobers Gymnasium at Wildey. Many luxury villas also have courts.

Jet Skiing

Barbados Blue at the Hilton Hotel in Barbados offers Jet Skiing. ☎ 246 434 5764, barbadosblue@caribsurf.com.

Waterskiing

 You can find vendors at just about any beach along the west or south coasts of Barbados.

Jet skiing

Submarine Tours

Barbados is a coral island and extending out from it are miles of coral reef. Wherever you have a reef, you have sea life and the reefs here are no exception. There is an incredible variety of fish, plants, crustaceans, and, just to make it really interesting, ship-

Atlantis

wrecks. Of course, the only way to see all this is to get under the water, but for many scuba diving is not an option, so **Atlantis Adventures** (☎ 246 436 8929, www.atlantisadventures.com/barbados) has come up with a way for you to get under the water without scuba diving, in fact without even getting wet. It is the *Atlantis* submarine.

From the base in Bridgetown, you take a launch out to the *Atlantis*, moored in the middle of the Caribbean. From the launch, you step down into the submarine and take your place on one of two benches that run the length of the submarine. Everyone has his or her own viewing porthole, and as soon as everyone is aboard, the hatch is closed and the voyage begins. The *Atlantis* descends to a depth of 50 feet (17 m) and silently glides along the reef. Curious fish swim up to the portholes and stare back at you.

After exploring the reef, the *Atlantis* descends to 150 feet (51 m) to view a shipwreck. The *S.S. Stavronikita* is 350 ft (117 m) long and sits upright on the ocean floor. Visions of *Titanic* and all the other undersea movies you've ever seen come back to you as the submarine circles the wreck, before returning to the surface to disgorge its group of excited undersea explorers.

The *Atlantis* is suitable for all ages but if you are in any way claustrophobic, you would be advised to sit this one out.

 Don't bother trying to take photos out of the portholes; they will just come out as a wash of blue. If you want a souvenir picture, they are available at the Atlantis office, or you can buy the book *Barbados Dive Guide* by Lucy Agace, which has more than 100 underwater photos.

Atlantis also offers a Power Snorkel Adventure. Using a handheld "scooter," you can take a guided tour to explore the underwater life and shipwrecks James Bond style!

Cooking the Bajan Way

Seafood dish (www.bookit.com)

The national dish of Barbados is cou-cou and flying fish. Cou-cou, made from cornmeal and okra, is served with fish, vegetables, rice or pasta. Flying fish are silvery blue fish about eight to 10 inches (18 to 22 cm) long. Kingfish, snapper, tuna, shark and barracuda are other popular fish that Bajans enjoy, and pork is the favorite meat. Barbados' climate is perfect for growing a wide variety of fruits including bananas, mangoes, sour sop, sea grapes, dunks, guavas, Bajan cherries, limes, oranges, tamarinds, sugar apples, sapodillas, pawpaws and mammee apples, as well as vegetables such as yams, sweet potatoes, eddoes, sweet cassavas, breadfruits, pumpkins, avocados and plantains.

Bajans use lots of seasoning; a favorite is made with onion, parsley, shallot, marjoram, thyme, garlic, clove, black pepper, white pepper, Scotch bonnet pepper, limejuice and salt. And, of course, they have their own hot pepper sauce, with Scotch bonnet peppers, fresh turmeric, shallots, dry English mustard, onions and vinegar, plus other ingredients that my mother in law would never tell me. If you like hot sauce, this is the hottest!

Pudding and souse is another island favorite. The "pudding" is a spicy dish made with sweet potato. The "Souse" is made from pig's head, feet, and tail boiled and served with onion, cucumber, herb, and pepper sauce.

Fishcakes made with salted cod are my favorite. If you are a tea drinker, eat some fishcakes then drink some tea. The spice in the fishcakes has an effect on your tongue that makes the tea taste just great! Pepperpot (a spicy stew made with a variety of meats, and conkies, a mixture of cornmeal, coconut, sweet potatoes, raisins, pumpkin, sugar and spices steamed on a banana leaf, are other popular dishes.

Preserves such as guava jelly, orange marmalade and green mango chutney, plus sweets such as guava cheese, tamarind balls, coconut sugar cake and fudge made from the local sugar, are all popular treats. But my favorite is Great Cake, a delicious blend of the finest fruit and rum. Pick it up in stores around the island or at the Mount Gay Rum shop.

Sightseeing

 Although Barbados is a small island, it has a rich history and, for those who want to get off the beach and spend some time exploring, there is plenty to see and do. In fact, you could spend every day for two weeks and still not see all there is to see.

Following are some of the most popular sites. Full descriptions can be found in the later "parish" sections of this book.

The Barbados Museum, St Michael. Housed in an 1815 British military prison, at the Garrison Savannah. ☎ 246 427 0201, fax 246 429 5946, admin@barbmuse.org.bb, www.barbmuse.org.bb.

The Harry Bayley Observatory, St Philip. Home of the Barbados Astronomical Society, built in 1963 on a 350-year-old plantation, and housing a 14-inch reflector telescope. The rum distillery, built in 1996, manufacturers ESA Field white rum and Alleyne Arthur Old Brigand labels. The heritage park has a theater and artists' studios. There is also a children's park and petting zoo on the grounds. ☎ 246 420 1977, fax 246 420 1976.

Folkestone Marine Park, St James. A protected reef with sections of the water set aside for research, and other sections used for snorkeling and water sports.

Gun Hill Signal Station, St George. Built in 1818, it was part of a six-station system used to warn of attack and to relay messages around the island.

Harrison's Cave, St Thomas. A limestone cave, reputed to be the largest of its kind in the Caribbean. Take a tram ride through the cave system and see the incredi-

Gun Hill Signal Station

ble stalactites suspended from the cave roof and stalagmites emerging from the ground.

Animal Flower Cave, St Lucy. Sea caves, home to "animal flowers," small yellow sea anemones that resemble flowers when their tentacles are open.

Barbados Wildlife Reserve, St Peter. A four-acre open-air zoo, home to both imported and native animals. Wander among green monkeys, wallabies, iguanas, peacocks, land turtles, and herons. Then visit the alligators and pythons safely behind glass. ☎ 246 422 8826.

Tyrol Cot Heritage Village, St Michael. Built in 1854 of coral stone, this is a fine example of period architecture. The former home of Sir Grantley Adams, the first premier of Barbados, and his son Tom Adams, Barbados' second premier, it's filled with their furnishings and memorabilia. The complex is home to a heritage village with chattel houses, a slave quarters and a rum shop.

Mount Gay Rum Visitors Center, Bridgetown. The world's oldest rum distiller. See how rum is produced, then see how it tastes! ☎ 246 425 9066.

Flower Forest, St Joseph. A 50-acre garden on the grounds of an old plantation. Stroll the paths and enjoy the flowers, both native and imported. ☎ 246 433 8152, fax 246 433 8365, ffl@sunbeach.net.

Chalky Mount, St Andrew. A small village home to a number of potters. Watch as they make pots in the traditional way then buy some straight from the kiln.

St Nicholas Abbey, St Peter. One of three remaining Jacobean mansions in the Western Hemisphere. Dating to the early 17th century, it is the oldest building on the island.

Francia Plantation House, St George. Designated as a house of architectural interest by the Barbados National Trust, it is a beautifully maintained plantation house. ☎ 246 429 0474, fax 246 435 1491.

Graeme Hall Nature Sanctuary, Christ Church. A Barbados National Environmental Heritage Site. A 3½-acre oasis with ponds and wading

Graeme Hall Nature Sanctuary

areas surrounded by white and red mangroves. ☎ 246 435 9727, fax 246 435 7078, admin@graemehall.com.

Mallalieu Motor Collection, Christ Church. A collection of vintage cars, including Bentleys, Daimlers, Humbers, Triumphs, and other unusual cars, not to be missed by any car lover. ☎ 246 426 4640, billm@ sunbeach.net.

Ocean Park, Christ Church. Barbados' newest attraction is a marine aquarium with attractions such as Freshwater Falls, Ray Pool, Shoreline Discovery Pond, Sea Lab & Classroom, Quarantine & Sea Rescue, Mangroves, Rocky Coast, Living Reef, Touch Pool, and Ocean Encounter. ☎ 246 420 7405, fax 246 420 7406, info@oceanparkbarbados.com.

Sunbury Plantation House, St Philip. A 300-year-old Plantation House featuring mahogany furniture, antiques, old prints, and a collection of horse-drawn carriages. After visiting the house, stroll through the mahogany woods and landscaped gardens. ☎ 246 423-6270, fax 246 423-5863.

Sunbury Plantation House

Barbados Heritage Tours

You can rent a car and tour the different sites at your own pace or there are a number of companies offering guided tours either as a group or individually. The following companies offer both.

Boyce's Tours, Grazettes Court, St Michael, ☎ 246 425-5366, fax 246 424-1455, tours@boycestours.com.

Glory Tours, #2 Western Ave, Fort George Heights, St Michael, ☎ 246 231-2932, tours@glorytours.org.

Hinkson's Tours, ☎ 246 424-1470, info@hinksonstours.com.

Cricket

Cricket in Barbados is not a sport... it's a national obsession! If you meet a Bajan and you're not sure what to talk about, just ask what they think of

Cricket team

the national team's chances and you can sit back and listen for the rest of the day. This doesn't just apply to men; ask any man woman or child and you'll get the same result.

Barbados is home to some of the world's greatest cricketers and many have been knighted for their service to the game and their country, including Sir Gary Sobers, Sir Frank Worrell, Sir Clyde Walcott, Sir Everton Weekes, and Sir Conrad Hunte.

The Kensington Oval is the main cricket stadium in Barbados, but on any weekend in any town or village there is almost certainly a game to be found. But this is nothing like England where you sit on the grass beer in hand and politely clap whenever a run is scored. No, this is the Caribbean and games include a DJ blasting out music to the crowd, and the crowd, as much a part of the game as the players, blasting horns, whistling, cheering, booing and providing a general air of noise and merriment.

Even better, if you don't want to leave the beach, there's a good chance a pick-up game will happen at any time and everyone is welcome to join in. However, chances are you'll be somewhere in the outfield (the ocean?) waiting for a stray ball to come your way and once you get up to bat be prepared to be quickly dispatched by some 12-year-old who will have you bowled out before you even have a chance to see the ball. But not to worry; there's always plenty of rum afterward to take your mind off the agony of defeat.

International teams often come through Barbados to play a Test Match or a One-Day International at the Kensington Oval. If this happens while you're there you have two choices – go to the game, or lie on the beach – everyone who works in Barbados will be, "out of the office for the day."

 For information about matches at the Kensington Oval, or other cricket information contact Barbados Cricket Association, ☎ 246 436 1397, www.cwcricket.com.

If you want to take a team to Barbados to play against local teams contact **Sporting Barbados**, ☎ 246 228 9122, www.sportingbarbados.com.

Horse Racing

The Barbados Turf Club celebrated its centenary in 2005. The club organizes three racing seasons every year – January to April, May to August, and October to December – with races taking place at the Garrison Savannah, two miles outside of Bridgetown.

The soldiers of the British Army used the Savannah,  originally a military parade ground, as a sports field. Then, in 1845, the officers of the British Regiment started using the parade ground to race their horses and today it is the home of horse racing in Barbados.

There are four major races on the Barbados racing calendar – the **Sandy Lane Barbados Gold Cup**, held on the first Saturday in March, and the three races of the Triple Crown: the **Banks Barbados Guineas** in April, the **Pinnacle Feeds Midsummer Creole Classic** in July, and the **United Insurance Barbados Derby** in August.

There are two completely different ways of enjoying a day at the races – the island version and the Gold Package version. Both are fun and it's probably worth making two trips to experience them both. In the island version, just hop on a bus or take a taxi to the grounds, pay your entry fee, join the locals in one of the three stands track-side, check the form, place your bets and enjoy the unique excitement and atmosphere of horse racing in the Caribbean. Or if you prefer something even more informal, take a picnic and relax under the tall trees that surround the track.

If you want to try the Gold Package, for $150 BDS ($75 US) per adult, half-price for children 12 and under, you will be treated to a day of pampered luxury and excitement. The day starts when you are picked up at your hotel and transported to the racetrack. Upon arrival, you will be ushered to your table in the air-conditioned "Finish Line Restaurant." Offering a commanding view of the track and with pari-mutuel windows right in the restaurant, guests spend the entire day in air-conditioned luxury. Admission includes a race program and a five-course meal. If you're lucky and pick a few winners, you may even get the whole day paid for out of your winnings.

There is also a play park for kids and vendors selling a range of Bajan dishes such as pudding and souse, rice and stew, fried fish and fish cakes.

To wash it all down there is soft drinks and coconut juice for the kids, beer, and fine Bajan rum for the adults.

 Barbados Turf Club, ☎ 246 426 3980, www. barbadosturfclub.com.

Rum Shops

Rum barrels

If you want a real Bajan experience, you have to make at least one visit to a rum shop. Rum shops are actually small bars found in every village and are social centers where residents gather to discuss politics, play dominoes, catch up on the latest news, gossip and... drink rum.

Some shops also act as grocery stores and are a good place to grab a snack, particularly cutters. Cutters are the Bajan equivalent of sandwiches, a round bun generously stacked with cheese, ham, fish or whatever.

First licensed in 1652, rum shops are often housed in original chattel houses brightly decorated in multiple colors and covered with distillery ads, logos and signs.

Many are located on main streets with outside tables, where you can sit just inches away from the buses and cars roaring past. Inside, the slap of dominoes on wood tables, a cricket match on the television and the constant ebb and flow of conversation provide a steady rhythmic background to the serious business of drinking.

Rum has historically been the lifeblood of the Caribbean. It was first invented in Barbados shortly after the British settled on the island in 1627. There are three distilleries still on the island, Mount Gay, Malibu, and ESA Field white rum/ Alleyne Arthur Old Brigand, all of

Typical rum shop (Rodney Nelson)

which are open for touring and tastings.

It is said there are 1,000 rum shops on the island. Some even say there are 1,500. Regardless, you'll easily find one to enjoy, and, if you know anything about cricket you can spend a whole day, and night, never running out of conversation or people to talk to.

Select Rum Shops

- The Watering Hole in Christ Church
- Lemon Arbour in St John
- Nigel Benn Auntie Bar in St. Andrew
- The Bird's Nest in St Michael
- The John Moore in St James
- The Fisherman's Pub in St Peter

Distilleries

Mount Gay, ☎ 246 425 8757, www.mountgayrum.com.

Malibu, ☎ 246 425 9393.

ESA Field white rum and Alleyne Arthur Old Brigand, The Rum Factory & Heritage Park, Four Square, St Philip, ☎ 246 420 1977, fax 246 420 1976.

Nightlife

 When the sun goes down the nightlife begins. Whether you're looking for a romantic dinner, dancing to the latest club music, a live show, or drinks and a live band, you can find it in Barbados.

Most of the nightclubs are in the St Lawrence Gap, or on Bay Street in Bridgetown. Most feature live entertainment, everything from calypso and reggae to R&B and jazz.

The Whistling Frog, at Time Out At The Gap, has party nights with karaoke and live music. St. Lawrence Gap, Christ Church, ☎ 246 420 5021, fax 246 420 5034, timeout@gemsbarbados.com.

Club Xtreme is a 10,000-square-foot state-of-the-art nightclub with the hottest DJs and the wildest parties. Worthing Main Road, Worthing, Christ Church, ☎ 246 228 2582, info@clubxtreme.net.

Harbour Lights is an open-air beachfront nightclub where the DJs spin the latest tunes, and you can dance under the stars. For a truly tropical evening, on Mondays and Fridays, the Beach Extravaganza Dinner Show offers dancing barefoot in the sand to the pulsating beat of a live calypso band, exotic free drinks, a barbecue dinner, and entertainment, including fire eating, limbo and Caribbean dancing, amazing stiltmen and the acrobatics of the green monkey. Marina Villa, Bay Street, St. Michael, ☎ 246 436 7225, fax 246 436 5069, contactus@harbourlightsbarbados.com.

The **Bajan Roots & Rhythms** show at **The Plantation** is a dinner and stage show presenting an authentic demonstration of West Indian culture. It is an all-inclusive extravaganza with thrilling choreography, music, song, dance and the red-hot excitement of a fire-eater and flaming limbo dancer. The Plantation Theatre, St. Lawrence Main Road,

Bajan Roots & Rhythms

Christ Church, ☎ 246 428 5048, fax 246 420 6317, plantationrest@ sunbeach.net.

The Boatyard in Bridgetown has something going on all day and all night at the beach club bar and nightclub. Bay Street, Bridgetown, ☎ 246 436 2622, fax 246 228 7720, Boatyard@sunbeach. net.

For something a little quieter, take a cruise along the coast with the **Harbour Master Starlight Dinner Cruise**, or charter a catamaran and celebrate a quiet evening for two. Tall Ship Cruises, The Shallow Draught Harbour, Bridgetown Port, Bridgetown, ☎ 246 430 0900, fax 246 430 0901, tallships@sunbeach.net.

 Or enjoy an evening of romance and fine dining at one of Barbados' many restaurants. Many sit right on the edge of the ocean and some provide live entertainment to complement the mood.

Agouti at the Barbados Wildlife Reserve (Rodney Nelson)

Traveling With Children

Small pitcher got wide ear hole.
(Be careful what you say in front of children who might understand far more than you think.)

Barbados is a great island for vacationing with kids. Safe beaches, particularly along the west coast, and numerous activities and attractions make for a holiday the whole family can enjoy. Submarine trips, wildlife reserves, nature sanctuaries, horseback riding, water sports, including snorkeling, kayaking, and swimming lessons, are all available.

Some hotels offer Kids' Club facilities, allowing parents to spend time alone without worrying, and it is easy to find babysitters at a cost of approximately $20 BDS ($10 US) per hour, plus transport home.

The following attractions are great for both adults and children. Make sure that children are well protected from the sun and heat and you will all enjoy a great time

★★Barbados Wildlife Reserve

The Wildlife Reserve (Farley Hill St Peter, ☎ 246 422 8826) is located in a natural mahogany forest, across the road from the Farley Hill National Park in the parish of St Peter.

Entering through the gates of the Barbados Wildlife Reserve you find yourself in a magical mahogany forest filled with green monkeys, ducks, turtles, tortoises, peacocks, otters, raccoons, agoutis, deer, macaws, porcupines, flamingos, parrots and pythons. Take a journey of discovery and wonder as you stroll through over one mile (1.6 km) of wooded trails winding through the forest.

All the animals, except the pythons and parrots, roam freely throughout the forest, so it is important to walk slowly and quietly. The animals are in their natural environment so, unlike animals in a zoo, you have the unique opportunity of seeing them behave naturally.

Brought to the island from Africa in the late 17th century, the green monkeys are now one of the biggest attractions at the reserve. The best time to see them is late afternoon when they come out to feed.

There is an exotic orchid collection, and an iguana sanctuary, where you can see an endangered species of Cuban iguana, a walk-in aviary, where the screeching macaws compete with other parrots to see who can make the most noise, and an information center where you can learn about the animals' habitats and history.

There are plenty of places to sit, rest, and just watch the animals. There is also a café and shop on-site where you can buy a snack and cold drink, which you may need, as it can get quite hot.

The entrance fee to the Wildlife Reserve includes admission to the adjoining Grenade Hall Forest and Signal Station, so be sure to visit once you've completed your tour of the reserve.

The admission fee is $11.50 adults, kids 12 and under $5.75.

Grenade Hall Forest & Signal Station

Built in the 1800s, the signal station is one of six towers erected at strategic points around the island. By using flags or semaphores, intelligence and other information could be relayed from Bridgetown to the north of the island. Restored to its original state, the interior of the tower now houses a series of exhibitions and historic artifacts.

Grenade Hall Forest encompasses a coral stone pathway with educational resources along the way that provide you with an opportunity to learn about, and appreciate, the natural environment.

Open daily from 10 am to 5 pm. Farley Hill, St. Peter, ☎ 246 422 8826.

Grenade Hall Signal Station

★★Harbour Master Cruise

The Shallow Draught Harbour, Bridgetown Port, Bridgetown, ☎ 246 430 0900, fax 246 430 0901, tallships@sunbeach.net.

The MV *Harbour Master* is a custom-built, floating entertainment center. 100 feet long, 40 feet wide and four decks high. It features a 70-foot water slide, dance floor, and air-conditioned restrooms with hot and cold fresh water showers.

Facing page: Wildlife Reserve resident

The Bajan Village Life Lunch Cruise captures the spirit of Barbados as local characters from the past entertain and take you back to old Barbados. The cruise also has cooking demonstrations, tasting sessions, a buffet lunch, interactive games, and an onboard Craft Village with artisans displaying their work.

MV Harbour Master

At the beach stop kids can play on a safe sandy beach, snorkel on a nearby reef, or the more adventurous can try the 70-ft water slide. Then, on the journey home, a live calypso band will entertain you.

★★★ Harrison's Cave

Harrison's Cave (www.barbados.gov.bb)

The Caves are located near the geographical centre of Barbados, in the parish of St Thomas.

The tour starts in the theater with an audio-visual show documenting the fascinating and unique geological history of Barbados, as well as the wonders of the cave.

After the show, accompanied by a guide and driver, you board the trams for the stunning ride underground. What follows is a spectacular journey through vast caverns, with waterfalls thundering over ledges into crystal-clear pools, and thousands of stalactites and stalagmites.

There is a Visitor's Centre that provides refreshments, handicraft shops, and an exhibit of Amerindian artifacts, excavated from sites around the island.

Children $7, adults $16.

Welchman Hall, St. Thomas, ☎ 246 438 6640, fax 246 438 6645.

★★Graeme Hall Nature Sanctuary

Entering the Graeme Hall Nature Sanctuary, an unspoiled view of the peaceful environment spreads out before you. The swamp's red and white mangrove trees provide a natural habitat for more than 40 species of birds, and are a temporary home for a large number of migrant and wintering water and shore birds. As you follow the winding path of the boardwalk, you get a close-up view of the mangroves and marine life. Placed on trees throughout the sanctuary, are information boards describing the flora and fauna. Green monkeys and mongooses can often be seen flitting along the path and through the trees, while several species of rare plants can be found in the swamp,

Stork at Graeme Hall Nature Sanctuary

including the button creeper (with pink stems and white flowers) and sedges (tall plants that grow over three feet (one meter) high. There is also an enclosed area, which is home to parrots, the scarlet ibis, and a large collection of flamingos.

The sanctuary is the perfect way to experience the unique beauty of a mangrove swamp. Located in the parish of Christ Church, it has the largest expanse of inland water in Barbados.

Christ Church, ☎ 246 435 9727, fax 246 435 7078, admin@graemehall. com.

★★Ocean Park

"Walk underwater without getting wet!"

Ocean Park, ☎ 246 420 7405, fax 246 420 7406, info@oceanparkbarbados. com, is a fully interactive marine aquarium, where kids and their families can discover the spectacular underwater world of Barbados.

Feeding demonstrations, a walk-through underwater tunnel, pools where children can touch and feed the fish, and 26 displays and exhibits that explain the undersea world provide a fascinating and interactive experience for kids of all ages.

Ocean Park

The park has a play area, "Shark Bites," restaurant & bar, souvenir shop and Pirate Adventure mini golf.

The Living Reef explores the diverse and exotic world of the coral reef and is home to a multitude of colorful reef fish including bonnethead sharks and the graceful, acrobatic cownose rays. The Touch Pool allows kids to pick up various creatures. The Ocean Encounter display is a 100,000-gallon salt-water aquarium housing the parks three nurse sharks, blacktip reef sharks and barracudas. Don't miss the "feeding frenzy" every day at 4 pm.

The Freshwater Falls showcases fish and animals from the Amazon River and beyond. You can buy small amounts of food to feed the fish.

Watch stingrays as they gracefully glide through the water

Open 9 am-6 pm daily – tickets are valid all day. Combo tickets with Mini Golf are also available. Adults $17.50/ $35 BDS, children four-12 $10/ $20 BDS, children under four free, seniors and students $12.50/$25 BDS.

Barbados Museum

St Ann's Garrison, ☎ 246 427 0201, 246 436 1956, fax 246 429 5946, admin@barbmuse.org.bb, www. barbmuse.org.bb.

The Barbados Museum, located at the Garrison, is housed in the former British Military Prison. There is a chil-

Barbados Museum

dren's gallery, 'Yesterday's Children,' which provides an informative and educational voyage back into Barbadian history. There are also special programs for children.

Disabled access. Open 9 am-5 pm Mon-Sat, 2 pm-6 pm Sunday. Closed on public holidays. Admission: adults $11.50, children $5.75.

★★Atlantis Submarine

Visions of *Titanic* and all the other undersea movies you've ever seen come back, as the submarine slowly descends and then makes its way to a sunken shipwreck. (See *Land of Adventure* for more details). ☎ 246 436 8929, www.atlantisadventures.com/barbados.

Atlantis Submarine

★★Adventure Beach at the Boatyard

Adventure Beach

This hotspot in Bridgetown has something for everyone. Kayaks, pedal boats, glass bottom boats, banana boat rides, rope swinging, ocean trampolines, beach volleyball and snorkeling. ☎ 246 436 2620, fax 246 228 1720.

★Power Snorkeling

An exciting snorkel experience that uses a special hand-held power "scooter," James-Bond style. You are outfitted with snorkel gear and the guide explains the proper use of the snorkel gear and power scooter. A 15-minute ride on a power catamaran takes you into historic Carlisle Bay, home to the famed wrecks *Berwyn* and *Cornwallis*.

Once you are comfortable with your snorkeling equipment, you receive your individual power scooter. The scooters are simple to use and safe to operate. After a few minutes orientation, your guide leads you on a fascinat-

Power snorkeling

ing tour over wrecks dating from the early 1900's.

Atlantis Adventure Center located at Shallow Draught, Bridgetown, ☎ 246 436 8929.

★Island Safari Adventure 4x4 Tours

ATV Safari

Adventure 4X4 Tours (☎ 246 429 3687 or 246 418 3687) and Island Safari (☎ 246 429 5337) provide off-road tours in Land Rovers and Patrol Safaris. You travel through 10 of the 11 parishes of Barbados, visiting areas not normally seen by visitors, particularly along the north and east coasts. Tours begin at 8. 30 am and include a number of scenic stops where rum and fruit punch is offered. Lunch is provided at a local restaurant and the tour drops you back at your hotel at about 3.30 pm.

 Note: The tours spend considerable time traveling off-road, along bumpy tracks and unmarked trails. They are not suitable for anyone with back problems and, at five hours, young children will probably get bored and tired. People with back, heart or physical conditions and women who are pregnant, should not participate.

Minimum age is five years old and an adult must accompany children five-12 years old.

This safari offers many stops, including two on the beach and an opportunity for a swim after lunch at the local beach.

8 am to 2:30 pm. Daily departures. Adults $77, children $47.50.

Another alternative is the **land and sea safari**. This tour starts with a 4 x 4 Safari exploring the countryside and eastern coastline, then switches to the *Tiami Catamaran* to ride the waves. Next you relax in the sun, or swim, and snorkel with turtles. All snorkel equipment is included. 8/ 8:30pm-3:30/4 pm every Saturday. Adults $117.50, children $60.

★Mini Buggy Safari & Swim

Foster's Funland in St Peter, is the headquarters of the Mini Buggy Safari and Swim adventure. The Mini Buggy is a two-seater, fully roll-caged, all-terrain vehicle with an extended wheelbase and 10-inch ground clearance. Its extra-large cockpit and all-terrain suspension make this a fun and safe vehicle to drive.

Upon arrival, your guide will take you through a short safety briefing and operating procedure. After selecting your helmets, you climb into your Mini Buggy and embark convoy-style for your tour through the rugged north coast. The guide determines the pace for the next hour of off-road fun while you enjoy the beauty of Barbados. Once off-road, you hardly see another person as you explore the landscape with the Atlantic Ocean on one side and the Scotland Hills of St Peter and St Andrew on the other.

After the safari, you take a coach to the west coast where you can enjoy a cool drink and a 30-minute swim at Paradise Beach.

Duration: 3½ hours. Includes helmet, tropical punch, sodas, and rum punch. Minimum age: five years. Cost $100 per buggy. ☎ 246 418 3687.

★Snuba

If you've never snorkeled, or even if you've never swum, you can Snuba. Snuba is a unique, shallow-water diving system that bridges the gap between snorkeling and scuba diving.It's great for families, children eight years and older, and seniors.

Snuba divers breathe underwater by means of a 20-foot airline, connected to a standard scuba tank mounted on a raft at the surface. The raft follows you as you move around underwater. Guided by a diving professional, you can swim close to the surface or descend to the ocean floor.

Snuba diving (surfsupusa)

Start in shallow water and take as much time as necessary to get comfortable breathing underwater. Once comfortable, you take a guided underwater tour. You'll feel as if you're swimming in an aquarium surrounded by tropical fish. A great experience for both young and old.

Contact **Ocean Adventures** at ☎ 246 438-2088, fax 246 438-3650, oceanadventures@sunbeach.net, www.oceanadventures.bb.

★★★Sea Turtle Project

Swimming with turtles is an amazing experience for both adults and children and will certainly be a highlight of your trip. Barbados is home to a large population of hawksbill and leatherback turtles. Once endangered

by over-fishing, these great creatures are now protected and monitored throughout the island.

Turtles are sociable and tend to stay in the same area, following a steady routine. They can be seen playing and feeding along the inshore reefs. In certain monitored areas, they are relatively tame, and have become accustomed to humans. You can swim with them as they feed among the coral. A good way to do this is with a sailboat tour and snorkeling picnic.

★★Catamaran Sailing

Sail along Barbados' calm, crystal-clear waters to a secluded bay, where you can swim with the sea turtles, stroll on the beach or sunbathe on deck. Explore a shipwreck where you can feed schools of tropical fish in the shallow waters, and discover a spectacular world of underwater life. Snorkeling gear is provided, and the crew can quickly teach you this easy skill. While anchored, a delicious lunch with wine and dessert is served onboard.

Heatwave catamaran

Cool Runnings Catamaran Cruises, ☎ 246 436 0911, fax 246 429 2596, info@coolrunningsbarbados.com.

Silver Moon Luxury Catamarans, 60 Clerview Heights, Stage 1, St Michael, ☎ 246 438 2088, fax 246 438 3650, oceanadventure@sunbeach. net, www.oceanadventures.bb.

Tiami Catamaran Cruises, Bridge House, Cavans Lane, Bridgetown, ☎ 246 427 7245, fax 246 431 0538.

Heatwave Sailing Cruises, ☎ 246 228 8142, 246 228 7720

Barbados Blue, Hilton Hotel, ☎ 246 434 5764, barbadosblue@caribsurf. net.

El Tigre Cruises, 28 Prior Park Terrace, St James, ☎ 246 417 7245, fax 246 421 7582.

Just Breezing Water Sports, Holetown, St James, ☎ 246 432 7645, fax 246 432 7062, contactus@justbreezingwatersports.com.

Good Times Watersports, 1st Avenue Lower Carlton, St James, ☎ 246 422 1900, info@goodtimesbarbados.com.

Kid Friendly Restaurants

There are numerous restaurants and cafés where children are welcome. The following are some that particularly cater to children.

Chefette operates 14 restaurants, two Barbecue Barns and nine drive-throughs. Located throughout the island they offer good fast food at reasonable prices. The menu includes rotis, pizza, chicken pieces and nuggets, burgers, salads, and sandwiches. They also offer a vegetarian menu. Seven of the Chefettes have Kids Zones, with slides, cars and rides.

The island may be the only place left in the world where there are no McDonald's!

Pizzaz serves pizza, burgers, and fish. It is located in Sunset Crest on the West Coast and has its own playground.

There are a few **KFCs** on the island and a number of pizza restaurants. The **Bean N' Bagel** cafés are good spots for breakfast and snacks throughout the day.

It is not hard to find places to take children out to eat in Barbados. While there are probably more along the south coast of the island than on the west coast, there are plenty there too.

Cocomos, in Holetown on the West Coast, has a special children's menu, and supplies crayons to play with. The children's menu includes flying fish fingers, burgers, chicken and chips, and jumbo hot dogs.

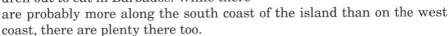

Culture, Art & Music

When yuh en' got horse, ride cow.
(Use whatever resources are available.)

Barbados was an English colony from 1627 right up until independence in 1966. It is the first island west of Africa and was a major stop in the slave trade. Thousands of slaves were shipped to Barbados, either to work on the sugar plantations or as a stop on the way to other islands and North America. The two influences, English and African, shape the society and create a uniquely Bajan culture. It shows up everywhere, from the schoolchildren in their school uniforms to the calypso heard throughout the island, and from the quintessentially English cricket matches, to the African-influenced art found in galleries and sold on the roadside.

Many of the festivals also serve to accentuate this fusion, from Crop Over, to the Celtic Festival. The religion is predominantly Anglican, but the gospel singing is like nothing you'll hear in an English church.

Music

Barbados is often called the music capital of the Caribbean. Many of the bands and singers have become popular way beyond the border – from Roy Haynes, one of the greatest jazz drummers, to 17-year-old Rihanna, whose massive worldwide hit *Pon De Replay* blasted out of radios and in clubs in the summer of 2005. The Merrymen of Barbados toured throughout North America, bringing a touch of sun everywhere they played. Other popular artists include The Mighty Gabby, David Kirton, Krosfyah, Arturo Tappin, and The Plantation Band.

Much of the music you hear in Barbados, although it did not originate on the island, has been adapted, influenced and improved by the island's musicians and composers.

Kid Site

Facing page: Monkey in the Barbados Wildlife Reserve (Rodney Nelson)

Calypso

Calypso originated in Trinidad. The rhythms are infectious but the lyrics often provide serious social commentary on the issues of the day. Bajan "Kaiso men have invented new rhythms, Ring Bang, derived from "Tuk" and Ragga Soca. The inventions of the Red Plastic Bag, a legendary Calypso band, have set Barbados apart from the calypso of other islands.

Soca

Barbados is the undisputed leader in "Soca," a more upbeat version of calypso. By continually inventing and incorporating new rhythms and new songs, Bajan musicians dominate the Soca world, locally and internationally.

Steel Pan

Steel bands are the sound of the Caribbean. Originally from Trinidad, steel bands can now be found everywhere. The pans, made out of old oil drums, are beaten into shape and tuned. Many schools in Barbados have added steel pan bands to their curriculum and some great musicians are graduating from the schools. Bands range in size from 10 to over 30 musicians and the music covers everything from calypso to classical.

Soca artist, Kimberley Inness

Tuk

Tuk bands are indigenous to Barbados. Tuk is an amalgam of British military marching music and African rhythms. The music evolved when slaves, using the drums of the British military, combined them with their own instruments and rhythms. Using drums and penny whistles, the group play rhythms, unique in both style and cadence, starting with a slow waltz, and then evolving into a march rhythm, before finally taking on the irresistible rhythms of Africa.

Roving groups of musicians, often dressed in comical attire and accompanied by local folk characters, dance and play their way through the crowds at the Crop Over festival and at Christmas and New Years.

Spouge

Spouge is a style of music created by Jackie Opel. It is a fusion of Ska and calypso, combined with sea shanties, spirituals, folk, hymns and classical music.

On a visit to Barbados, you can hear music from all over the world. Jazz, opera, R&B, classical, calypso, reggae and gospel are all featured in the various festivals and clubs around the island. You can hear local artists alongside international stars at the Jazz festival, Holders season, Gospelfest and numerous other festivals.

Enjoy local music and discover the history of Barbados at **Bajan Roots and Rhythms**. Or, head to **The Plantation Garden Theatre** and hear The Plantation Band, one of the best bands on the island playing music that varies from the cultural rhythms of the Caribbean, to the hits of Motown.

Terencia TC Coward

Bajan Roots and Rhythms, The Plantation Theatre, St. Lawrence Main Road, Christ Church, ☎ 246 428 5048, fax 246 420 6317, plantationrest@sunbeach.net.

Bajan artists have gained exposure and recognition throughout the Caribbean and the world. While you're in Barbados, enjoy the sights, feel the sun, and let the music move you.

Art Galleries

Barbados is home to an enormous range of artists and art galleries, everything from the smallest one-man foundry in the world, at the home of Bertalan, who makes metal sculptures, to Chalky Mount, where almost the whole village is involved in the manufacture and sale of pottery, to the Barbados Art Gallery, home of the national collection. You can find something for every taste and often meet the artists themselves.

The Art Foundry, Heritage Park, St Philip, ☎ 246 418-0714, fax 246 435-6361. The largest professional art gallery in Barbados, The Art Foundry exhibits the best of contemporary Caribbean art. Housed in a 17th-century coral-stone building in Heritage Park, the gallery displays, and offers for sale, paintings, sculptures, original prints, photographs, installation art and fine crafts. Open 9 am-5 pm on weekdays, and by appointment.

Barbados Arts Council, Pelican Village, Bridgetown, ☎ 246 426 4385. A forum and outlet for local artists to display their work, the setting showcases work by seasoned artists as well as newcomers. Exhibitions rotate monthly.

Barbados Gallery Of Art, The Garrison, St Michael. Opened in 1996, this is the home of the island's national collection. Featuring both visiting and permanent exhibits, the permanent displays rotate, so a variety of works can be viewed. Some prints are available for sale.

The Gallery's public hours are Tuesday through Saturday 10 am to 5 pm. There is a minimal admission fee. It is open year-round except for Barbadian public holidays.

Information about public programs and tours of the temporary exhibitions is available by calling ☎ 246 228-0149 Monday-Saturday during business hours.

Bertalan (sculpture), Marine Gardens, Christ Church. Contact the Kirby Gallery, ☎ 246 430 3032. Bertalan owns and operates the smallest, and perhaps only, one-man foundry in the world. His gallery and workshop are an integral part of his home, which you will find nestled in a little residential area just off the south coast main road. His metal sculptures are beautiful and definitely worth viewing. Bertalan displays his work in his garden and the studio areas of his home.

Beyond Aesthetics Gallery, 34 Regency Park, Christ Church, ☎ 246 228 0485. Original art and limited edition prints by John W.F. Walcott, and floral creations by Mary Walcott.

Earthworks Pottery

Earthworks Pottery, Edgehill, St Thomas, ☎ 246 425 0223. Goldie Spieler and her son David specialize in functional art pottery. Their work is unique and very Caribbean. You will find everything from individual showpieces to entire dinner place settings. They create art pieces as well as functional artistic pottery such as coffee mugs, plates and containers.

Freedom Fine Art Gallery, Shop # 10, Chattel Village, Holetown, St. James, ☎ 246 432 7047. A showcase for contemporary Bajan and Caribbean art.

Gallery of Caribbean Art, Speightstown, St. Peter, ☎ 246 419 0858, and The Hilton, Needhams Point, St. Michael, ☎ 246 434 5765. Various exhibitions showing the talent and diversity of Caribbean art.

Gang of 4 Art Studio, The Cottage, Springvale Plantation, St. Andrew, ☎ 246 438 7883. Contemporary Caribbean art and sculpture featuring the work of Gordon Webster, Lillian Sten, Aziza and Ras Bongo Congo-l.

Kirby Gallery, The Courtyard Hastings (☎ 246 430 3032); The Boatyard Bridgetown (☎ 246 430 3033). The gallery contains a collection of original works by many top local artists. It has a wide selection of regional works in all types of media, and in styles ranging from realistic to abstract. The gallery also carries a selection of prints alongside the fine art collection.

The Launching
(Virgil Broodhagen, Kirby Art Gallery)

Mango's Fine Art Gallery, Speightstown, St Peter, ☎ 246 422 0704, fax 246 422 0296, info@mangosart.com. Mango's exhibits the work of Michael Adams. The works depict Creole and island life, botanical gardens and waterfalls from around the world. Open evenings or by appointment.

Medford Mahogany & Craft Village (Lower Barbarees Hill, St Michael, ☎ 246 427-3179) is the most recognized center for Bajan mahogany souvenirs and gifts. Owned by self-taught artist Dr. Reggie Medford, the three shops feature hand-carved birds, boats, fish, clocks and other crafts. Visitors are encouraged to watch and photograph the craftsmen as they work.

On The Wall, Tides Restaurant, Holetown, St James, ☎ 246 424 8329. Local and regional art exhibited on the walls of the bar, courtyard and reception areas of the restaurant.

Pelican Village, Bridgetown. Located on the outskirts of Bridgetown, it is a great place to browse and purchase local art and crafts. (See St Michael)

Potter's House, Shop Hill, St Thomas, ☎ 246 425 3463. A collection of works by various local artists and craftspeople, the gallery is located next to Earthworks Pottery at Shop Hill.

Rain Dance (On the Wall Gallery)

Queen's Park Gallery, Queen's Park, Constitution Row, Bridgetown, St. Michael, ☎ 246 427 2345. The venue for many of the island's public art, craft and photography shows and a major venue for national shows and exhibitions.

Verandah Art Gallery, Bridgetown, ☎ 246 426 2605. This upstairs gallery features original work by many of Barbados' top artists, carvers and sculptors. There is also work by Haitian artists, and local batik, ceramics and custom jewelry pieces.

Wild Feathers, St Philip, ☎ 246 423 7758. The studio-home of Geoffrey and Joan Skeete, who specialize in carvings and drawings of Caribbean birds. Their son, John and his wife, Monica's work are also displayed. Geoff's carvings and Joan's watercolors, prints and note cards are all on sale.

Winston Kellman Studio, by appointment, The Cottage, Little Buckden Plantation, St. Joseph, ☎ 246 433 2101, dekellmanart@hotmail.com. This studio presents the work of local artist Winston Kellman, who specializes in watercolor and charcoals. His free-form landscapes have a simple yet compelling quality.

Zemicon Gallery, Hincks St, Bridgetown, ☎ 246 430 0054. A contemporary gallery, exhibiting some of the best local artists. Open Tuesday to Friday 10 am-4 pm or by appointment

Art at Wild Feathers

Festivals

Throughout the year, Barbados hosts a number of festivals that showcase the depth and variety of its history and culture.

The **Jazz Festival** in February features a range of international and local artists at various locations on the island. Sit in the grounds of a ruined plantation house and listen to the music washing over you as some of the world's best musicians create intricate harmonies and complex rhythms.

Or, join in the celebrations of **Crop Over**, a five-week-long summer festival dating from the 1780's, when Barbados was the largest producer of sugar, and slaves celebrated the end of the sugar cane season. The festival begins with the ceremonial delivery of the last canes and the crowning of the King and Queen of the Festival

Bridgetown Market celebrates the festival with calypso music and Tuk bands wandering through the crowds as they shop for food and local crafts.

The Grand Kadooment

The festival continues with **Cohobblopot**, a huge carnival featuring the Kadooment bands displaying their elaborate costumes, while calypso bands perform.

"Queen of the Bands" at Cropover

Children can participate in the Kiddies Kadooment, where they can join their friends, dressed in colorful costumes and parade in front of the judges.

One of the main features of the Crop Over is calypso. Calypsonians are organized into "tents" (Conquerors, Untouchables, House of Soca, Pioneers, Stray Cats, etc) and compete for prizes and titles, including the Party Monarch, the Road March Monarch and the Pic-O-De-Crop Monarch.

The grand finale is the Grand Kadooment. The carnival parade features large bands with members dressed in elaborate costumes depicting different themes. The designers compete for the *Designer of the Year* prize while partiers dance along with the parade from the National Stadium to Spring Garden.

The weeklong **Holetown Festival** in February commemorates the settlement of Barbados in 1627. Highlighting culture, history, and arts and

"King Shango" at Cropover

crafts, the festival features street parades, fashion shows, concerts, music and theater.

With over 100 different religions practiced in Barbados it is no surprise that there is a festival celebrating their music. Gospel artists from Barbados, the Caribbean, and around the world congregate to sing and celebrate in styles ranging from Reggae and Calypso to Jazz and Soul. You don't need to be a Christian; you don't even need to be religious to enjoy this spiritual and uplifting music!

With the arrival of Spring comes **Holders Season** featuring opera and musical theater performed outdoors at Holders House. New and emerging artists are featured alongside world-renowned performers such as Luciano Pavarotti and the London Symphony.

The artists, the musicians, the poets, playwrights and writers, along with the festivals, concerts and other performances all contribute to the cultural life of the island. So, visit for the sun, sand and sea, but be sure not to miss the music, art and culture.

Bridgetown

Bridgetown & the South

Bridgetown

Yuh can' stop yuh ear from hearing, but yuh can stop yuh mout from talking.
(Don't gossip.)

When the British landed on Barbados, it was uninhabited, but a primitive bridge was discovered over the Careenage in Bridgetown. It is believed that the Arawak, a people indigenous to the Caribbean, had constructed the bridge before being wiped out. The area was originally called Indian Bridge, then the Town of St Michael, and finally Bridgetown.

Two new bridges, the Chamberlain Bridge and the Charles Duncan O'Neil Bridge, have since replaced the original one.

The first settlers arrived in Carlisle Bay at the mouth of the Constitution River in 1628. Since that time, the city has grown and, like many other British cities, has been described as being planned after a long day in the local pub! By the mid-1660's there were more than 100 drinking houses, which worked out to about one house for every 20 residents or, to put it another way, 100 drinking houses for every 1 city planner!

Over the years, the city has been the victim of a number of fires, which burned down large portions of the city. In 1668, 80% of the city was destroyed, and in 1766, 26½ acres were destroyed, including 1,140 buildings and all the public offices.

Bridgetown is the only city outside of North America that George Washington visited. The house where he stayed has been reno-

George Washington House

vated, and is now known as the George Washington House. It is open to the public and you can visit it in the Garrison Historic Area.

Bridgetown is the capital city of Barbados and is on the south west coast in the parish of St Michael.

Shopping

Bridgetown is the main shopping center in Barbados and is home to a large and varied selection of shops. You will need to take your passport with you in order to take advantage of the tax-free shopping. If you are planning a purchase of high-end jewelry, precious stones, electronic or photographic equipment, the shops in Barbados offer some great duty free deals, some even sell at wholesale prices. Broad Street is the main shopping

Bridgetown shopping area (portreviews.com)

street and is home to DaCostas Mall the biggest shopping mall in Bridgetown. With more than 35 stores, it makes a great destination for the start of a day's shopping.

Bridgetown street vendor (portreviews.com)

The best time to go to Bridgetown is just after 9 am so you can miss the rush hour traffic and still be early enough to miss the midday heat. If you are out and it's too hot the shops and Malls are all air-conditioned, or you can head to the careenage and sit outside catching the breeze off the water while sipping something cool.

Shops in DaCostas Mall include **Tiffany & Co** known worldwide for their famous blue box that is sure to hold a fine piece of jewelry. Another store known across the Caribbean for its jewelry is **Little Switzerland**. Designer pieces from Baccarat, Baume & Mercier, Breitling, ESQ, Lalique, Lladro, Movado, Omega, Rado, Raymond Weil, Tag Heuer, and Tissot, are just some of the names they carry.

If your tastes are a little simpler **Ganzee** carries more than 300 designs of 100% cotton T-shirts. For clothing check out **Up Beat,** they offer a wide assortment of styles for men, women, and children, and a range of locally manufactured swimwear in a wide variety of bright, tropical colors.

Flamboya has a line of clothes, manufactured in Barbados, featuring hand-painted and hand-dyed tropical scenes on natural fabrics.

At **The Runway,** you can buy designer clothes and accessories at tax-free prices. Prada, Dior. Gucci, Versace and Armani are just some of the names you will see.

Finally, visit **Dingolay** for a selection of international clothing, shoes, bags, sarongs, accessories

Shops in the Cruise Terminal
(Barbados Tourism Authority)

and their own line of Dingolay clothing designed and made in Barbados.

And when you need to take a break from all that shopping, there are two food courts offering a large selection of lunches and snacks.

Also on Broad Street is the **Colombian Emeralds International** flagship store. The world's foremost emerald jeweler, they carry emerald jewelry at prices 20-50% less than US and European stores. They also carry diamonds from DeBeers and watches from, Omega, Ebel, Raymond Weil, Tag Heuer, Rado and Gucci. All purchases come with a Certified Appraisal and a free 90-day insurance replacement plan.

Diamonds International, the leading loose diamond, diamond jewelry and watch retailer in the Caribbean with over 80 stores throughout the region, has two locations on Broad Street and one at the Cruise terminal. Pick out your diamond or precious stone and they will design and create your very own unique piece of jewelry. You will also find watches from Audemars Piguet, IWC, Piaget, Cartier, Breitling, Ebel and Chopard.

The Royal Shop carries a selection of watches from, Rolex, Chopard, Girard-Perregaux, Longines, Movado, Seiko, Tissot and Citizen, and a selection of jewelry and figurines.

Cave Sheppard and **Harrison's** offer a wide variety of china, crystal, jewelry, perfume, liquor, clothing, electronics, and cameras.

If you're looking for bargains visit **Jewelers Warehouse** in the Norman Centre. Everything is 50% off regular pricing, appraisal included.

If you're not shopped out by now visit **The Galleria Mall**, and check out **Earth Mother Botanicals**, which produces the finest, uniquely Caribbean skin care products, including Embolic Sun Bloc and After Sun.

Your final stop on Broad Street is a shop no woman can resist – **Sunny Shoes.** This little shop will make custom shoes right on the spot, everything from sandals to dress shoes.

Leaving Broad Street, head to the waterfront Careenage, and visit **Colors of De Caribbean**. This store is known throughout the Caribbean

Bridgetown & the South

The Careenage

for sophisticated casual wear with a tropical flare. Look for fine hand-painted clothing made from imported fabrics, linen and silk and designer **Nefertari's** distinctive bold images of nature.

For the cigar lover a visit to Bridgetown wouldn't be complete without visiting **The House of Cuban Cigars**, next to the Waterfront Café on the Careenage.

Heading south out of Bridgetown, past the Careenage is **Bay Street**, where more unique shops can be found.

Cotton Days Designs by Carol Cadogan features hand painted clothing and accessories. **Cotton Days Designs** are made in Barbados from Sea Island cotton.

Dingolay, (see above) also have a store on Bay Street.

 Listings in this book with one star (★) are highly recommended. Those earning two stars (★★) are considered exceptional. A few attractions, resorts and restaurants rate three stars (★★★), which means they should not be missed.

Sightseeing

★★The Parish Church

The parish church of St Michael is on St Michael's Row in Bridgetown. The original church on this site was built in 1665; the current one dates from 1784. (For complete description see *St Michael*, page 94).

St. Michael's Parish Church

Central Bridgetown

River Road/Hwy 6

Crumpton

Queen's Park

Hwys 3, 4, & 5

Maidens

ichlow's

Church St

St. Michael's Row

Jordan's

Bus Terminal

Fairchild

O'Neale Bridge

Minibus Terminal

③

⑤

④

Spry

Bridge St

Dottins

Amens

Marhill

Rickett

Inner Basin

Bay Street/Hwy 7

Shurland

Farnell

Roebuck

Palmetto

②

Chamberlain Bridge

Independence Square

Parfitt

Magazine Ln-Hwy 2

Pinfold

⑥

James

High St

Middle St

Shepherd

Wharf

Cavans

Pierhead

⑧

Synagogue Lane

Colerdige

Victoria St

Henry

Broad

Philadelphia

Prince William

The Careenage

Caribbean Sea

Swan

Milk Market

McGregor

Tudor

Baxter's Road

Nile

Hincks

P

Reed

Suttle St.

Prince Alfred

P

Chapel

Lower Broad

Bus Terminal

Princess Alice Hwy

P

P

Harts

St. Mary's Row

⑦

Cumberland

P

Hwy I

Heliport

N

HUNTER PUBLISHING

500 FEET

150 METERS

1. National Heroes Square (Trafalgar Square)
2. Public Buildings
3. St. Michael's Cathedral
4. Central Bank Building
5. Frank Collymore Hall
6. Jewish Synagogue
7. St. Mary's Church
8. Waterfront shops & restaurants

P = CAR PARK

Parliament Buildings

Parliament

The Parliament Buildings were built in 1871, in a Neo-Gothic style. The West Wing was completed in 1872, and the East Wing in 1873. A tower was erected in the East Wing to accommodate a clock and a peal of bells, but in 1884 the clock tower had to be dismantled because the subsoil couldn't support the weight of the structure. In 1885, the clock and bells were relocated to their present position in the West Wing.

The upper floor of the East Wing houses the chambers and offices of the Legislative Council (the Senate) and the House of Assembly. The windows in the Senate depict the armorial bearings of past Presidents of Council and Speakers of the Assembly.

The West Wing houses public offices. Its stained glass windows depict British sovereigns from James I to Queen Victoria (and include Oliver Cromwell). On the main stairways of the West Wing are two stained glass windows, with the Biblical quotation, "Render to Caesar the things that are Caesar's". They were originally situated in the East Wing, over the Customs Department!

National Heroes Square

Originally called Trafalgar Square, with a statue of Lord Nelson erected in 1813, it predates the statue and square of the same name in London by 30 years. It was renamed National Heroes Square in 1999 to honor the national heroes of Barbados.

The Cenotaph, commemorating Barbadians killed in

National Heroes Square (www.barbados.gov.bb)

the two World Wars, was brought to Bridgetown on the SS *Intaba* in 1925. The names of the fallen from WW II were added in 1953.

The fountain in the square was built to commemorate the first running water piped in from Benn's Spring.

Queens Park

Queens Park was established over 90 years ago, on land that was bought in 1782 by General Gabriel Christie, who commanded the British troops in Barbados. The following year, he built Kings House, later during the reign of Queen Victoria, renamed Queen's House, as a residence for the army commanders-in-chief. Two additional buildings, The Retreat and The Pavilion, were constructed as quarters for senior staff officers.

When the British Garrison withdrew (1905-11), the property was taken over by the Bajan government and turned into a park. It was opened in 1909.

Bridgetown Synagogue

The Bridgetown Syna-gogue, built in 1654, is one of the oldest in the western world. Destroyed by a hurricane in 1831, it was rebuilt but fell into disrepair. In 1983, it was restored to its present state with its beautiful Gothic arches, and it is now a Barbados National Trust-protected building and an active synagogue.

Bridgetown Synagogue

Public Library

The Bridgetown Library on Coleridge Street is one of the many neoclassical libraries funded by Andrew Carnegie.

Montefiore Fountain

John Montefiore gave the Montefiore Fountain to the city in 1865, in memory of his father. Its original location was on Broad Street, where it served as a public drinking fountain. It was moved to its present location in front of the library in 1940, but is no longer operational.

Law Courts

Next to the library and adjoining the police station stand the law courts. The courts originally housed the jail, the courts, and the legislature, leading to the famous quote by Henry Coleridge, "His Majesty's Council, the General Assembly, the judge, the juries, the debtors and felons, all live together in the same house."

If you were to attend a court hearing today, you would see the same wigs and robes that have been worn in British courts for the last several hundred years.

Broad Street

The street was originally called Cheapside, then Exchange Street, New England Street and finally Broad Street. The impressive buildings that line the street are evidence of the city's importance and the wealth that flowed through it.

The Careenage

The Careenage (stab3)

The Careenage carves Bridgetown in two. During the rainy season, the constitution river flows into the Careenage and on into Carlisle Bay. Most of the charter fishing boats, yachts and dive boats operate from here. It was originally the main port, but has since been replaced, by the deep-water harbor, where the cruise boats berth. It is a great place to walk, shop, or catch a meal at the Waterfront Café.

Independence Arch

At the southern end of the Chamberlain Bridge stands the Independence arch. It was built in 1987 to commemorate 21 years of independence. The two pillars are decorated with reliefs of a pelican and flying fish, the two symbols of Barbados. Overhead is the coat of arms and the motto, "Pride and Industry."

The Queens Park Baobab Tree

There are two stories about the baobab tree in Queens Park. The first says it was brought to Barbados from Guinea around 350 years ago. The second says the area was originally a swamp; a seed blown from Guinea 1,000 years ago took root! Either way it is the largest tree of its kind in the Caribbean. Its circumference of 61½ ft (18 m) takes 15 adults with outstretched arms to cover! Another tree,

The Queens Park baobab tree

only slightly smaller, can be found on Warren's Road in St Michael. The trees are listed in the Seven Wonders of Barbados.

Adventures on Foot

Walking Tour of Bridgetown

Start at the **Independence Arch**, at the south end of the Chamberlain Bridge. Go north across the bridge to **National Heroes Square**, and the **Parliament** buildings. From the Parliament buildings walk east on St. Michael's Row, to **St.**

The Independance Arch (www.sunnybarbados.com)

Michael's Cathedral. Continue east to **Queen's Park**, and visit the playground to see the 300-year-old **baobab tree**. Go back along Constitution Road to St. Michael's Row and turn right on Marhill St., then right again on Palmetto St., left on Bruce Alley and you arrive at the **Bridgetown Synagogue**.

From the Synagogue, head west on James St. and north on Coleridge St. and you come to the public library, the law courts and the central police station. From the police station go south on Prince William Henry Street till you come to Broad Street. On the far west end of the street is the **Mutual Building**, a large green building with a silver dome built between 1894 and 1895. Walk east until you come to **DaCostas Colonnade**, a building with a pink and white façade that looks like a wedding cake. It is home to DaCostas Mall. After exploring the Mall, head south to the **Careenage**, and stop in at the **Waterfront Café** for a well-deserved cool drink by the water.

Adventures on Water

★★Deep Sea Fishing

 The best fishing is from December to April when wahoo, dorado, white and blue marlin, sailfish, yellow and black fin tuna are found in the waters around Barbados. Marlin pass by the island in September/October but the best months are February, March and April. Wahoo, barracuda, dolphin, marlin and sailfish are in the waters all year. Tuna are usually caught in the winter months. Most tropical species of shark are also present year-round.

Fishing is mostly on the South and West Coasts. The West Coast is protected from the prevailing easterly trade winds and is ideal for those with poor sea legs.

Barbados has a number of charter companies who will take you out for a day or half-day of deep-sea fishing. The charter captains have their favorite spots and, although there are no guarantees, there are always great opportunities!

Cannon Charters is a family-owned and -operated deep-sea big-game fishing company. They charter a 42-ft Hatteras, equipped with Penn International gold reels powered by twin 430-hp Diamond series Cummins diesel engines. They are ideal for comfortable fishing and cruising. All safety equipment is provided. Whole-day, half-day or shared charters. Tackle and bait provided. Included in the charter:

- Experienced crew
- Complimentary drinks and snacks
- Transportation to and from the boat

Contact Kathy Roach, ☎ 246 424-6107, fax 246 421-7582.

Predator Sportfishing is also a family-owned and -operated business. The captain has been fishing since he was old enough to hold a rod and reel. His numerous tournament successes include heaviest wahoo by points in both the 1996 and 2000 Mount Gay Rum/Mutual International

Tournament. He also claimed heaviest wahoo in the 2000 MGR/MIT and heaviest blue marlin by points in 1991.

Predator offers a fishing charter out of Bridgetown for wahoo, dolphin (mahi mahi), sailfish, marlin, tuna, barracuda and others. You fish in a classic, fully customized Bertram 25, with top-of-the-line electronics, a wide selection of quality tackle, plus full Coast Guard-approved safety equipment and insurance coverage. If you're not an experienced angler, they are happy to teach you.

Whole-day or half-day trips are available. Inshore/offshore fishing. Troll offshore for wahoo, dolphin (mahi mahi), sailfish, marlin, tuna and barracuda. Or, fish inshore on a reef or wreck for grouper and snapper. Shark fishing is also available. They are the only local outfit that offers light tackle as an option. They have a wide variety of tackle, from Penn International 50 VSWs to 6-lb spinning outfits, so you can match gear to your taste and skill level.

An inshore light tackle (trolling) trip is a popular choice among anglers with kids as it provides for regular action from tuna, jacks, barracuda, mackerel and more.

Quality bait and tackle provided, along with drinks & snacks.

The trip can be customized to suit your interest.

Predator Sportfishing encourages catch-and-release for billfish.

Contact Christopher Burke, ☎ 246 228-2774 (home), 246 230-1845 (boat).

IOU Charters is captained and crewed by its British owners Martyn and Angie. Angie has many years of catering experience in the UK, which ensures that you are well looked after and provided with some of the best snacks afloat, including freshly made cutters and a wide

IOU

selection of drinks. Martyn, at 63 years of age, can claim over 45 years of seagoing experience and has captained commercial fishing vessels up to 65 ft.

IOU is a specially built 36-ft Sports Fisherman, with full toilet facilities, a large sundeck, spacious cockpit with sun awning and plenty of seating both in the cockpit and on the flybridge. They encourage your participation by involving you in re-baiting the lines, steering the vessel and com-

I love my wahoo (IOU Charters)

ing up to the bridge, where the navigational instruments are explained. IOU recently underwent a major refit. Most of the fishing is trolling using outriggers and downriggers with well-tried and tested lures incorporating deadbaits. Sometimes they will drift with live baits. Reef fishing can be done but they require prior notice to arrange bait and special anchors.

They use short, stand-up rods, which allow you to handle big fish easily; lines are 50 to 80 lbs and they have recently re-equipped with Okuma 50W graphite lever drag reels. They use wind on leaders so you can play a big fish right to the boat.

☎ 246 429 1050, cell 246 238 9638, sunshine@sunbeach.net.

Honey Bea Charters provides a deep-sea fishing and coastal cruise service on a sleek 40-ft Cabin Cruiser Honey Bea 111. They employ an experienced captain accompanied by a professional angler mate. Charters are generally four hours (half-day) or eight hours (full day) for groups up to nine people.

Honey Bea 111 is a 40-ft custom-built sports avenger vessel, powered by twin 6-354 Perkins diesels with a freshwater shower and two cabins, including two heads. Safety equipment is included on-board. Fishing equipment includes five Penn Rods and Todd fishing chairs. ☎ 246-428-5344

Services provided by Honey Bea include:

- A dependable and comfortable boat.
- Transport to and from the boat berth.
- Light refreshments and alcoholic beverages, soda, beer, rum punch, sandwiches, snacks, etc.
- Fresh bait and well-maintained fishing tackle and equipment.
- Teaching how to fish for varieties of saltwater trophy fish such as wahoo, mahi-mahi (dorado), marlin, tuna, etc.
- Filleting of fish.

 For **submarine tours**, see *Land of Adventure, page 43.*

★★Power Snorkeling

For a unique underwater experience, try power snorkeling, offered by **Atlantis Adventure Center**. Using a hand-held "scooter," James Bond-style, glide through the water visiting the wrecks of the *Berwyn* and *Cornwallis* in Carlisle Bay and then explore the delicate beauty of the coral reef.

Power snorkeling (www.knownworld.com)

The power snorkel scooter is simple and safe to use and operate. Your guide instructs you in the use of the gear, and then takes you on a 15-minute ride on a power catamaran to Carlisle Bay. As soon as you are comfortable with the gear and its use, your guide takes you on a fascinating 30-minute guided tour. Participants must be in good physical condition and weigh less than 230 lbs. This tour is not suitable for children aged 11 years and under.

Monday to Saturday, 9, 11 am, 1, 3 pm. Pick-up from most hotels is available. Cost $57. Contact Atlantis Adventure Center, The Shallow Draught, ☎ 246 436 8929, fax 246 436 8828.

★★The Boatyard

The Boatyard is located on the outskirts of Bridgetown at Carlisle Bay. Its sandy white beaches, calm waters and tropical atmosphere, make it a great spot to relax. The wide range of activities, also make it a great spot to have fun. The boatyard comprises beachfront dining at the South Deck Grill, coastal cruises, water sports, snorkeling, scuba diving, and beach facilities at the boatyard Beach Club, Sharkey's Bar for a cool beer or exotic cocktail, the Shark Shak for souvenirs, and the Boatyard Night Club for live entertainment.

Freshwater showers, change rooms, beach games, and free shuttles to the cruise ships are all provided. Open 365 days a year.

The Boatyard is on Carlisle Bay, Bay Street, ☎ 246 436 2622/228 8142, fax 246 228 7720.

Adventures in the Air

Helicopter Tours

Bajan Helicopters offer a flight-seeing tour, taking you from Bridgetown in the southwest, past the beautiful beaches and luxury hotels along the Caribbean to the west. You fly over the rugged cliffs and pounding waves of the north and east, then inland over gullies, cane fields, villages,

Bajan Helicopters (www.funbarbados.com)

forests and other points of interest. Flying in air-conditioned comfort in five-passenger jet helicopters, you get a new appreciation for the island and its treasures.

Take your camera and video recorder and go home with a unique souvenir of the island. Prices start from $97.50 per person.

Bajan Helicopters, The Bridgetown Heliport, ☎ 246 431-0069, fax 246 431-0086, info@bajanhelicopters.com.

Cultural Excursions

Verandah Art Gallery

Located in the renovated Old Spirit Bond Mall overlooking the Careenage, Verandah features original work by local and international artists, carvers and sculptors. There is an interesting selection of work by Haitian artists, as well as batik, ceramics and custom jewelry. ☎ 246-426-2605.

Zemicon Gallery

Zemicon features original art works by leading artists in Barbados. Tue-Fri 10 am-4 pm or by appointment. Hincks St, ☎ 246 430 0054.

Spectator Sports

★★Cricket

Just to the west of the city is the 120-year-old **Kensington Oval**, home to international cricket in Barbados. Cricket at the Oval began in 1882 with the Pickwick Cricket Club. The first international match was played in 1895, and the first test match was played in 1930 when the West Indies and England played to a draw.

The Oval was rebuilt for the 2007 Cricket World Cup. It seats 28,000 and the area around the stadium has undergone a US$45 million redevelopment.

The Oval also hosts other events, including football, hockey, athletics, and concerts.

If there is a game playing while you are on the island you will be treated to a lively, not-to-be-missed, event. The Bajans take the game very seriously and certainly won't just sit and clap politely!

★★Horse Racing

There are three racing seasons – January to April, May to August, and October to December. Organized by the Barbados Turf Club, races take place at the Garrison Savannah, two miles outside of Bridgetown.

There are four major races on the Barbados racing calendar – The Sandy Lane Barbados Gold Cup, held on the first Saturday in March, and the three races of the Triple Crown: The

Race at the Barbados Turf Club (Junior Franklyn)

Banks Barbados Guineas in April, the Pinnacle Feeds Midsummer Creole Classic in July, and the United Insurance Barbados Derby in August.

There is a play park for kids and vendors selling a range of Bajan dishes, soft drinks and coconut juice for the kids, and beer and fine Bajan rum for the adults.

For a complete description, see *Land of Adventure*.

Barbados Turf Club, ☎ 246 426 3980, www.barbadosturfclub.com.

Where to Stay

Sweetcane Guest Apartments

Bridgetown is a great place to visit and explore, but there are no hotels or guesthouses other than the Sweetcane, which is on the edge of the city. Sweetcane offers four furnished apartments, one studio, two one-bedrooms, and one two-bedroom, in a residential area on the edge of Bridgetown. They are on the bus route for access to the rest of the island. Clean and affordable if you are on a very tight budget. $40 per person per night. Whitehall, St Michael, ☎ 246 424 0255.

Where to Eat

★The Waterfront Café

There are few restaurants in Bridgetown. The Waterfront Café is the best place to eat and has entertainment most nights. Otherwise, there is only a Chefette and the food court at the Broad Street Mall. The Waterfront Café has an all-day menu that includes local and regional foods such as flying fish, jerk chicken, cou cou, pepper pot, curry and shrimp, or international foods such as ceviche, samosas, and hamburgers. Entrées $12-$20. The Careenage, ☎ 246 427 0093, fax 246 431 0303, waterfrontcafe@sunbeach.net, www.waterfrontcafe.com.bb.

Nightlife

Most of the nightlife happens just a few miles away in Christ Church and St Michael, but Bridgetown does have some of it own hot spots.

★★Boatyard Bar & Grill

The beachfront Boatyard Bar & Grill on Bay Street has drinks, dancing, and live music four nights a week. Bay Street, ☎ 246 436 2622, fax 246 228 7720, boatyard@sunbeach.net, www.theboatyard.com.

★★Harbour Lights

Party at Harbour Lights

Also on Bay Street, they have live music, dancing and a Caribbean barbecue. There is a patio overlooking the ocean and they serve hot dogs, hamburgers, fish, and chicken. Monday, is beach party night; the cover charge of $49 includes transportation to and from your hotel so there is no problem getting home late at night. Marina Villa, Lower Bay Street, ☎ 246 436 7225, fax 246 436 5069, contactus@harbourlightsbarbados.com, www.harbourlightsbarbados.com.

★ The Waterfront Café

Sitting on the Careenage, the Waterfront Café has entertainment every night, and Tuesday features a Caribbean buffet with a live steel pan band. The Careenage, ☎ 246 427 0093, fax 246 431 0303, waterfrontcafe@sunbeach.net, www.waterfront-cafe.com.bb.

View from the Waterfront Café

★★ Baxters Road

For an authentic Bajan night out, head to Baxters Road late on Friday or Saturday night. Bajans run all the bars, and you can pub-crawl the street taking in the atmosphere and action until dawn. Plan to sleep in late the next day!

Bridgetown & the South

St. Michael

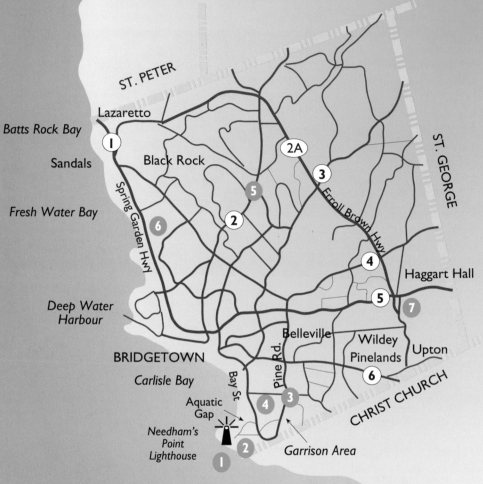

ST. PETER

Batts Rock Bay

Lazaretto

Sandals

Black Rock

Fresh Water Bay

Spring Garden Hwy

Errol Brown Hwy

ST. GEORGE

Haggart Hall

Deep Water Harbour

BRIDGETOWN

Carlisle Bay

Bay St

Pine Rd.

Belleville

Wildey Pinelands

Upton

CHRIST CHURCH

Aquatic Gap

Needham's Point Lighthouse

Garrison Area

Caribbean Sea

N

HUNTER PUBLISHING

2 MILES

3 KILOMETERS

1. Charles Fort
2. St. Anne's Fort
3. Barbados Museum
4. Barbados Gallery of Art
5. Tyrol Cottage Heritage Village (Tyrol Cot)
6. Mount Gay Rum Visitor's Center
7. Bussa Roundabout (Emancipation Monument)

St Michael

Yuh can' be in de church an' de chapel too.
(You can't be in more than one place at the same time –
another way of saying, mind your own business.)

The parish of St Michael is in the southwest of the island, with Christ Church to the south, St George to the west, St Thomas, and St James to the north. St Michael is home to Bridgetown, the capital. Bridgetown is the center of commercial activity on the island and houses the Deep Water Harbor and seaport.

Shopping

The main shopping area is Bridgetown. (For a description, see the Bridgetown chapter).

★Pelican Craft Center

The Pelican Craft Center

Harbour Rd, Bridgetown, ☎ 246 427-5350. Just outside of Bridgetown, on the Princess Alice Highway, is the Pelican Craft Center, a collection of workshops where craftspeople create and sell their work. It is one of the best places to buy unique pieces of art, and to see craftsmen creating pieces in glass, wood, batik, baskets, jewelry, metal, and pottery. There are also a number of shops, a wine bar and bistro, and a restaurant.

Every week, during the tourist season the center hosts the Pelican Dooflicky Carnival. This parade and show encourages visitors to join in with the entertainment.

Shops At The Center:

Carved wooden figures at the Pelican Craft Center

Pelican Variety Shoppe (Snacks, drinks, ice cream, toiletries, pharmaceuticals and film)

Tulis Batik Barbados (Original batik shirts, wraps, scarves, wall hangings, pictures and greeting cards)

Wintex Tees (T-shirts, polo shirts, hats, sunglasses and belts)

Islandcrafts (B'dos) Ltd. (Basketry, pottery, glass art, woodcraft, dolls, wire sculpture)

Bagnall's Point Gallery & Annex (Various exhibitions)

Collectors' Treasures (Pottery vases and ornaments, sundresses, cotton shirts, hand-painted stones)

Second Hand Rose (Recycled articles including books, dinnerware, lamps, furniture, linens, and pictures)

The Monkey Pot (Painted pottery, jewelry, souvenirs, hand-painted dresses and ties)

Scheper's Cork & Bottle Wine Bar & Bistro (Open-air dining and courtyard barbecue every Friday night)

The Barbados Crafts Council (Assortment of crafts from members of the council)

Roslyn of Barbados (Clay figurines, straw handbags, woven placemats, antique maps, books, masks)

Tortuga (Rum cakes, alcoholic beverages, key chains, postcards, etc.)

Art Whiz (Ceramic jewelry boxes, mirrors, lamps, cushions)

Medford Craft Gallery (Mahogany figurines, clocks, trophies, sculptures, key chains)

Gift Line (Shell crafts, jewelry, bathroom accessories, figurines and bead craft)

The Barbados Arts Council (Art gallery and shop of the Council, artwork and prints by island artists)

Artforms (Golden Calabash) (Mahogany sculpture, bowls, chambered boxes, and sea washed glass jewelry)

Hewitt's Metal Art (Forged metal figurines, clocks, candleholders, wall decorations)

Pottery at Pelican Craft Center

The Clay Gallery (Pottery items, including dinnerware, plant pots, wind chimes and candle shades)

Diane Crafts (Dolls of every description plus magnets, Christmas tree decorations and bags)

DeShakk Boutique (Cotton dresses, skirts, blouses, shirts, beach towels and wire craft)

Island Flavours & Gift Baskets (Rum cakes, sauces, sweets, syrups, gift baskets)

Cou-Cou Village Restaurant and Bar (Local cuisine with an island flavor. Dine indoors or in the courtyard. Karaoke every Friday night)

Workshops At The Center (Building #2, Ground Floor)

Indigenous Potteries (Production studio of one of the island's leading potters where you can see wheel throwing, mould-making and slab work)

Harwood Woodworks (Mahogany woodwork, mortar pestles, fruit/salad bowls, coasters and bud vases)

Pelican Prototype workshop (Model-making)

Val's Manufacturing (Sewing shop, offering sundresses, shirts, children's clothing and bags)

Mena's Arts and Crafts (Resin-moulded souvenir chattel houses, rum shops and wall plaques)

First Floor

Golden Calabash (Father and son team of wood sculptors)

Palona's (Artist and ceramic sculptor)

Skeete's Art Studio (Hand-painted figurines, oil paintings and souvenirs)

Building #3, Ground Floor

Ann's Craft Center (Straw handbags, purses, hats, cotton shirts)

Roots and Grasses (Woven baskets, planters, Khus-khus rugs, laundry baskets, bread baskets and exotic basket sculpture by Ghana-trained Barbadian basket weaver)

Bags from Ann's Craft Center

First Floor
Caribbean Cigar Co. Inc. (Watch Cuban cigars being made by hand)

Building #6, Ground Floor
Fine Art Framing Ltd. (Professional art framers and gallery)
Glass Creations (Watch glass blowers as they create interesting pieces)

First Floor
Hooper Garment Company (Textiles and apparel, including women's sleepwear and clothing, men's shirts, pillowcases, cushion covers, and custom-made pieces)
Tropical Weavers Ltd. (Loom weaving and handbag manufacturing – Home of "Exstrawdinary" baskets and handbags)

Medford Craft World

Medford Mahogany and Craft Village, located just outside Bridgetown, is the center for genuine Barbadian mahogany souvenirs and gifts. Owned by artist Dr. Reggie Medford, the three shops feature an array of hand-carved birds, boats, fish, clocks and other local crafts. You can watch, and photograph the craftsmen as they work.
Medford Craft Village, Lower Barbarees Hill, St Michael, ☎ 246 427-3179.

 Listings in this book with one star (★) are highly recommended. Those earning two stars (★★) are considered exceptional. A few attractions, resorts and restaurants rate three stars (★★★), which means they should not be missed.

Sightseeing

★★ The Parish Church

St. Michael's Parish Church

Built in 1784, St Michael's Cathedral is noted for its arched roof, which at one time was the widest in the world. The original wood church, built in 1641, on the site now occupied by Saint Mary's Church, proved too small, so a Col. William Sharpe donated the new site. The new church, built of stone, was destroyed by a hurricane in 1780. A third church was built in

1784. It could hold 3,000 worshippers and was the largest church outside of Europe. Severely damaged by a hurricane in 1831, it was repaired and is substantially the same church you see today. Built of coral stone in the classical style, it features the English tre-foil in the clerestory windows. It has galleries on three sides, with the organ, one of the best in the West Indies, in the west gallery. The Chapter Room is over the south porch and the Choir and Clergy Vestries over the north.

In 1938, a Chapel of the Blessed Sacrament was added. Covered with wallaba shingles, the roof of the Chapel is designed in the shape of an upturned boat. A small marble font situated at the western end of the Cathedral dates from 1680, and a number of monumental tablets and works of sculpture can be found on the walls. The bells in the Tower are no longer rung.

★Malibu Beach & Visitor Centre

Just to the north of Bridgetown is one of the most famous distilleries on the island. In business since 1897, and set on a beautiful white sand beach, the Malibu Beach & Visitor Centre offers visitors two options. An all-inclusive package that includes transportation to and from your hotel, a tour of the distillery, lunch at the beachside grill, four rum cocktails, and use of a beach chair. The second option includes the distillery tour, one rum cocktail, and use of a beach chair. Whichever option you choose, you should plan to spend an hour or two or even the whole day on the beach,

Malibu Beach Visitor Centre

where you can relax or enjoy a range of water sports after the tour. There is a small restaurant and beach bar, serving lunch and rum punch, as well as changing rooms, and showers.

Mon-Fri 9 am-5 pm. Admission $33, including lunch and transportation from your hotel. Basic tour $10; day pass $40.

Malibu Beach & Visitor Centre, Brighton, Black Rock, St Michael, ☎ 246 425 9393.

★Mount Gay Rum Tour

Mount Gay is the world's oldest rum distiller. As early as 1655, Barbados was producing 900,000 gallons of rum each year. The history of rum is also the history of Barbados. The tour starts with a 15-minute video that gives a brief history of the island and explains the traditional processes of rum-

Mount Gay Rum distillery bar

making – refining, ageing, blending & bottling, and the ancient craft of barrel assembly. Then, to finish the tour, you get a taste of the rum in the distillery bar. There is also a restaurant with a shady veranda overlooking the ocean, where you can enjoy traditional Bajan cuisine while sipping rum cocktails.

45 minute tours 9 am-3:45 pm Monday to Friday. Admission $6. Special luncheon tours available.

Mount Gay Rum Tour Experience, Mount Gay Rum Visitors' Centre, Spring Garden Highway, Bridgetown, ☎ 246 425 9066, fax 246 425 8770.

★★ Tyrol Cot House & Heritage Village

Constructed in 1854, this was the home of Sir Grantley Adams, the first premier of Barbados and the only Prime Minister of the Federation of the West Indies. The home is also the birthplace of his son, Tom, the second Prime Minister of Barbados. Tyrol Cots' mix of

Tyrol Cot

Palladian and tropical architecture, restored by the Barbados National Trust, is filled with the Adams' antique furniture and memorabilia.

Next to the house is The Heritage Village, which features a number of chattel houses, displaying the work of traditional craftsmen and artists. The village is a faithful replica of a 1920s Bajan village, which graphically shows the difference in lifestyles between the landowners and the workers. The chattel houses are typical of the island. Their size was dictated by the fact that farm workers did not own the land on which they lived and, if they changed employment, their house had to be small enough to move to the next estate.

There is also an 1820s stone and straw slave quarters, a blacksmith's museum, a carriage house and stables, an original outhouse, and a traditional Rum Shop serving sandwiches, fish cakes, and, of course, rum!

Leather goods, ceramics, pottery, clothing,

Tyrol Cot interior

artworks, and local confections can all be purchased at the village.

Open Monday to Friday, 9 am to 5 pm; $11.50 for adults, children half-price.

Tyrol Cot Heritage Village, Codrington Hill, St Michael, ☎ 246 424 2074, fax 246 429 9055.

★★Baobab Trees

There are two enormous baobab trees in St Michael, the largest at Queen's Park, the other, only slightly smaller, at Warren's Road. There are different theories as to how and when they arrived here. One says a seed from Guinea was blown here over 1,000 years ago and took root. The other theory suggests they were brought to Barbados in 1738, making them about 250 years old. Whatever theory is correct, they are enormous, one with a circumference of 44½ feet (13.6 m), the other in Queen's Park 51½ feet (18½ m). It takes 15 adults with outstretched arms to envelop its circumference! These two Baobab trees are among the "Seven Wonders of Barbados."

The Bussa Emancipation Statue

Bussa was the leader of a slave uprising in 1816. The rebellion, known as the Bussa Rebellion, was the first in Barbados since

The Emancipation Statue

1692. Born free in Africa, captured and brought to Barbados as a slave in the late 18th century, he led a band of 400 freedom fighters into battle at Bayley's on Tuesday April 16. He was killed in the battle and the uprising was defeated.

The statue created by Bajan sculptor Karl Broodhagen, was unveiled in 1985, 169 years after the revolt. In 1999, Bussa was named a national hero of Barbados. The statue stands on the Bussa roundabout on the Earl Barrow Highway. The inscription reads: Lick an Lock-up Done Wid/Hurray fuh Jin Jin (Queen Victoria)/De Queen come from England to set we free/Now Lick an Lock-up Done Wid,/Hurray fuh Jin Jin. This was what the slaves' chanted when apprenticeship was finally abolished in 1838.

National Ordnance Collection of Barbados

During the 17th & 18th centuries, Barbados was an important military base for the British, who imported an enormous number of cannons into the island. As needs and armaments changed, and conflicts ended, the cannons were abandoned. The government recently made a decision to gather them together, and create a National Ordnance Collection of all the old guns on the island – more than 400 were collected!

Ordnance Collection (Ian Clayton, AXSES Inc)

They were found everywhere – on beaches, in gardens, buried under fortifications, and even embedded in the sides of buildings. Charles Trollope, an English apple farmer (who also happens to be a world authority on ordnance), was invited to Barbados to catalogue the collection. He arrived armed with copies of the Royal Armoury archives from the Tower of London. The British, like the Spanish with their bullion, kept meticulous records of all cannons shipped to and from the West Indies. The oldest cannon was cast in 1620, the youngest, and the rarest was cast in 1870. It was called the Victoria Gun and is the first rifled muzzle loader made in England. Besides the English cannon, guns from Sweden, Spain and Holland have all been found.

You can see 26 of the most important pieces in the collection, mounted in front of the Main Guard House in the Garrison Savannah.

For further information on the National Ordnance Collection of Barbados, Contact: Major Michael Hartland, The Main Guard House, The Garrison, St Michael, ☎ 246 426 8982, fax 246 429 6663.

Mallalieu Motor Collection

If you love vintage cars take some time to visit the Mallalieu Motor Collection. Bill Mallalieus' collection of automobile accessories and vintage cars includes Bentleys, Daimlers, Humbers, Triumphs, and other unique cars. Entry fee $5 US. Open every day.

Mallalieu Motor Collection, Pavilion Court, Historic Garrison, ☎ 246 426-4640.

Adventures on Foot

Hiking

The Barbados National Trust organizes Sunday walks at 6am and 3:30 pm The hikes are listed in the newspaper, or you can obtain a schedule for $2.50 from the National Trust, ☎ 246 426 2421, fax 246 429 9055.

Adventures on Wheels

★Island Safari

Island Safari of Barbados offers a variety of 4X4 Jeep Safari Tours. Tours take you through the gullies, forests, and out-of-the-way spots on the island that are inaccessible to ordinary vehicles. You can also do a tour of Rum Shops, or combination tours on land and sea.

The Adventure Safari takes you to the east and northeast, where you will see some of the most magnificent sites on the island. The Discovery Safari visits hidden bays and beaches. The Land and Sea Safari explores the island on land and on water. Or take the Jeep Safari and Kayak Adventure. And, for a real taste of the island, take the Rum Shop Safari (must be 18 or older).

Island Safari

Adventures on Water

Beaches

 ★★Pebbles Beach. Located on the South Coast, it has a children's play area, benches for picnics and a lifeguard on duty. It is a beautiful beach for swimming, and the one next door, on the other side of the Hilton Hotel, is a turtle-nesting beach. You are quite likely to meet a turtle or two while you're swimming. You can pet and swim with them.

![Brownes Beach photograph]

Brownes Beach (www.barbados.org)

★★Brownes Beach. Continues from Pebbles Beach and into Carlisle Bay. It is a great beach for swimming, with disabled access, and a lifeguard on duty.

★Carlisle Bay. A crescent-shaped bay with a man-made underwater park. Shipwrecks make it great for scuba diving. It is a popular beach with both locals and visitors. The Boatyard provides most of the beach activities. After paying the entrance fee you can use the beach chairs, umbrellas, kayaks, pedal boats, ocean trampolines, giant iceberg climb and slide, beach volleyball, showers, and the bar and restaurant.

★Drill Hall Beach. A large beach with beautiful pink sand on the South Coast. It is a favorite surf spot, because of its shallow reef. There are strong waves, which makes it not very safe for swimming, but there is a lifeguard on duty. They have a car park and plenty of trees and picnic tables

★★Brandon's Beach. A large beach, just off the Spring Garden Highway, with beautiful sand and great water for swimming. There are changing facilities with toilets and showers, a volleyball net, picnic tables and plenty of trees for shade. You can rent beach chairs, umbrellas, kayaks and other non-motorized water sports equipment, and there is a lifeguard on duty as well as beach security personnel.

Weisers on the Beach offers international and Barbadian cuisine with prices ranging from $8-$24.

★★**Brighton Beach**. At the opposite end of the bay from Brandon's, with the same white sand and calm clear water.

Carlisle Beach

Scuba Diving

 St Michael is home to numerous dive shop operators, and Barbados offers some spectacular diving on reefs and wrecks. The following is a list of some of the operators.

The Dive Shop Ltd. Founded in 1965, it is a PADI, NAUI and ACUC Training Facility. They have classes for beginner, intermediate and advanced levels. Offering over 20 dive sites on both the West and South Coasts, dives are from 10 to 130 feet, including shallow and deep reef dives. Also offered are antique bottle dives, and a multitude of shipwrecks, including a 70-foot WWI French tugboat sunk in 1919 and the *Stavronikita*, a 365-foot wreck. All dive packages include transportation to and from your hotel or the Cruise Terminal.

The Dive Shop Ltd., Pebble Beach, Bay Street, St Michael, ☎ 246 426 9947, fax 246 426 9947, www.divebds.com.

Barbados Blue Water Sports. They offer a wide range of water sports including jet skiing and boogie boarding, snorkeling, and PADI certified scuba diving. Located at the Hilton Hotel they arrange snorkeling over wrecks, scuba lessons by PADI certified instructors, swimming in the endangered turtle habitat, and hand-feeding rainbow-colored fish over beautiful coral reefs.

Barbados Blue Water Sports, The Hilton, Grand Bay, St Michael, ☎ 246 434 5764, www.divebarbadosblue.com.

Rogers Scuba Shack. Owned by Roger Hurley, winner of the 1997 Award for Tourism. Roger has lived on Barbados all his life and is a highly experienced dive instructor.

Rogers Scuba Shack, The Boatyard Complex, Bay Street, St Michael, Barbados, ☎ 246 436 3483, fax 246 417 0003, www.rogers-scubashack.com.bb.

Sailing

Heat Wave Sailing Cruises. *Heatwave*, is a luxury 57-foot catamaran designed to give the ultimate sailing experience. Licensed to sail with a maximum of 60 passengers, they normally sail with around 35, to ensure maximum comfort, relaxation and enjoyment. Daily lunch cruises, plus the Sunday Wet & Wild cruise, a combination of water sports and sailing.

The boat can also be chartered privately.

Heat Wave Sailing Cruises, Royal Mail Building, Cavans Lane, St Michael, Bridgetown, ☎ 246 429-9283, fax 246 430-0293.

★★ Snorkeling

Heat Wave Sailing Cruise

Ocean Adventures provides individual attention to ensure the snorkel tour will be one to remember. Previous experience is not necessary as professional guides provide instruction and supervision.

A 3½-hour trip along the West Coast takes you to two separate snorkel locations. At the first, a guided underwater tour of a living reef provides an opportunity to see corals, an amazing variety of fish and reef creatures, perhaps even an elusive octopus. Then, for the underwater experience of a lifetime, swim with the turtles, learn about their lives and habits and get up close with these fascinating creatures.

Ocean Adventures

Tours include snorkeling equipment, drinks such as rum punch and beer after snorkeling and light snacks. Groups up to 32 guests welcome. Ocean Adventures, #69 Clerview Heights, Stage 1, St Michael, ☎ 246 438 2088, fax 246 438 3650, www.oceanadventures.bb, oceanadventure@ sunbeach.net.

★Kayaking

Kayaking with Ocean Adventures

For an unforgettable experience, join **Ocean Adventures** (see above) for a day out on the water in an ocean kayak. A powerboat ride along the West Coast, past white sandy beaches, through crystal-clear water and over colorful reefs takes you to the location for the trip

At rest stops along the way, the guides will tell you about the island. When you reach Turtle Bay, you board the raft and relax with a cool drink while learning about the turtles and their living habits. You can accompany the guides into the water and watch as they feed them. Then enjoy a complimentary rum punch and beer as you return along the coast.

Ocean Adventures uses ocean kayaks, which have scupper holes in the cockpit to direct water out and keep the kayak from being swamped. The kayaks are stable and virtually unsinkable. The "sit-on" kayak allows the paddler to enter and exit the kayak easily and paddle without feeling confined. Double kayaks have three moulded seat wells, making it easy for solo or tandem paddling. They also have room for a third passenger, perfect for family paddling!

★Snuba

For something a little different, try snuba, a unique shallow water diving system that bridges the gap between snorkeling and scuba diving. It is safe, easy and does not require certification. Snuba divers breathe underwater by means of a 20-foot airline connected to a scuba tank, mounted on a raft at the surface. Even if you have never snorkeled, or can't swim, you can snuba. Snuba is perfect for couples, families and children eight years and older. You start in shallow water, then, once you feel comfortable, take a guided underwater tour. Contact **Ocean Adventures** for details (see above).

Other Water Adventure Guides in St Michael

Adventureland Water . . . . ☎ 246 429-3687
Atlantis Submarines . . . . ☎ 246 436-8929
Barbados Yacht Club . . . . ☎ 246 427-1125

Cultural Excursions

★★Red Clay Pottery

Red Clay Pottery

Located at Fairfield Cross Roads, they have a diverse selection of dinnerware, terracotta pots and other pieces. Watch the potters as they make these unique pieces.

Red Clay Pottery, Fairfield House, Fairfield Cross Roads, ☎ 246 424 3800, fax 246 424 0072.

The Barbados Gallery of Art

The Barbados Gallery of Art is home to a national collection and features both visiting and rotating permanent exhibits. The Gallery is open Tuesday through Saturday 10 am to 5 pm, except for public holidays.

Information and tours of the exhibitions are available by calling ☎ 246 228-0149 Monday-Saturday during business hours.

The Barbados Gallery of Art, Garrison, St Michael, ☎ 246 228 0149.

★Barbados Museum

The Barbados Museum, at the Garrison, is housed in the former British Military Prison. The prison's upper section was built in 1817, the lower section in 1853. It became the headquarters of the Barbados Museum and Historical Society in 1930. The galleries and collections include Barbadian history, Amerindian and African culture, furnishings of an 18th-century plantation house, a children's gallery "Yesterday's

Children," which pro-
vides an informative
and educational voy-
age back into
Barbadian history,
European decorative
arts such as glass,
ceramics, and silver
and a collection of
antique maps, prints
and paintings. There
are special programs
for children, and a ref-
erence library avail-
able for research

Barbados Museum display

The Museum Shop
carries a wide range of
West Indian books, reproductions of maps, and Barbadian crafts and jewelry. The Café offers lunches, teas, and snacks. Disabled access.

Open 9 am-5 pm Monday-Saturday, 2-6 pm Sunday. Closed on public holidays. Admission: adults $14BDS, children $5BDS.

Barbados Museum & Historical Society , St Ann's Garrison, %% 246 427
0201, 246 436 1956, fax 246 429 5946, admin@barbmuse.org.bb, www.
Barbmuse.org.bb.

Spectator Sports

Cricket and horseracing are two of the main spectator sports in St
Michael. **Kensington Oval** for cricket and the **Garrison Savannah** for
horseracing are both described in the Bridgetown chapter.

Where to Stay

Arjan Apartments

The complex consists of four two-bedroom units, and six one-bedroom units. Each has air-conditioned bedrooms, kitchen with
microwave, toaster, and oven, fridge, and cable television. The
rooms are basic but clean and quite livable, located on the outskirts of
Bridgetown, five minutes by car from Brandon's Beach.

Rates range from $50 per night per person.

Arjan Apartments, 1st Avenue, Accommodation Road, Spooners Hill, St
Michael, ☎ 246 438 6112, fax 246 425 1266, arjan@caribsurf.net.

Blue Ocean Realty

For short- or long-term villa rentals and sales, Blue Ocean Realty is a member of the Barbados Estate and Valuers Association (BEAVA) and has co-brokering relationships with all agents on the island, providing access to every property in Barbados.

Blue Ocean Realty, PO Box 1010E, Bridgetown, St Michael, ☎ 246 256 6550, info@blueoceanbarbados.com, www.blueoceanbarbados.com.

Freshwater Bay

Freshwater Bay apartments

Ten apartments set in a private garden fronting on the Caribbean, 10 minutes from Bridgetown.

Rates in winter: sea view one bedroom $150 per night (based on two sharing); sea view two bedroom $160 to $185 per night (based on four sharing); inland view $85 per night. Rates in summer: sea view one bedroom $85 per night (based on two sharing); sea view two bedroom $135 to $155 per night (based on four sharing); inland view $70 per night.

Freshwater Bay, St Michael, ☎ 246 424 8119, halashley@caribsurf.net.

★★Grand Barbados Beach Resort

On beautiful Carlisle Bay stands the luxurious 134 room Grand Barbados Beach Resort. Recently renovated and upgraded, each room has a private balcony with panoramic views, richly appointed with Italian marble floors, pastel walls, vibrant colorful fabrics, and bathrooms with marble

Grand Barbados Beach Resort

vanities. The first five floors are standard guest rooms with garden or ocean views. The sixth and seventh floors are devoted to the corporate traveler and include wireless high-speed Internet access, work desk and complimentary daily newspaper.

There are also five deluxe suites at the end of the 260-foot (87-m) Victorian pier. Sitting right over the water, the luxurious suites are perfect for honeymooners, or for anyone seeking luxury and seclusion. Each suite has a spacious bedroom with luxurious linens, a separate sitting room with custom-crafted mahogany furniture, and a large bathroom finished in granite and marble. From the private balcony, you can watch schools of fish swimming in the clear water.

Grand Barbados Beach Resort, Carlisle Bay, St Michael, ☎ 246 426 4000, fax 246 429 2400, 800 814 2235 from US.

★★★ The Hilton

A five-star resort with 350 ocean-view guestrooms. All rooms have private balconies, separate shower units, high-speed Internet access, and cable TV. The hotel is built on Needham's Point peninsula and has two great beaches. There is a large swimming pool and whirlpool complex, fitness center, three tennis courts, and a 'Kidz' paradise club. The resort has a number of restaurants and bars, ranging from a beach bar to a gourmet restaurant.

The Hilton

I once stayed in the old hotel, which has been demolished. It left a lot to be desired but the beaches were spectacular. The beaches remain the same, and now the hotel is as impressive as the beaches.

Rates from $300 per night (single or double occupancy).

The Hilton, Needham's Point, St Michael, ☎ 246 426 0200, fax 246 434 5770, info.barbados@hilton.com, www.hiltoncaribbean.com.

Intimate Hotels of Barbados

The Intimate Hotels of Barbados, also known as "The Small Hotels of Barbados," is a non-profit company formed under the umbrella of the Barbados Hotel & Tourism Association (BHTA). It represents over 45 unique Barbados properties, including small hotels, apartment hotels, apartments, villas and guesthouses. You can book the property through them. Rates are affordable and perfect for travelers on a budget.

Intimate Hotels of Barbados, 4th Avenue Belleville, St Michael, ☎ 246 436 2053, fax 436 3748, information@intimatehotelsbarbados.com, www. intimatehotelsbarbados.com. In Europe, ☎ 49 211 405 6 506, europe@ intimatehotelsbarbados.com. In Canada, ☎ 905 315 9037, fax 905 915 9038, canada@intimatehotelsbarbados.com. In the UK, ☎ 011 44 1252 783715, uk@intimatehotelsbarbados.com. In Jamaica, ☎ 876 960 0600, fax 876 960 0601.

Island Inn

A 26-room all-inclusive hotel less than a mile from the center of Bridgetown, and a short walk to the beach and Carlisle Bay. There is a restaurant/bar and a cobblestone courtyard where you can relax with a cooling drink. Rates from $90 summer, $100 winter.

Island Inn, Aquatic Gap, St. Michael, ☎ 246 436 6393, quaint@caribsurf. com.

Nautilus Beach Apartments

With 14 rooms on Carlisle Bay, one mile from Bridgetown. Rates from$88 summer, $117 winter.

Nautilus Beach Apartments, Bay Street, St. Michael, ☎ 246 426 3541, nautilusbeach@caribsurf.com, www.nautilusbeach.com.

Villa #5 at Freshwater Bay

Villa #5

A cozy two-bedroom, two-bath beach-style bungalow that can sleep up to six people plus a baby or young child. The master bedroom has a king-sized bed, the second bedroom has two twin-beds, there is a queen-size pull out couch in the living room, and a fold away bed or crib is available on request. There is also a fully equipped kitchen and a patio with BBQ. A laundry room is also available.

Beach at Villa #5

Rates in winter: one-two people from $120 per night; three-four people from $140 per night; extra person $15 per night. Rates in summer: one-two people from $180 per night; three-four people from $220 per night; extra person $20 per night.

Villa #5 at Freshwater Bay, St Michael, ☎ 246 437 1200, fax 246 426 7845, conserv@caribsurf.com, www.freshwaterbaybarbados.com.

Where to Eat

 The five-star Hilton at Needham's Point is home to three great places to eat:

★★**The Careenage Bar & Grill** – Gourmet food.

★★**The Lighthouse Terrace** – A casual indoor/outdoor eatery serving breakfast, lunch and dinner.

★★**The Water's Edge Beach Bar** – A relaxed setting for snacks and cocktails.

The Hilton, Needham's Point, St Michael, ☎ 246 426 0200, fax 246 434 5770.

Careenage Bar & Grill

Barbecue Barn

Barbecue Barn's two convenient locations, Rockley in Christ Church and the centrally located Warrens, offer casual fast-food dining at affordable prices.

They have appetizers, platters of steak, chicken, fish, burgers or roast beef grilled and served with sides and garnishes. Or try their turkey and roast beef wraps, free beverage refills, and self-service salad bars.

Barbecue Barn, Warrens, St Michael, ☎ 246 436 5000, fax 246 429 4378, chef@chefette.com, www.barbecuebarn.com.

★Brown Sugar

Set in a restored traditional Bajan home surrounded by fern-covered patios and water gardens Brown Sugar is the place for authentic Bajan food. Try the all-you-can-eat buffet lunch or enjoy local entertainment most evenings. Buffet lunch Monday to Friday, $22.50, Sunday $27.50. Children under 10 half-price, under five free. Dinner Monday to Sunday. Starters $6-$13, main courses $17-$39.

Brown Sugar, Aquatic Gap, Bay Street, St. Michael, ☎ 246 426-7684.

Fast Food

Kentucky Fried Chicken, St. Michael, ☎ 246 424 9268.

Chefette Restaurants, various locations. Roti, pizza, chicken, sandwiches, salads.

Chicken Barn, St. Michael, ☎ 246 421 2276. Barbecue, chicken, burgers.

Nightlife

★★Harbour Lights

Harbour Lights Beach Extravaganza
(Rodney Nelson)

Harbour Lights is an open-air beachfront nightclub where the DJs spin the latest tunes, and you can dance under the stars. For a truly tropical evening, on Mondays and Wednesdays the Beach Extravaganza Dinner Show offers dancing barefoot in the sand to the pulsating beat of a live calypso band, exotic free drinks, a Bar-B-Que dinner and the best of local entertainment, including fire eating, limbo and Caribbean dancing, amazing stiltmen and the acrobatics of the green monkey.

Wednesdays and Fridays are Club Nights. Each night has its own theme, from Beach Parties with free drinks to top live bands. Pay one entry fee, and drink free all night – rum, vodka, gin, beer, rum punch, soft drinks, and juice, free until 2am

For certain shows you must be 18 years or older. Check in advance.

Harbour Lights, Marina Villa, Bay Street, St Michael, ☎ 246 436 7225, fax 246 436 5069, contactus@harbourlightsbarbados.com, www. harbourlightsbarbados.com.

★★Harbour Master Cruises

Take a Starlight Dinner Cruise on the MV *Harbour Master*, a custom-built, one-of-a-kind floating entertainment center, 100 feet long, 40 feet wide and four decks high. Enjoy welcome cocktails, a buffet featuring a mix of Bajan and international cuisine, followed by a spectacular floorshow, including belly dancing, tropical dancers and a limbo act.

After the show, dance to a live band and the resident DJ, or spend time on the Calypso deck under the stars in the night sky as the boat makes its way back to port.

Harbour Master Cruises, The Shallow Draught Harbour, Bridgetown Port, Bridgetown, ☎ 246 430 0900, fax 246 430 0901, tallships@sunbeach. net, http://tallshipscruises.com.

★Lucky Horseshoe Saloon & Steakhouse

Open 24 hours a day, the Lucky Horseshoes, one in Christ Church and one in St Michael, are loud Wild-West-themed bars, featuring one-armed bandits, music videos on dozens of screens and a constant party atmosphere.

Lucky Horseshoe Saloon & Steakhouse, Worthing Main Road, Christ Church, ☎ 246 435 5825.

Waterfront Café

See Bridgetown chapter.

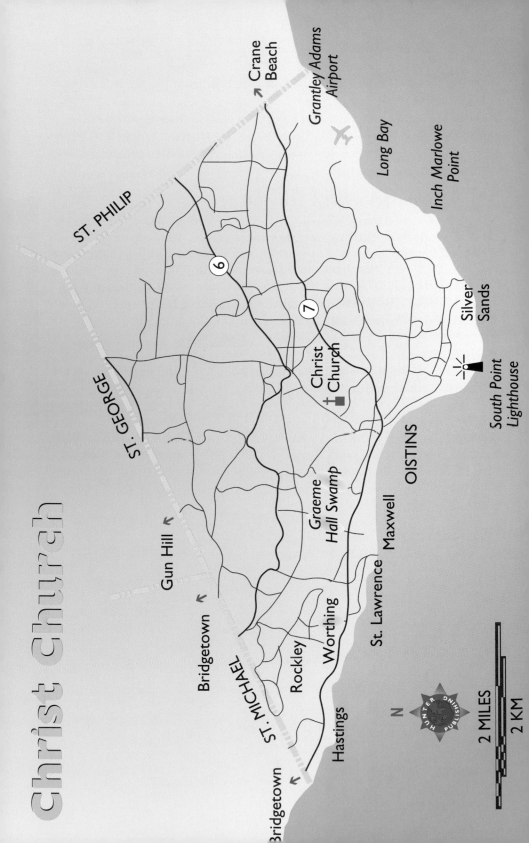

Christ Church

ST. PHILIP

ST. GEORGE

ST. MICHAEL

Bridgetown

Gun Hill

Bridgetown

Hastings

Rockley

Worthing

St. Lawrence

Maxwell

Graeme
Hall Swamp

OISTINS

Christ
Church

6

7

Crane
Beach

Grantley Adams
Airport

Long Bay

Inch Marlowe
Point

Silver
Sands

South Point
Lighthouse

N

2 MILES

2 KM

HUNTER PUBLISHING

Christ Church

Wha' evah in de ole goat in de kiddie.
(Children inherit the traits of their parents.)

Christ Church is the south-ernmost parish, bordered by St Michael to the west, St George to the north, and St Philip to the east. Grantley Adams Airport is in this parish, and it is one of the most developed parts of the island, with numerous restaurants, nightclubs, hotels, and bars. The beaches are generally safe for swimming, but can have strong currents and occasionally strong waves. There are lots of water sports on the south coast,

including windsurfing, kite surfing, wake boarding, snorkeling, jet skiing, and a host of others.

St Lawrence Gap, usually referred to as "The Gap," is the major tourist destination on the whole island, and many of the most popular clubs, bars, and restaurants can be found there.

Also in Christ Church is **Oistins**, which is a major fishing center and home to the "Friday Night Fish Fry," which is one thing you don't want to miss while you're in Barbados.

Another area is **Hastings**, one of the busier areas on the island, with lots of hotels, vacation homes, restaurants, boutiques and all types of shops, many right on the beach.

Oistins Fish Fry (Rodney Nelson)

Shopping

Some of the best shopping on the island can be found in Christ Church. There are shopping malls, specialty stores, street vendors, and souvenir shops.

Just off the ABC Highway is the **Sheraton Centre Mall**, housing about 70 stores, a Cineplex with six theaters, and a large food court. It's a great place to visit in the middle of the day to escape the heat of the midday sun.

The **Vista** shopping complex is a relatively new addition; there are a number of interesting stores, including a **Cave Shepherd** duty free store, selling cosmetics, electronics, cameras, liquor, cigars, and clothing at savings of up to 40%.

In Hastings are the **Hastings Plaza**, the **Quayside Centre**, and the **Shak Shak Complex**. You can find duty-free fragrances, clothing and leather goods at **Harrisons** in the Hastings Plaza and swimwear and surf gear at **Lazy Days & Island Waves** in the Quayside Centre.

In St Lawrence Gap, is the **Chattel House Village**. The shops, which are all replicas of traditional chattel houses, sell souvenirs, gifts, and clothing.

The two floors of **Walkers Caribbean World** are stocked with gifts from around the world, Bajan crafts, furniture and home accessories, and there

is a café overlooking the beach.

Along the sidewalk, you'll find artisans and jewelry makers selling handmade goods.

Hastings Plaza, Berwin Hasting Main Road, ☎ 436-8171.

Quayside Centre Mall, ☎ 246 429-9080.

Walkers Caribbean World, St Lawrence Gap, ☎ 246 428-1183, fax 246 420-4520.

Chattel House Village

Sightseeing

★★ The Parish Church

The original parish church was built in 1629 near Dover Beach. The present church, built in 1935, is the fourth on the site, the previous ones being destroyed by fire, flood, or hurricane.

In the graveyard is the famous **Chase Vault**. The vault housed a number of coffins, but each time the vault was opened, the coffins had been moved.

An investigation in 1820 could find no explanation for this mystery and the last time the vault was opened, the coffins were found strewn around the vault, some lying down, others standing upright! Ultimately, it was decided to move the coffins, and bury them individually. The vault was then sealed.

South Point Lighthouse

Christ Church Parish Church

South Point Lighthouse

South Point Lighthouse is located at Atlantic Shores, the most southerly point of the island. It was the first lighthouse in Barbados, originally shown at the Great Exhibition in London in 1851, and then shipped to Barbados where it was reassembled in 1852.

Made of cast iron and standing 89ft (30m) tall, it was restored in 2004, and is still operational. The lighthouse site is open to the public, but the lighthouse itself is closed.

★★★ St Lawrence Gap

In the middle of the south coast is a one-mile (1.6-km) strip of road famous for its restaurants, bars, shops, hotels and nightlife. The St Lawrence Gap, or the Gap, as it's better known is a focal point for both visitors and locals.

With bars along the waterfront, street parties, karaoke and live bands, nightclubs and restaurants catering to all tastes, and the constant bustle of tourists shopping by day and partying by night, St Law-

St Lawrence Gap at night

Bellini's Restaurant

rence Gap is the party center of Barbados.

Entering from the Worthing entrance to the Gap, **Bellini's**, on the right, offers some of the best Italian cuisine anywhere on the island. Farther down, also on the right, is **Pisces**, its spectacular setting and superb seafood making it a favorite destination for that special night out. Just past Pisces is **Josef's**, its stunning cliff-side setting and tables set in manicured gardens making this a great place for a romantic dinner under the stars.

A little farther along, on the left, is the **Ship Inn**, the island's original pub. With great pub food, a DJ, live bands and numerous happy hours, the Ship Inn is the place to drink and dance the night away. Across the road is Harlequin, an intimate hotel with a terrace overlooking the excitement on the street below.

Josef's Restaurant

During the day, there are street vendors, water sports, and sometimes even a soccer match on the field outside the oddly named hotel, **Time Out At The Gap**, where you can sit and drink a beer or piña colada while watching 22 crazy men running up and down the field in the heat of the midday sun.

But it's after dinner that the Gap really comes alive and the bars and nightclubs arc home to a constant stream of visitors dancing the night away to the sounds of reggae, soca, old school, calypso, hip hop, and the latest sounds from the clubs of New York and London.

- **Bellini's,** ☎ 246 420 7587
- **Pisces,** ☎ 246 420 5730
- **Josef's,** ☎ 246 420 7638
- **The Ship Inn,** ☎ 246 420 7447
- **Harlequin,** ☎ 246 420 7677
- **Time Out At The Gap,** ☎ 246 435 9473

Adventures on Foot

Hiking

The Barbados National Trust organizes Sunday walks at 6 am and 3 pm. The week's hike is listed in the newspaper, or you can obtain a schedule for $2.50 from the Barbados National Trust, ☎ 246 426 2421, fax 246 429 9055.

Golf

The Barbados Golf and Country Club and The Rockley Golf Club are both in Christ Church and open to the public.

★★**The Barbados Golf and Country Club**, originally built in 1974, is graced with mature trees, two lakes and coral waste bunkers. Redesigned in 2000 by Ron Kirby, it is a challenging yet rewarding course, suitable for players of all levels. Sanctioned by the PGA European Tour, the 18-hole, 6,905-yard, par-72 course hosted a PGA Seniors Tournament and the Barbados Open in 2000 and 2001. It features a clubhouse, bar and restaurant, a pro shop, and electric trolley and pull cart rentals, shoe rentals, bag drop and lockers, a practice chipping and putting

Barbados Golf & Country Club

green, warm-up nets, private lessons, and tournament facilities.

Green fees for 18 holes, $67.50; for nine holes, $40.50. Three-day unlimited golf pass, $167.50; seven-day unlimited golf pass, $350.

Golf lessons, one hour, $25.

Barbados Golf Club, Durants, ☎ 246 428 8463, fax 246 420 8205, admin@barbadosgolfclub.com.

Rockley Golf Course, 5,610 yards, par 70, is the oldest golf club in Barbados. Its nine holes with fairways from 170 to 430 yards are suitable for all ages and abilities. Its moderate price and friendly staff make this a favorite with locals and visitors. There is a bar and restaurant for after-round celebrating or commiserating. It features nine holes, with alternative tees for 18, a clubhouse, bar and restaurant, a pro shop, electric trolley and pull-cart rentals, a practice driving area, warm-up nets, private lessons, and tournament facilities.

Green fees for 18 holes, $48; nine holes, $37.

Club Rockley Barbados, Worthing, ☎ 246 435-7880, fax 246 435-8015.

Adventures on Water

Beaches

 There are numerous beaches along the south coast, which are well worth visiting. You could go to a different one every day and not see them all. Following are some of the best.

★**Accra Beach**. Set in a beautiful bay. The water is calm, making it great for swimming or sunbathing. There are toilets and showers, a children's playground, and bars selling snacks and drinks. You can also rent beach chairs, umbrellas and boogie boards. There are licensed vendors operating from beach huts selling beachwear, crafts and gifts.

★**Coconut Court Beach**. A white sand beach protected by a coral reef, making it safe for swimming. You can rent beach chairs, umbrellas and boogie boards. The beach lies in front of the Coconut Court Beach Hotel, which has a restaurant and bar.

★**Rescue Beach**. An often-deserted beach set in a quiet bay, great for sunbathing and swimming with that special someone. There is a beach bar where you can get drinks and snacks.

★**Dover Beach**. As busy as Rescue Beach is quiet! Jet skiing, beach volleyball, Hobie Cat sailing, children's playground, windsurfing, hair braiding, and vendors selling crafts and jewelry. The water is great for swimming and safe for children. Buy a coconut from one of the roadside vendors and drink the milk straight out of the shell. There are toilets, showers, picnic tables, and a lifeguard on duty.

★★**Enterprise Beach**. Otherwise known as Miami Beach, this is a great one for families. It's a big white sand beach with calm water, great for swimming, and with plenty of trees for shade. There are vendors selling beachwear, T-shirts, and jewelry, and a snack van selling fishcakes and drinks.

They have toilets and showers, and you can rent beach chairs and umbrellas. A lifeguard is on duty.

★**Freights Bay**. One of the top surf spots on the south coast. There is no lifeguard on duty and no amenities. You must be relatively fit to get down the stairs to the beach.

It is safe to swim, but the currents can change and create big waves.

★**Inch Marlow**. There are several small bays at Inch Marlow, some good for surfing, some for swimming. The area, also known as Kayak Point, is a popular kayaking destination. It is a great fishing and diving spot due to the rocks that dot the water. Night fishing is very popular, as is diving for octopus. It is safe for swimming but there is no lifeguard on duty. There is a beach bar at Surfer's Point, as well as toilets and showers.

★★Maxwell Beach. A beautiful gold sand beach, calm seas, benches to sit and enjoy the view or eat a picnic lunch, and a wooded area behind the beach where you can hide from the sun or hunt for red crabs.

There are hotels facing the beach, where you can stop in for lunch or a drink. You can rent beach chairs and umbrellas, and buy crafts and jewelry from the local vendors. A lifeguard is on duty, making it a great place to bring the whole family.

★Oistins Beach. Oistins is a busy beach with fishing boats coming and going. There are picnic tables, food stalls and rum shops. This is very much a business beach for the fishing industry. It is safe for swimming but you have to watch out for fishing boats. There is no lifeguard, but there are showers and toilets and it's great for kids who can watch the day's catch being brought in and the fish being prepared.

★★Sandy Beach. Officially known as Worthing Beach, this is a beautiful, wide beach with an offshore reef, which makes the water very calm, great for swimming and a popular area for people learning to windsurf. There are plenty of trees for shade, picnic tables, beach bars and vendors, as well as toilets and showers. You can also rent beach chairs and umbrellas.

On Sunday evenings, there is a BBQ and rum punch party, popular with both locals and visitors. A great beach, definitely worth a visit.

★Silver Rock Beach. A beautiful beach, with sand banks and safe for swimming, though the water can be quite rough. A great beach for wind-

St Lawrence Beach

surfing and kite surfing, but there are no lifeguards on duty so care must be taken, as the coast is susceptible to strong currents, depending on the time of year.

There is a children's playground and picnic tables shaded by trees. For a snack or a drink, there is a rum shop nearby and the Round Rock restaurant above the north end of the beach. There are also toilets and showers.

★**Silver Sands Beach**. The sea can be quite rough here; there are strong undercurrents and no lifeguard, which makes it suitable only for strong swimmers. There is a T Club Mistral shop on the beach where you can rent windsurfing equipment or take wind- and kite surfing lessons. The cost for lessons is $60 half-day, $75 full-day, or $285 for a week. The Silver Sands Hotel sits right on the beach and has a bar and restaurant.

★**St Lawrence Beach**. A calm beach at St Lawrence Gap with lots of shallow reefs, home to a variety of plants and sea life. Great for snorkeling, bodysurfing, boogie boarding and, for the less athletic, a good spot for shelling. Lots of restaurants and bars are close by.

★**Welches Beach**. Located west of Oistins, this beach has been extensively renovated. The waters are very calm, making it great for swimming, although there is no lifeguard on duty.

Scuba Diving

The waters around Barbados are perfect for scuba diving, with visibility between 80 and 98 ft (29-33 m) for most of the year. There are more than two dozen dive sites between the western and southern coasts.

For a complete list of companies offering scuba diving, see *Land of Adventure*, page 40.

Surfing

 Barbados has the Caribbean's most consistent surf conditions with steady swells all year round, and a water temperature that never drops below 77°F/25°C. South Point on the south coast is home to many surfing competitions.

Windsurfing

November to July are the best months for windsurfing. The consistent wind and sea conditions on the south coast make it popular with windsurfers. Silver Rock Beach is the venue for the **Barbados Waterman Festival**, held every February. Between Maxwell and Hastings, there are ideal conditions for beginner and intermediate windsurfers. The best place to learn windsurfing is Sandy Beach, also known as Carib Beach. It has a shallow lagoon, calm water, and is protected by an offshore coral reef.

Previous page: Welches Beach

Waterworld

Located next to the Bougainvillea Hotel, Waterworld is the place for adventure on the water. Take a boat trip and snorkel with the turtles ($75), reef and wreck snorkeling ($40), take the Banana Boat Ride ($15), jet ski ($50 per half-hour), go waterskiing or wake boarding ($25), try Hobie Cat sailing ($150) or surfing ($25-$40 per day).

Surf lessons are available at $180 for a six-hour course, windsurfing is $160 for six hours, kite surfing lessons are $100 for one session, $150 for two, or three sessions for $190. Sessions are between one and two hours each. And, if you're an experienced surfer, you can rent surfboards for $25 per hour.

Eco-Tourism

Graeme Hall Nature Sanctuary and **Ocean Park Marine Aquarium** (see *Traveling with Children*, page 57-58).

Spectator Sports

Next to Time Out At The Gap is the **Dover Playing Field.** Visiting cricket teams often play matches here against local teams. Soccer and basketball games are frequently played as well and you are usually welcome to join in.

★★Horse Racing

There are four major races on the Barbados racing calendar – The Sandy Lane Barbados Gold Cup held on the first Saturday in March, and the three races of the Triple Crown – The Banks Barbados Guineas in April, the Pinnacle Feeds Midsummer Creole Classic in July, and the United Insurance Barbados Derby in August.

Races are held at **The Savannah**, which was originally a military parade ground. In 1845, the officers of the British Regiment started using the parade ground to race their horses and today it is the home of horse racing in Barbados.

For complete details, see *Land of Adventure*, page 49.

Where to Stay

There is a wide range of accommodations in Christ Church, ranging from inexpensive apartments and guesthouses to luxury hotels and resorts.

★ Accra Beach Hotel & Resort

Accra Beach Resort's prime beachfront location includes 3½ acres of lush gardens. The hotel has 146 rooms offering ocean, pool or island views, including six luxurious Penthouse Suites. It has a large swimming pool with a shallow bank for lounging and a swim-up bar; there is a fully equipped gym, gourmet restaurants, banquet and conference facilities, and a great beach for swimming and sunbathing.

Accra Beach Hotel & Resort

Rates from $185 summer, $195 winter.

Rockley, Christ Church, ☎ 246 435-8920, fax 246 435-6794, www. accrabeachhotel.com.

Adulo Apartments

Adulo has 10 comfortable apartments, furnished studios or two-bedroom fully equipped units with patios overlooking a tropical garden. Each fully equipped unit comes with a private bathroom and kitchenette containing basic cooking utensils. All units are outfitted with telephones and have access to maid services and laundry facilities.

Rates for studios $60 a day in winter, $50 a day in summer; two bedroom apartment are $85 a day in summer, $75 a day in winter.

☎ 246 426-6811.

Affinity Villas

Tastefully refurbished one-bedroom villas set in a tranquil location. Amenities include a fitted kitchen, AC and ceiling fans, TV, CD/DVD player and separate living area.

$560-$900 per week.

☎ +44 787 944 0853 (in the UK).

Amaryllis Beach Resort

Amaryllis Beach Resort

Guests can select from 150 hotel rooms, wheelchair accessible rooms, studios, deluxe studios, one-bedroom suites, two-bedroom suites. All rooms were completely renovated in 2003.

Rates from $139 summer to $236 winter, double occupancy.

☎ 246-438-8000, www.amaryllisbeachresort.com.

Angels Annexe Guesthouse

Situated in a quiet residential area, six minutes walk to Accra Beach and 10 minutes to St Lawrence Gap. The Guesthouse has three double bedrooms, one with a double and a single bed. All rooms have ceiling and floor fans and TV. The kitchen is fully equipped, and the patio area is equipped with a sun lounger, chairs and a dining table

The house can also be rented as a complete unit, offering a spacious three-bedroom apartment that can sleep eight people. Long-term rental is also available at discounted rates. Free pick up from the airport included. Rates are $40 per night including breakfast; $120 per night for the entire house.

Dayrells Road, Christ Church, ☎ 246 437 3749, angel_metatron@sunbeach.net.

★Barbados Beach Club

Air-conditioned studio rooms include bathroom, telephone, satellite TV, hairdryer and private balcony with views of the ocean, pool, or gardens. The all-inclusive resort offers meals in three restaurants, low-key evening entertainment, tennis, mini-golf, and non-motorized water sports.

Rates from $130 in summer or $165 in winter, double occupancy.

Barbados Beach Club

Maxwell Coast Road, Christ Church, ☎ 246 428-9900, fax 246 428-8905, www.barbadosbeachclub.com.

Blue Orchids Beach Hotel

An intimate hotel on Worthing beach, featuring 31 rooms, including studios and one- and two-bedroom air-conditioned apartments, with kitchenette, baths and balconies. There is a restaurant, shop, and water sports are available.

Rates from $112 in summer, $170 in winter.

Blue Orchids Beach Hotel

Blue Orchids Beach Hotel, Worthing, Christ Church, ☎ 246 430 8057, blorchids@ caribsurf.com, www.blueorchidsbarbados.com.

★★★Bougainvillea Beach Resort

Bougainvillea Beach Resort

The Bougainvillea Beach Resort is a luxurious, oceanfront all-suite resort, featuring 138 spacious suites, from studios, one- and two-bedroom deluxe suites to penthouse apartments. It sits in a stunning location on one of the island's most beautiful beaches, with a landscape of lagoon pools, cascading waterfalls and lush gardens.

Rates from $155 summer, $232 winter.

Maxwell Coast Road, Christ Church, ☎ 246 418 0990, fax 246 428 2524, www.bougainvillearesort.com.

Following page: View from Bougainvillea Beach Resort (Rodney Nelson)

Butterfly Beach Hotel

With 75 rooms, an oceanfront location, a swimming pool, restaurant, and beach bar. Rates from $90 in summer, $120 in winter.

Butterfly Beach Hotel, Maxwell Main Road, Christ Church, ☎ 246 428 9095, reservations@butterflybeach.com, www.butterflybeach.com.

Carib Blue Apartments

Just two minutes from Dover Beach, and four minutes from St Lawrence Gap, the 18 tastefully furnished suites

Butterfly Beach Hotel

here include studios and one- or two-bedroom apartments with fully equipped kitchenettes, en-suite bathrooms and a private balcony with a view of Dover Beach or the courtyard.

Rates start from $48 per night.

60 Dover Terrace, Christ Church, ☎ 246 428-2290, fax 246 428-5140, www.caribblueapts.com.

Cherry Tree Apartments

A Cherry Tree Apartment

Located about five minutes from Maxwell Beach and seven minutes from Dover Beach, in a beautiful park. There are 10 studios, each of which sleeps two people. The studios have a small kitchenette, two beds, safe deposit box, shower/toilet, balcony or terrace. Four of the studios can accommodate an extra bed for a child. summer rates from $33 per night, winter rates from $45, double occupancy, VAT inclusive. Minimum rental is five nights.

Dover, Christ Church, ☎ 246 822 1267.

Coconut Court Beach Hotel

A 3-star hotel featuring 120 rooms with private balconies overlooking the Caribbean. Rates from $157 summer, $189 winter.

Coconut Court Beach Hotel, Hastings, Christ Church, ☎ 246 427 1655, jfield@coconut-court.com, www.coconut-court.com.

Coconut Court Beach Hotel

Croton Inn

With seven rooms on the South Coast, the Croton Inn is a cozy and intimate guesthouse with a quiet, homey atmosphere, five minutes from the beach, restaurants, shopping and entertainment. Public transportation is at the door. Rates from $30.

Croton Inn, Maxwell Main Road, Christ Church, ☎ 246 428 7314, stay@crotoninn.com.

★Divi Southwinds

The Divi Southwinds Beach Resort sits between a half-mile stretch of pure white sand beach and St Lawrence Gap. The resort offers spacious beachfront, pool-view, and garden-view suites with full kitchens. There are two restaurants, plus an open-air beachfront café, poolside lounge, tennis courts and on-site fitness room. Rates from $164 summer, $254 winter.

Divi Southwinds

St Lawrence, Christ Church, ☎ 800-367-3484, fax 246-428-4674, www.divisouthwinds.com.

Dover Beach Hotel

Dover Beach Hotel (TripAdvisor)

Offering 59 rooms, set right on beautiful Dover Beach, the hotel has a swimming pool, and a restaurant/bar. Rates from $80 summer, $110 winter.

Dover Beach Hotel, St. Lawrence Gap, Christ Church, ☎ 246 428 8076, resdover@ caribsurf.com, www.dover-beach.com.

Golden Sands Apartment Hotel

It has 27 rooms set between St. Lawrence Gap and Oistins, and close to a wide range of shops and restaurants. Golden Sands has a swimming pool and restaurant, and is one minute from the beach.

Rates from$80 summer, $120 winter.

Golden Sands Apartment Hotel, Maxwell, Christ Church, ☎ 246 428 8051, goldsand@ caribsurf.com, www.goldensandshotel.com.

Golden Sands

Inchcape Seaside Villas

Six spacious houses on the white sand beach of Silver Sands, with tropical gardens and ocean views, tastefully furnished and well equipped. Self-contained two-bedroom/two-bathroom houses with maid/cook and one-bedroom apartments. Amenities include satellite TV, stereos, telephone, Internet access, fax machine, airport pick up/drop-off, special taxi service, rental car arrangements, and special golfing rates at Royal Westmoreland and Barbados Golf Club.

Rates from $80 to $450.

Inchcape Villa

Inchcape, Silver Sands, Christ Church, ☎ 246 4287006, fax 246 4204748, www.inchcape.net.

Kingsland Palace Guest House

With 11 rooms, a small, friendly guesthouse in a residential neighbour-hood offering West Indian hospitality and cooking – breakfast, lunch and dinner are available. All rooms are air-conditioned and have bathrooms, a small fridge and TV. Public transportation is right outside the door, a short ride to beaches and shopping. Rates from $40.

Kingsland Palace Guest House, 446 Kingsland Drive, Christ Church, ☎ 246 420 9008, kingsland446@yahoo.com.

★★★ Little Arches

I can't think of a better place for a romantic getaway than Little Arches. This privately owned 10-room boutique hotel is an adults-only hideaway just steps from Miami Beach. King-size beds and air-conditioning are standard, and the oceanfront suites feature private oversized whirlpool spas and terracotta terraces.

Meals are served in-room, poolside or alfresco in the rooftop restaurant.

Little Arches

The hotel's **Cafe Luna** is the top-rated Zagat choice for best hotel dining experience, rated number one for Mediterranean food and number three for best food overall in Barbados in 2006/7.

Luxury Ocean Suite from $336 per night, Ocean Deluxe from $244, Garden Suite from $244, Garden Superior from $212, Garden Standard from $192. Rates are per room per night, single or double occupancy

Enterprise Beach Road, Christ Church, ☎ 246 420 4689,

Little Arches pool area

fax 246 418 0207, paradise@littlearches.com.

Little Bay Hotel

The hotel sits directly on the beach, in St Lawrence Gap; it has 10 rooms, including seven studios and three one-bedrooms. All have an ocean view and are equipped with a king-size bed, kitchenette, telephone, cable television, air-conditioning and ceiling fan. Each studio sleeps two. The one-bedrooms have a sleeper sofa and sleep four. Rates from $100 summer, $110 winter.

St Lawrence Gap, Christ Church, ☎ 246 435 7246, fax 246 435 8574, little_bay@caribsurf.com, www.littlebayhotelbarbados.com.

Long Beach Club

Long Beach Club

Take a short drive from Bridgetown along the south coast and you'll come to Long Beach. This beach, and hotel of the same name, although just minutes away, remains undiscovered by the majority of visitors to the island. The hotel, built in the 1950s, is somewhat past its prime but for the person who wants to get away from the crowds and traffic this is the ideal spot. Privately run, the rooms, although modest, feature balconies and a small kitchen, so after a trip to the supermarket you can lock yourself away and just spend time between your room, the swimming pool, the bar, and the beach.

There is a swimming pool on the grounds and an open-air restaurant. The food is modest and the entertainment, such as it is, low key. Upstairs is a small library, stocked with an eclectic selection of books, left behind by previous visitors. The beach itself is aptly named, stretching away for miles, and usually deserted. It is one of the undiscovered gems in Barbados.

The only way to reach the hotel is to drive or take a taxi, so if you plan to tour the island or even just visit the local bars and restaurants you will need to rent a car or take taxis wherever you go. The people who stay at Long Beach usually want to relax and unwind. If you want to party this is not the spot for you!

But if you want to spend some time away from the rat race, read a few books, or maybe even write one, then this might just be the ideal location for you. But get there soon before someone decides this place should be demolished and a luxury Superclub should be built in its place.

☎ 246 428 6890, fax 246 428 4957.

Maresol Beach Apartments

The Maresol apartment complex is at the end of Dover Beach. The seven buildings housing the apartments are surrounded by a tropical garden, elevated about three feet above sea level and protected by a low seawall.

There are spacious one- and two-bedroom apartments, some with two bathrooms, all with patios or balconies, 13 comfortably furnished apartments with full kitchens, seven apartments situated directly on the sea, four apartments with sea views, accommodation for the physically challenged, maid service and direct access to a 1,500-ft (50-m) white sand beach.

Maresol Beach Apartments

Weekly rental rates from $500.

Dover Beach, Christ Church, ☎ 246 428 9300, fax 246 428 9300, maresolapt@caribsurf.com, www.maresolbeach.net.

Maraval Guesthouse & Apartments

Offering budget accommodation. Apartments and guesthouse are on the beachfront with a sea view. Short- and long-stay options available.

Rates from $40 per night per room.

Worthing,Christ Church, ☎ 246 435 7437, fax 246 435 7437, www. maravalbarbados.com.

Melrose Beach Apartments

It has 14 rooms, just 50 yards/50 m from the beach, and close to supermarkets, stores, banks, restaurants, and nightclubs. Fully equipped kitchenettes, TV, and air-conditioned bedrooms. Rates from $90 summer, $105 winter.

Melrose Beach Apartments, Worthing, Christ Church, ☎ 246 435 7984, info@melrosebeach-apt.com, http://melrosebeach-apt.com.

Meridian Inn

This 16-room apartment hotel is situated at the quiet end of St Lawrence Gap. Choose from three ground-floor, six first-floor and six second-floor units, or the penthouse on the top floor of the hotel. Units have either one

Meridian Inn (hotelrentalgroup.com)

queen size or two twin beds, air-conditioning, ceiling fan, private balcony, private bath with shower, kitchenette, daily maid service, and cable television.

Spring/summer/fall rates are $59 per night, winter rates are $89. Extra person $20 per night. Special rates for group and long-term stays. Minimum seven nights stay, rates based on double occupancy.

St Lawrence Gap, Christ Church, ☎ 246 428 4051, fax 246 420 6495, meridianinn@sunbeach.net, www.meridianinn.com.

Monteray Apartment

There are 21 studio and one-bedroom apartments, each with private patio and two- or three-bedroom cottages. There is a freshwater pool and a restaurant. Centrally located between the airport and Bridgetown within walking distance of nightspots, restaurants, shops and Dover Beach. Studio $85, one-bedroom $95.

Monteray Apartment, 2nd Avenue, Dover, Christ Church, ☎ 246 428 9152, monteray@caribsurf.com.

The Nook

A quiet property with seven rooms on the south coast. The apartments are fully furnished and fully equipped, just a short walk to the popular Rockley beach, shopping, restaurants and public transportation. Relax at the pool and enjoy the garden setting. Rates from $70.

The Nook, Dayrells Road, Rockley, Christ Church, ☎ 246 427 6502, nookbdos@sunbeach.net.

Ocean Spray Apartments

Listen to the sound of the waves from your bedroom in this 15-room complex close to Oistins fishing village. Units feature kitchenette, TV and phone. Rates from $75 summer, $95 winter.

Ocean Spray Apartments, Inch Marlow, Christ Church, ☎ 246 428 5426, oceanspray@sunbeach.net.

Ocean Spray Apartments

Oleander Beach Apartments

Oleander Beach Apartments is a new property overlooking the ocean. Five of the eleven units are town houses. Walking distance to supermarkets, nightlife and a variety of restaurants serving fast food and local cuisine. Rates from$120.

Oleander Beach Apartments, Worthing, Christ Church, ☎ 246 430 9630, oleanderbeach@sunbeach.net.

Pirate's Inn

The Pirate's Inn offers 22 comfortable self-contained studios and one-bedroom units. All rooms are equipped with full bathroom, hot and cold water, balcony or patio and self-contained equipped kitchen. Rates from $90 summer, $120 winter.

Hastings, Christ Church, ☎ 246 426 6273, fax 246 436 0957, reservations@pirates-inn.com.

Point View Apartments

Point View Apartments are in a quiet residential area close to two white sand beaches – Silver Sands and Long Beach. Both are excellent windsurfing beaches. The property has eight one-bedroom apartments, and one two-bedroom apartment, all with private patios. winter rates start from $75 per night, summer rates from $50.

Inch Marlow, Christ Church, ☎ 246 428 7301, 246 428 3586, pointview@caribsurf.com.

Point View Apartments

Rainbow Beach Hotel
(hotelrentalgroup.com)

Rainbow Beach Hotel

Set on Dover Beach in the heart of St. Lawrence Gap, with 45 rooms. Air-conditioned accommodation includes one-bedroom suites with patio, kitchenette, and lounge, or studios equipped with microwave, toaster-oven, fridge, and coffeemaker. Rates from $87 summer, $92 winter.

Rainbow Beach Hotel, St. Lawrence Gap, Christ Church, ☎ 246 428 5110, info@rainbowreef.com, www.rainbowreef.com.

★Rockley Plum Tree Club

Originally built more than 25 years ago, the recently renovated Plum Tree Club offers guests all the advantages of a genuine hideaway, without the disadvantages of remoteness. A cluster of 40 one- and two-bedroom self-contained apartments, each with its own private patio offers a choice of views overlooking the golf course, swimming pool or the landscaped gardens.

Plum Tree Club pool

The living rooms come with ceiling fans and the bedrooms are air-conditioned. Kitchens are equipped with a microwave, toaster oven, and coffee percolator. All apartments have cable television, telephone, and safety deposit boxes. Housekeeping is provided.

Play golf or tennis, relax around the pool, or take a free shuttle to Rockley Beach. The Sugar Reef Restaurant has a full bar and is open for lunch and dinner, offering live entertainment.

Disabled access.

Summer rates, April 15-December 15, one bedroom $100, less 10%, two bedrooms $160; winter rates, one-bedroom $130, two bedrooms $240. Extra adults charged from $15 to $20 per night. Children under 12 stay free.

Rockley Golf Course, Christ Church, ☎ 246 435 7606, fax 246 435 8282, plumtree@rockley.com.bb, www.rockley.com.bb.

★★Rosalie Apartments

The ultimate in adult luxury accommodation. Luxury one- and two-bedroom apartments are air-conditioned, with satellite TV, a private patio and heated Jacuzzi. Situated in an exclusive residential area on the South Coast just 20 minutes from St Lawrence Gap and 15 minutes from the airport.

Rosalie Apartments

A representative will greet you at the airport and chauffeur you to the five-star holiday apartments.

13 Seaside Drive, Atlantic Shores, Christ Church, ☎ 246 420 3832, fax 246 420 3832, www.rosalieapartments.com.

Rostrevor Apartment Hotel

A family-oriented hotel with 61 rooms directly on Dover Beach in St. Lawrence Gap, minutes away from shops, nightclubs and restaurants. Rates from $57 summer, $90 winter.

Rostrevor Apartment Hotel, St. Lawrence Gap, Christ Church, ☎ 246 428 9298, rostrevor@caribsurf.com, www.rostrevorbarbados.com.

★Round Rock Apartments on Sea

An uncrowded, intimate hotel with 13 rooms, two minutes from Silver Sands Beach, with two restaurants serving great West Indian food. Rates from $65. Round Rock Apartments on Sea, Round Rock Road, Christ Church, ☎ 246 428 7500, roundrck@caribsurf.com.

★Sandy Bay Beach Club

Round Rock Apartments

An all-inclusive 129-room hotel on a beautiful beach, protected by a coral reef. Within walking distance of the restaurants, shops, and nightclubs of St. Lawrence Gap. Rates from $282 summer, $355 winter.

Sandy Bay Beach Club (wheretostay.com)

Sandy Bay Beach Club, Worthing, Christ Church, ☎ 246 435 8000, vacation@sandybaybeachclub.com, www.sandybeachbarbados.com.

Sea Breeze Beach Hotel (hotelrentalgroup.com)

Sea Breeze Beach Hotel

The Sea Breeze Beach Hotel is located directly on two white-sand beaches offering "Superior Rooms," "Superior Studios" and two-bedroom apartments, all with air-conditioning. There are two freshwater pools, a three-Jacuzzi garden spa, a well-equipped air-conditioned fitness room, non-motorized water sports, outdoor games area with shuffleboard, croquet, table tennis, pool table, basketball, volleyball and a gift and souvenir shop. There are three restaurants, the Fish Pot Beach and Pool Bar, the Pavilion Restaurant featuring barbecues and themed buffet dining and the elegant Mermaid Restaurant.

Rates are from $125 per night. All-inclusive packages available.

Maxwell Coast Road, Christ Church, ☎ 246 428-2825, fax 246 428-2872, www.sea-breeze.com.

Shonlan Airport Hotel

Minutes away from the airport and close to most major roads the hotel has 13 units – singles and doubles, as well as one- and two-bedroom apartments. Rates from $65.

Shonlan Airport Hotel, Coventry Terrace, Christ Church, ☎ 246 428 0039, shonlan@cariaccess.com.

★South Beach Resort & Vacation Club

South Beach Resort is located directly opposite Rockley Beach. An ultra-modern boutique resort offering 49 luxurious suites at great rates, including deluxe studios, one- and two-bedroom suites, penthouses and deluxe honeymoon suites. Rates from $132US for two in summer or $198 for two in winter.

Rockley at Accra Beach, Christ Church, ☎ 246 435-8561/69, fax 246 435-8954, www.southbeachbarbados. com.

South Beach Resort

Southern Heights

Five minutes drive from St Lawrence Gap, Southern Heights offers 12 comfortable air-conditioned one-bedroom apartments. The living and dining rooms are fully furnished, and include cable TV, telephone, and ceiling fan. Kitchens have a refrigerator, stove, and microwave.

Winter rates (December 15 to April 15) $95; summer (April 16 to December 14) $76, based on double occupancy. Extra person $50. Children under 12 free, 12-16 $25.

8 Amity Lodge, Christ Church, ☎ 246 435 8354, fax 246 228 0753, reservations@southernheightsbarbados.com.

★★Southern Palms Beach Club

Set on five acres of tropical gardens on Dover Beach, the Southern Palms has 92 rooms, two freshwater pools, tennis, miniature golf, windsurfing, and boogie boarding. The Garden Terrace restaurant serves Caribbean cuisine, and there's a steelband to provide entertainment. Rates from $145 summer, $230 winter.

Southern Palms Beach Club (hotelrentalgroup.com)

Southern Palms Beach Club, St. Lawrence Gap, Christ Church, ☎ 246 428 7171, reservations@southernpalms.net, www.southernpalms.net.

Southern Surf Beach Apartments

Southern Surf rooms are fully furnished and include air-conditioning, cable television, twin beds in the studio apartment (king bed on request), two double beds in the deluxe studio apartment, fully equipped kitchenette, and daily housekeeping. All rooms can accommodate an extra bed. St Lawrence Gap is about a half-mile away.

Studio apartment summer rates from $70 per night; deluxe studios from $85 per night.

Rockley Beach, Christ Church, ☎ 246 435 6672, 786 522 1977 (from the US), fax 246 435 6649, southernsurf@sunbeach.net, www.southernsurfbarbados.com.

Time Out at the Gap

This "party central" hotel has 76 rooms, local entertainment three times a week, and a restaurant/bar with large screen TV, pool tables, and dart boards. Rooms are air-conditioned with mini-fridges, satellite TV, radio, hairdryers, irons and ironing boards. Rates from $145 summer, $200 winter.

Time Out at the Gap, St. Lawrence, Christ Church, ☎ 246 420 5021, reservations@gemsbarbados.com, www.gemsbarbados.com.

★★★ Turtle Beach Resort

Turtle Beach is a first-class all-suite hotel featuring 164 junior and one-bedroom suites. Set in six acres of lush tropical gardens and sitting on a stunning white sand beach, it has three natural pools and is a great destination for families, couples and honeymooners. Complimentary activities include water

Turtle Beach Resort (wheretostay.com)

sports, tennis, a state-of-the-art gymnasium, and a kids' club. Rates from $434 summer, $664 winter.

Turtle Beach Resort, Dover, Christ Church, ☎ 246 428 7131, Barbados. reservations@eleganthotels.com, www.eleganthotels.com.

Yellow Bird Hotel

Features 20 rooms set on the beach in St. Lawrence Gap, close to shops, restaurants and nightclubs. Studio apartments all have kitchenettes and air-conditioning. Rates from $80 summer, $120 winter.

Yellow Bird Hotel, St. Lawrence Gap, Christ Church, ☎ 246 435 8444, info@yellowbirdbarbados.com, www.yellowbirdbarbados.com.

Where to Eat

★ Apsara

As you step into Aspara you are transported to India. It is decorated like an elegant Indian home, you can choose to eat inside or outside on the verandah overlooking the gardens. If you love Indian food you'll love the seekh kebabs, tandooris and other specialties. Open for lunch and dinner Monday to Sunday in winter, in summer, Monday to Friday for lunch, Monday to Saturday for dinner. Lunch $29.50, dinner starters $10-$20, main courses $7.70-$47.50.

Apsara, Worthing, Christ Church, ☎ 246 435 5446.

★★ Aqua Restaurant & Lounge

With a menu described as "Bajan Fusion Cuisine," executive chef Michael Hinds combines international and Bajan cuisine and serves it to happy customers at this ultra-modern oceanside restaurant. After dinner relax at the late-night lounge, which doesn't close until the last person leaves. Open for lunch Sunday to Friday, for dinner every day.

Aqua Restaurant & lounge, Hastings, Christ Church, ☎ 246 420 2995.

Barbecue Barn

Barbecue Barn's two convenient locations, Rockley in Christ Church and the centrally located Warrens, offer casual fast food dining at affordable prices. There are

Aqua Restaurant

appetizers, platters of steak, chicken, fish, burgers or roast beef grilled and served with sides and garnishes. Or try their turkey and roast beef wraps, free beverage refills, and self-service salad bars.

Rockley, Christ Church, ☎ 246 436 5000, fax 246 429 4378, chef@chefette. com, www.barbecuebarn.com.

★Bay Bistro

Bay Bistro is part of the Yellow Bird Hotel, located directly across the street from Little Bay. Offering Southern Caribbean and British food with live blues and jazz, they are famous for their Full Monty British breakfast, steak & chips, seafood gumbo, Bajan paella, seafood medley, surf & turf, curries, pasta, and roast beef and Yorkshire pudding all day Sundays. Open daily for breakfast, lunch and dinner. Sip cocktails at Sunset Happy Hour from 5 to 7 pm each evening. They have 65 cocktails on offer.

Yellow Bird Hotel, St Lawrence Gap, Christ Church, ☎ 246 426 0059, fax 246 435 8522, info@baywatchbarbados.com, www.baywatchbarbados.com.

★★Bellini's Trattoria

Set on a Mediterranean-style veranda on the main floor of the Little Bay Hotel, Bellini's specializes in Italian food and fresh local seafood. Entrées from $22 to $34.

St Lawrence Gap, Christ Church, ☎ 246 435 7246, fax 246 435 8574.

Bellini's (shoestringbarbados.com)

Bert's

Worldwide sports coverage on the large-screen satellite TVs. Try the stone-fired pizza with an island cocktail on the side, or Bajan and international dishes served with a cold beer. Open for lunch and dinner. Starters $4-$10, main courses $9-$25.

Bert's, Rockley, Christ Church, ☎ 246 435 7924.

★Bistro Monet

Whether you eat inside or out, the international menu at this intimate bistro offers something for everyone at an affordable price. But you are right on a busy road if you sit outside. Open for dinner. Average price for lunch or dinner $30.

Bistro Monet, Hastings, Christ Church, ☎ 246 435 9389.

Bubba's Sports Bar

See *Nightlife.*

Bubba's Sports Bar, Rockley, Christ Church, ☎ 246 435-7924, info@bertsbarbados.com.

★★★Café Luna

I like this place so much I almost don't want to tell anyone about it in case it becomes too popular and I won't be able to get a reservation! The restaurant sits on the roof of the Little Arches Hotel, overlooking Enterprise Beach, and is possibly the most romantic place in the whole of Barbados. Zagat listed Café Luna as the top-rated hotel dining experience, rating it tops for Mediterranean cuisine, and third-best restaurant for excellence in food overall for 2006/7. To complete the romance, book a room for the night in this great boutique hotel. Starters $10-$14, main courses $25-$40.

Café Luna
(definitivecaribbean.com)

Café Luna, Little Arches Hotel, Enterprise Beach Road, Christ Church, ☎ 246 428 6172, paradise@littlearches.com.

★★★Champers Restaurant & Wine Bar

One of the leading restaurants on the South Coast, overlooking Accra Beach, this consistently excellent spot is both classy and romantic. The extensive menu features the best local produce, beautifully presented, and includes deep-fried Camembert, Parmesan-crusted barracuda, and grilled lobster. There is also a bar with a bistro menu and critically

Bridgetown & the South

acclaimed artwork on the walls. The restaurant is not suitable for young children. Lunch $11-$19; dinner $11-$37.50.

Champers Restaurant & Wine Bar, ☎ 246 434 3463, champersinc@caribsurf.com.

★★David's Place

Great Bajan food served next to the ocean. Open for dinner Tuesday to Sunday. Starters $7-$15, main courses $19-$42.50.

David's Place, St. Lawrence Main Road, Christ Church, ☎ 246 435 9755.

★The Garden Terrace

Overlooking the beach, this friendly restaurant serves a buffet lunch on Sunday, accompanied by a steelband, buffet dinner on Monday with a live band for dancing, and a barbecue under the stars on Thursdays with a live steelband. Saturday night's à la carte dinner is accompanied by music from a local band. Open for breakfast, lunch, and dinner. Lunch $5-$17.50, dinner starters $5-$10, main courses $16-$34.

The Garden Terrace, Southern Palms Beach Club, St. Lawrence, Christ Church, ☎ 246 428-7171.

★Harlequin

Affordable, family-friendly, international, seafood, and vegetarian dishes. Starters $6-$14, main courses $15-$50.

Harlequin, St. Lawrence Gap, Christ Church, ☎ 246 420-7677, www.harlequinrestaurant.com.

★★★Josef's

Josef Schwaiger, one of Barbados' best known chefs, and chef/patron Thomas Harris joined together to create one of the best dining experience in Barbados. The menu is international haute cuisine with a fusion of Caribbean and Asian flavors. Originally a plantation home on the water, the restaurant retained the original structure with just slight modifications. The dining area nestles between the garden of the home and the ocean. There are 10 waterfront tables, and about 20 others with views of the Caribbean. Two gazebos are slightly elevated on the edges of the garden and are perfect for a private and romantic meal.

Open for dinner nightly from 6:30 to 10 pm.

St Lawrence Gap, ☎ 246 420 7638, josefsrestaurant@hotmail.com.

Lucky Horseshoe Saloon & Steakhouse

See *Nightlife*.

Lucky Horseshoe Saloon & Steakhouse, Worthing Main Road, Christ Church, ☎ 246 435 5825.

★Luigi's Restaurant

Opened in 1963, it is the best-known Italian restaurant in Barbados, using only the best products, such as homemade pasta, cheese from their own cheese factory, and meats and wine imported from Italy. A family-run restaurant with an extensive menu and a homey atmosphere. Open Monday to Saturday 6:30-9:45 pm.

Dover, Christ Church, ☎ 246 428 9218, reservations@luigisbarbados.com, www.luigisbarbados.com.

★Mama Mia's

An Italian deli and pizzeria on Hastings Main Rd. Run by the same family as Luigi's. Try the grilled panini with meat and cheeses imported from Italy, classic Italian dishes, salads, the Italian pizza baked in an authentic wood-burning oven and, to finish off, dessert cake or gelato, made in Italy and imported weekly. Mama Mia is also a deli where you can buy Italian meats, cheeses, and other deli foods. Open Monday to Saturday 8:30 am-9 pm.

Hastings Main Road, Christ Church, ☎ 246 434 3354, fax 246 228 8693, info@mamamiadeli.com, www.mamamiadeli.com.

★★Ocean's

Nestled at the edge of Little Bay, in St Lawrence Gap, with a great view of the Bay, their specialty is seafood, but they also have vegetarian dishes, pasta, steaks, poultry and lamb. Open seven days a week.

☎ 246 420-7615, fax 246 418-0188, reservations@oceansbarbados.com, www.oceansbarbados.com.

★★Opa

A family-owned and -operated oceanfront Greek restaurant. Great souvlaki and moussaka. Open for lunch and dinner. Average meal about $10.

Opa, Hastings, Christ Church, ☎ 246 435 1234.

★★★Pisces Restaurant

There are many excellent restaurants in Barbados, large numbers of which are located close to, or right on, the water's edge and Pisces is one of the best. This landmark, sitting on the edge of the water in St Lawrence Gap, has been in business for over 30 years and has been an island favorite since its opening in 1972.

Entering the restaurant is like entering a rainforest. Extensive indoor gardens featuring an array of tropical plants and flowers that provide a cooling respite from the tropical heat. The Maitre d' shows you to your table, and there are no bad tables.Whether you want an ocean view or an intimate tropical garden setting, every seat is beautiful. Since there are so many other ocean-view restaurants in Barbados, you might want to ask for one of the interior tables. The service is friendly and unhurried, perfect for a romantic rendezvous, or a family celebration.

The menu, as would be expected, features a wide array of Caribbean fish and seafood, supplemented with a selection of meat and poultry dishes, then a mouth-watering selection of Caribbean-style deserts. The restaurant is recognized by AAA/CAA for its innovative preparation and presentation of the finest foods, so you'll definitely want to take a day off from your diet!

Pisces is only open for dinner, from 6 pm, and is not inexpensive. Prices for starters are $7-$15, and main dishes are $21-$55. But for a special night out this is one restaurant not to be missed. Dress, as in most Bajan restaurants, is elegantly casual, and reservations are recommended.

☎ 246 435 6564, piscesrestaurant@caribsurf.com.

Players Sports Bar

See *Nightlife*.

Players Sports Bar, Worthing Main Road, Christ Church, ☎ 246 426 3596.

★★★ The Restaurant at Southsea

Restaurant at Southsea
(barbadosbarbados.com)

Opened in 2003, they won the Barbados Restaurant of The Year in 2004 and 2005, a Four Diamond rating by the AAA Association, and were voted one of the top 66 new restaurants in the world by *Condé Nast Traveler.*

The restaurant is built in a traditional Barbadian home, overlooking a bay in St Lawrence Gap. Serving international cuisine, it has an outstanding wine list and the Caribbean's most extensive vintage rum collection.

Ask for a seat on the verandah!

St Lawrence Gap, Christ Church, ☎ 246 420 7423, restaurant-southsea@caribsurf.com, www.therestaurantatsouthsea.com.

★Sweet Potatoes

Their sign says "Good Old Bajan Cooking" and that's what they serve. Before or after dinner, head to the bar and sample from their long list of cocktails.

Sweet Potatoes, St. Lawrence Gap, Christ Church, ☎ 246 435-9638.

★★Tamnak Thai

Sharing the same building as Aspara, Tamnak Thai is on the first floor. Tamnak Thai means "House Fit For A King," and when you enter you will see why. In the elegant dining room or outside on the verandah, feast on satays, hot, hot, hot, green curries, and a selection of seafoods. Open for lunch and dinner, Monday to Sunday. Starters $12.50-$30, main courses $27.70-$47.50.

Apsara on the ground floor & Tamnak Thai on the floor above (barbadosbarbados.com)

Tamnak Thai, Worthing, Christ Church, ☎ 246 435 5454.

★★Thirty-Nine Steps Bistro & Wine Bar

Pasta, steak, fish and gourmet pizza paired with a glass of wine from their extensive list is what you can expect at this informal and affordable bistro. Open for lunch Monday to Friday, dinner Monday to Saturday.

Thirty-Nine Steps Bistro & Wine Bar, Chattel Plaza, Hastings, Christ Church, ☎ 246 427-0715.

★★Zafran

For the authentic taste of classical Indian, Persian, and Thai cuisine visit one of Zafran's four dining areas (smoking or non-smoking) and check out their curries, tandoori, and vegetarian selections. Located in the former US embassy, they are open for dinner every day. Three-course lunch $19, dinner $19-$40.

Zafran, Worthing Main Road, Worthing, Christ Church, ☎ 246 435 8995

Fast Food

Kentucky Fried Chicken, Hastings Oistins, Sheraton Centre, Christ Church.

Chefette Restaurants, various locations in Christ Church. Roti, pizza, chicken, sandwiches, salads.

Chicken Barn, Worthing, Christ Church, ☎ 246 435-7428. Barbecue chicken, burgers.

Nightlife

They say, "Entertainment in Barbados starts in St Lawrence Gap!" And it's not difficult to see why, the Gap has an enormous range of bars, restaurants and other attraction to suit every taste.

★★ The Plantation Theatre

Bajan Roots & Rhythms

The Bajan Roots & Rhythms show at The Plantation is a dinner and stage show representing the best of West Indian culture. An all-inclusive extravaganza featuring music, song, dance, fire-eating and a flaming limbo dancer. The buffet includes a wide range of Bajan entrées, salads and desserts.

St Lawrence Main Road, Christ Church, ☎ 246 428 5048, 246 420 6317, plantationrest@ sunbeach.net.

The Whistling Frog

The Whistling Frog, at Time Out At The Gap, has party nights with Karaoke, and live music.

★ Jam Rock Café & Grill

The Jam Rock Café Music Bar and Grill is a great place to eat as well as party. Different nights feature different music everything from top 40 to alt rock, salsa and hip-hop. Some nights feature live bands playing reggae and calypso.

☎ 246 420 7615.

★Café Jungles Tree House

Loud music in a jungle setting, great DJs and a Saturday night Coyote Ugly party with dancing on the bar.
St Lawrence Gap, ☎ 246 437 1127.

★Café Sol Mexican Grill & Margarita Bar

A little splash of Mexico in Barbados! The best Margaritas on the island served in glasses rimmed with sugar instead of salt. Sombreros on the walls, a great patio, and slow service – just like Mexico!
St Lawrence Gap, ☎ 246 420 7655.

★McBride's Pub & Cookhouse

Popular with both locals and visitors, the music ranges from reggae to hip hop, and karaoke to live bands. Always crowded, always loud!
St Lawrence Gap, ☎ 246 435 6352.

★Mojo

If you like rock music from the 60s on, then you'll love Mojo. Located in a renovated two-story house on Worthing Main Road, the décor consists of photos of rock stars from the 60s. Expect friendly service, cheap drinks and big crowds.
Worthing Main Road, ☎ 246 435 9008.

Players Sports Bar

Open 24 hours a day, featuring slot machines and multiple TVs both inside and on the verandah, showing sports from around the world. Cheap drinks and friendly service make it a favorite for sports lovers.
Worthing Main Road, ☎ 246 426 3596.

★Red Rooster Pub & Grill

Features live music from steel pan to alternative rock four nights a week, and a great happy hour. The Red Rooster is popular with both locals and visitors.
Garrison Historical Area, Hastings Main Road, ☎ 246 435 3354.

★Pravda Lounge

A sophisticated bar with great décor and great music. A good place to go for drinks, before or after dinner. The bar has a dress code; shorts are not allowed.
St Lawrence Gap, ☎ 246 420 7617.

★★ The Reggae Lounge

The Reggae Lounge is an open-air nightclub where you can dance under the stars, surrounded by natural, tropical vegetation with DJ's playing music from, reggae and calypso to rhythm and blues. Saturday nights features live music from Biggie Irie and the Mo'Lava Band.

Doors open at 9 pm. ☎ 246 435 6462.

The Ship Inn

The Ship Inn, proclaimed as "The Original Pub," has been going strong since 1974. Live music, live sports, plenty of good food and a DJ and live bands playing several nights a week.

The Captain's Carvery has a traditional Bajan buffet and is open for lunch and dinner. The restaurant offers an à la carte menu, and Barnacle Bill's BBQ has fresh char grilled fish and chicken, sandwiches, burgers and hot dogs.

St Lawrence Gap, ☎ 246 420-7447, fax 246 420-7661.

★ After Dark

After Dark is popular with both visitors and locals; the bartenders, standing behind the longest bar on the island, are friendly and generous. The outdoor dance floor features live music with popular local bands such as Square One and Coalishun playing calypso, soca, and reggae. The main room has DJ's spinning hot dance tracks, while the Jazz Club is more laid-back.

St Lawrence Gap, ☎ 246 435 6547.

★ Club Xtreme

Just a short distance from The Gap on the Worthing Road is Club Xtreme, a 10,000-square-foot state-of-the-art nightclub with the hottest DJs and the wildest parties. The club is divided into three zones – The Xtreme zone is where the dance action happens. The latest lighting, special effects lasers and state of the art sound all come together to keep the party pumping. The Game zone has the latest arcade games, pool and air hockey, so when you don't want to dance you can play. The Chill zone is a special room away from the noise and the crowd, a place to hang out with friends.

Worthing Main Road, Worthing, Christ Church, Barbados, ☎ 246 435-4455, fax 246 228-3344.

★★★Oistins

Oistins is one of the most popular attractions in Barbados. On a Friday evening, from around 6 pm onwards, hundreds of locals and visitors congregate here to enjoy freshly cooked fish, sample local rum and enjoy Caribbean music. The food is cheap – around $7.50

Friday night at Oistins

per plate, including fish, salad, macaroni pie, sweet potato, rice and peas. Buy some rum or a beer at one of the rum shops, find a seat at a picnic bench, listen as music fills the air, get up and dance if you hear a song you like, and enjoy the experience.

Music is geared toward the older generation at one end, while at the other end the music is more up-to-date, from disco through to hip-hop.

Bert's

If you're looking for a sports bar, there are two in Christ Church. Bert's, in Rockley, features state-of-the-art satellite sports coverage, a wall-size projection TV in the bar, and 24 plasma screens located throughout the restaurant and poolside. The menu includes North American and Bajan food, and pizza from a stone-fired pizza oven. Happy hour: 4:30-6 pm daily. Open seven days a week from 11:30 am.

Rockley, Christ Church, ☎ 246 435-7924, info@bertsbarbados.com.

Bubba's Sports Bar & Restaurant

This has two satellite dishes, three 10-ft screens, and 12 additional TVs. Catch the NFL, NBA, hockey, Formula One racing, and Premier League soccer. Bubba's fully air-conditioned two floors allow smoking on the main floor, better known as "The Pit" and is smoke-free on the second level.

They have an à la carte menu, great for adults and families, and serve breakfast on Sundays between 8 and 10:30 am.

Rockley Main Road, Christ Church, ☎ 246 435-6217, fax 246 435-8732, bubbas2@caribsurf.com.

Lucky Horseshoe Saloon & Steakhouse

Open 24 hours a day, the Lucky Horseshoes, one in Christ Church and one in St Michael, are loud Wild-West-themed bars, featuring slot machines, music videos on dozens of screens and a constant party atmosphere. Worthing Main Road, Christ Church, ☎ 246 435 5825.

If you want your nightlife a little quieter, enjoy an evening of romance and fine dining at one of the many great restaurants (see *Where to Eat*). Many sit right on the edge of the ocean and some provide live entertainment to complement the mood.

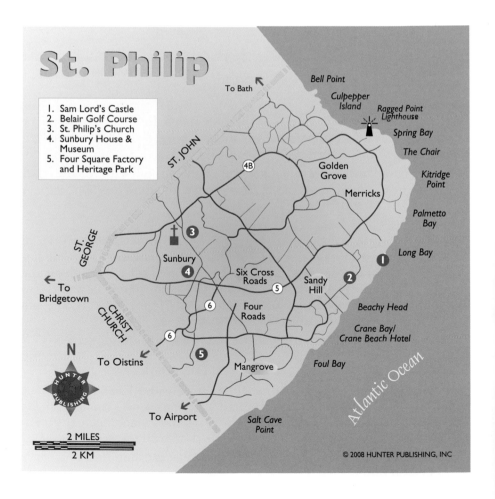

St. Philip

1. Sam Lord's Castle
2. Belair Golf Course
3. St. Philip's Church
4. Sunbury House & Museum
5. Four Square Factory and Heritage Park

© 2008 HUNTER PUBLISHING, INC

St Philip

Dead man can' run from 'e coffin.
(It's impossible to escape one's responsibilities.)

Located in the south east of the island, bordered by St George to the north west, St John to the north, and Christ Church to the west. The largest of the 11 parishes, it is relatively flat with the largest area of crop cultivation. There are no large cities. The largest commercial and residential area in St Philip is Six Cross Roads, which consists of a roundabout and neighborhood, where six roads converge.

Sightseeing

★★ The Parish Church

Just off highway 4B in Cottage Vale is St Philip's parish church. The original church on the site, built before 1649, was replaced in 1786, and again in 1831. The present church, built in 1836, was restored, after being gutted by fire in 1977.

St Philip Parish Church

★Ragged Point & East Point Lighthouse

Ragged Point Lighthouse

East Point Lighthouse is at Ragged Point, the easternmost point of the island. It offers a spectacular view of almost the entire East Coast of Barbados. Built in 1875, its white stone tower rises 97 feet (29½ m). It sits above the cliffs and is the most picturesque lighthouse in Barbados. Just off the coast is Culpepper, a tiny island that can be reached at low tide.

★Sunbury Plantation House

The original house was built in 1660. In the 1816 slave rebellion, the property sustained considerable damage. It was restored, and then in 1995 the house was destroyed by fire, but has now been restored once more to its former glory.

Unlike most stately homes, every room in Sunbury House is open for viewing. It houses an impressive collection of antiques, china, glassware and antique prints. The grounds surrounding the house are home to the largest collection of horse-drawn carriages in the entire Caribbean region!

You can enjoy snacks and drinks in the Courtyard Restaurant, surrounded by tropical gardens and woodlands.

Open daily from 10 am until 5 pm.

Sunbury Plantation House, ☎ 246 423 6270.

Sunbury Plantation House

Sunbury Plantation House bedroom

★Oughterson House & Zoo

Once the center of a large sugarcane plantation, Oughterson House is a Barbadian Great House of both architectural and historic interest. The house consists of an original 18th-century two-story block and a 19th-century single-story addition at the front. The ground floor is open to the public and contains some interesting antiques.

The former outbuildings and paddocks have been adapted to house a collection of birds, reptiles and mammals from around the world. The tanks in the remains of the old syrup factory are used for breeding tropical fish. Visitors can walk through the nature trail around the orchard. The zoo, although small, has a wide range of animals, including tapirs, squirrel monkeys, two species of capuchin monkey, marmosets, armadillos and agoutis. There are five different species of macaw and various species of South American caiman (alligators), four different species of boa constrictors, along with zebras, grey parrots, Barbados green monkeys and many more. Open 9 am-5 pm daily.

Oughterson House & Zoo, Nr. Bushy Park, ☎ 246 423-6203, fax 246 423-6167.

Four Square Rum Factory

The Four Square Rum Factory is one of the oldest rum distilleries on the island. It is set on eight acres of landscaped park in the heart of sugar cane country. There is a children's play area and petting zoo. You can take a guided tour of the rum factory, which has pictures detailing the rum process from past to present. There is a large art and craft center, a gift shop, a restaurant selling light snacks and refreshments, and an amphitheatre.

 Note: When I visited the factory, there was no one around, except one sleepy worker on the second floor. I wondered through the factory and then the grounds. Maybe it would be better in the high season, but when I was there, I found little to recommend it.

Adventures on Foot

Hiking

 The Barbados National Trust organizes Sunday walks at 6 am and 3:30 pm The hikes are listed in the newspaper, or you can obtain a schedule for $2.50 from the National Trust.
Barbados National Trust, ☎ 246 426 2421, fax 246 429 9055.

Adventures on Water

Beaches

 Although often not safe for swimming, the East Coast beaches are some of the nicest on the island, if not the world. Because there is often a strong breeze coming off the ocean, you may be unaware of the heat and it is easy to get sunburned. Make sure you use lots of sunscreen!

★★★**Bottom Bay**. Park at the top of the cliff, climb down the steps, and you come to... Paradise! Coconut palms, soft white sand, gentle breezes and the sun glinting off the blue-green sea – you have arrived at Bottom Bay

The bay is spectacular, and the sea,

Bottom Bay

although rough with strong currents, is suitable for strong swimmers.

There are no amenities, no outlets selling food or drink, and no lifeguards. The beach is often quite deserted, so leave the kids behind, take a picnic and your significant other and enjoy a taste of paradise.

★★★**Crane Beach**. Crane Beach is rated as one of the top 10 beaches in the world by *Lifestyles of the Rich and Famous*! The Crane Beach Hotel is a grand coral mansion perched atop tree-shaded dunes. Pink-tinged sand, steady breezes and a restless sea combine to create the best beach on the island.

Crane Beach at dusk

The sea is rough but is excellent for body boarding and safe for strong swimmers. Boogie boards, umbrellas, and beach chairs can be rented, and when you get hungry, climb the steps to L'Azure Restaurant at the Crane Beach Hotel.

If you park at the hotel there is a $25 BDS ($12 US) per person entrance fee redeemable at the bar or restaurant.

Foul Bay

★★★**Foul Bay**. A beautiful long, open expanse of beach, home to a small fleet of local fishing boats, on a ruggedly gorgeous stretch of coastline. The waves are big and break onshore, so there is a strong undertow at times. Never swim alone and make sure everyone is a strong swimmer. It is a great spot for body boarding, but there is no lifeguard, so don't allow children in the water. There are no amenities, no beach chairs, nowhere to buy food or drinks. However, there is a shower and toilets. A number of weddings have been performed on the beach.

★★★**Ginger Beach**. One of Barbados' best-kept secrets. This beautiful beach with hidden caves, white sand, swaying palm trees and blue water is often deserted, so it's perfect for a romantic picnic. The water is rough with strong undercurrents and there is no lifeguard on duty, so don't swim alone.

You have to climb down a rough set of stairs to get to the beach, and there are no amenities, so you must bring everything you need with you.

★★**Harrismith Beach**. On the cliff above the beach the burnt-out ruins of a grand mansion stands silent guard. The steps down to the beach are quite rough and steep but, once you arrive, you won't be disappointed.

There are no amenities, no lifeguard and swimming is dangerous, but there are shallow pools between the rocks at low tide where you can wade.

★★**Sam Lord's Beaches**. Sam Hall Lord, a colorful character from Barbados' past, built Sam Lord's Castle. Apparently, Mr. Lord placed lanterns in the coconut trees in order to lure ships onto the nearby reefs. Once the ships were grounded, he went out with a group of men, looted the ships and stored the booty in tunnels under the castle. For many years, the castle was a luxury hotel but it ran into financial difficulties and closed its doors in 2003.

Since its closing, beach access has been difficult, with many of the old walkways down to the beach overgrown. But it's worth the effort to get there. There are lots of benches and what used to be a beach bar and concrete dance floor. The sea is very rough and too dangerous for swimming. The area is quite isolated, so be sure to leave the beach before dark, as the climb up is not easy.

Skeetes Bay

★★**Skeetes Bay**. Swimming is safe here but there is no lifeguard on duty. You can fish from the jetty and, if you don't catch anything, there is a fishing complex where you can buy fresh fish. Early in the morning, you can watch the fishing boats leave, and then watch them return later. Toilets and showers are available.

Where to Stay

★★★ The Crane Beach Hotel

After landing at Grantley Adams Airport take the road less traveled and drive east. You will come to a place that just may be Paradise. At the end of a long drive, and surrounded by 40 lush acres, is The Crane Beach Hotel, sitting 50 feet above Crane Beach, rated one of the 10 best beaches in the world.

The Crane Beach Hotel is not a sterile, modern hotel, but a grand coral mansion, with the main villa dating from 1790 and the resort itself, the oldest continuously operating resort in the Caribbean, dating back to 1887.

Luxurious, but laid-back, the Crane's rooms and suites feature four poster mahogany beds, marble bathrooms, coral walls, and balconies overlooking the rest-

Crane Beach pool at sunset

less Atlantic Ocean. If you can drag yourself from the luxury of your room, just a few steps away is the restaurant **L'Azure**. White tablecloths, candlelight and a soft guitar complement the culinary pleasures of L'Azure, brought to you by its Michelin-starred chef. If you prefer something a little more exotic, head over to **Zen**, where the Thai and Japanese chefs serve sushi, while you sit in front of a wall of glass and watch the sea pounding against the rocks 50 feet below. Or, if you just can't pull yourself away from your room, you can order breakfast served on your own private balcony.

But, at some point, you have to leave your room and head off to the beach. Surrounded by rugged cliffs, lapped by the turquoise ocean, and caressed by a constant breeze, the white sand beach is heaven in the Caribbean. Take a book, rent a beach chair and umbrella and while away the day or, if you're feeling adventurous, rent a boogie board and body surf the waves.

If you don't ever want to leave, and you certainly won't be the first, you can now take ownership of the recently developed residences. You can own for a week, a month, or outright and, with less than seven residences per acre, and more than half a mile of ocean frontage, you may never have to leave this unique oasis of privacy and tranquility again.

The Crane, St Philip, ☎ 246 423 6220, fax 246 423 5343, reservations@ thecrane.com, www.thecrane.com.

Latoyas Guest House

A small but comfortable guesthouse with one- , two- , and three-bedroom units, 15 minutes from the airport and five minutes from Bottom Bay. Units have fridge, stove, microwave, and TV.

Rates for one bedroom $40, two bedrooms $80, three bedrooms $100 per night.

Latoyas Guest House, Cole, St Philip, ☎ 246 428 3853, 246 253 8448, latoyas_holiday_villas@yahoo.com.

Lindale Apartments

Sitting room in Lindale apartment

Studio, budget apartment, four bedrooms, three baths, two kitchens, dining area, TV, and patio, plus two two-bedroom self-contained apartments. Close to Crane Beach and Foul Bay, as well as on a main bus route.

Rates for studios $35 per day single occupancy, for rooms $20 per person, based on minimum four sharing. Upper floor: Studios $40 per day single occupancy, $45 double occupancy; two-bedroom apartment $50 double occupancy, $10 per day per extra person.

Lindale Apartments, St Martin, St Philip, ☎ 246 423 4233, linb@ caribsurf.com.

Khus Khus Apartments

Two family-owned furnished apartments with air-conditioning, cable TV, Internet access, and fully fitted kitchens, in a quiet residential area within walking distance of Crane Beach. $40 per night single, $60 per night double.

Khus Khus Apartments, 82 Union Development, St Philip, ☎ 246 243 1396, fluffy71255@yahoo.com.

Where to Eat

Chefette Restaurant

Fast food restaurant great for kids and adults, menu includes pizza, roti, chicken, sandwiches, salads, and ice cream.

Chefette Restaurant, Six Roads, St. Philip, ☎ 246 416 8480.

★★★ L'Azure

The Crane Beach hotel is home to two fabulous restaurants, L'Azure, and Zen. Both have spectacular views over Crane Beach. L'Azure offers an international and Caribbean menu, and is open for breakfast, lunch, and dinner. It has live background music in the evening. On Sundays, there is a Gospel Breakfast, a great way to start your day, with live Gospel choirs performing. Following breakfast is a Bajan buffet lunch.

L'Azure

★★ Sunbury Plantation House

Dining al fresco at Sunbury Plantation House

Have lunch or tea at a 300-year-old plantation house. Or, for something really special, have the Planters Candlelight Dinner, a five course meal served on the 200-year-old mahogany dining table. The evening includes cocktails before dinner, a tour of the house, the five-course meal with wine, followed by liqueurs and coffee in the drawing room. This is a great way to spend a special night out. A Sunday brunch is also served.

The Planters Candlelight Dinner is $75 per person. The Brunch is $29 per person.

Sunbury Plantation House, 6 Cross Road, St Philip, ☎ 246 423 6270, fax 246 423 5863, sunbury@caribsurf.com, www.barbadosgreathouse.com.

★★★ Zen

Zen is a beautifully decorated restaurant offering authentic Thai and Japanese cuisine. For complete privacy there are a number of tatami rooms; just close the screen doors and dine in splendid isolation. There is also a sushi bar with large glass windows overlooking the beach.

L'Azure & Zen, The Crane, St Philip, ☎ 246 423 6220, fax 246 423 5343, info@thecrane.com.

Nightlife

The only nightlife in St Philip are the restaurants at **Sunbury Plantation House** and **The Crane**. However, **Christ Church**, with its restaurants, bars and clubs is the main center for nightlife on the island, and is just a short cab ride away.

St. James

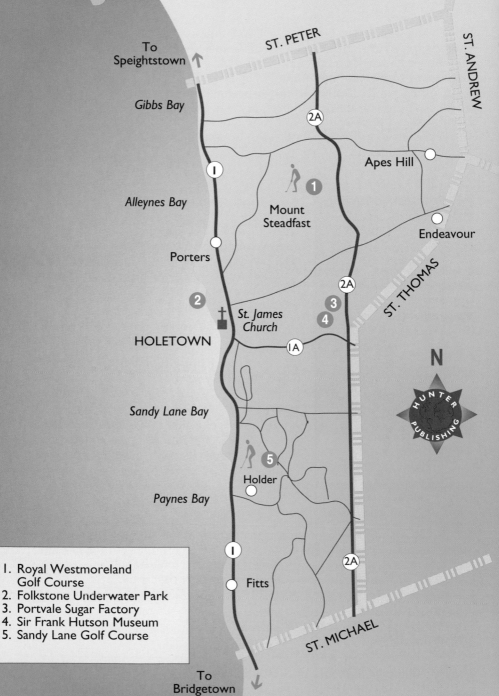

To Speightstown

ST. PETER

Gibbs Bay

ST. ANDREW

2A

Apes Hill

Alleynes Bay

①

Mount Steadfast

Endeavour

Porters

②

2A

ST. THOMAS

③

④

St. James Church

1A

HOLETOWN

Sandy Lane Bay

⑤

Holder

Paynes Bay

Fitts

2A

ST. MICHAEL

N

HUNTER PUBLISHING

1. Royal Westmoreland Golf Course
2. Folkstone Underwater Park
3. Portvale Sugar Factory
4. Sir Frank Hutson Museum
5. Sandy Lane Golf Course

To Bridgetown

2 MILES
2 KM

The West Coast
St James

De higher de monkey climb, de more 'e show 'e tail.
(The more you show off, the more your faults are seen.)

The parish of St James is bordered by St Peter to the north, St Andrew to the east, St Michael to the south, and St Andrew to the southeast.

Originally known as the gold coast, with the development of many luxury hotels and residences, and the influx of the rich and famous, it is now called the platinum coast. Tiger Woods chose the Sandy Lane Hotel as the site for his wedding, and Hollywood stars can sometimes be seen emerging from their luxury houses along the coast.

The first British settlers landed here in 1625 in Holetown. Originally

known as Jamestown, it came to be called Holetown because of the off-loading and cleaning of ships in the small tidal hole near the town. This is the site of the annual Holetown Festival, celebrating crafts, music, and history!

St James is one of the major tourist areas in Barbados, combining world-class shopping, with luxury hotels, and beautiful beaches lapped by the Caribbean.

In some ways, however, it is a victim of its own success. Traffic jams are common and the peace is continually interrupted by sounds of building, as new luxury homes and hotels go up on every spare inch of beachfront property. It is interesting to note the contrast between multi-million-dollar properties butting up against run-down chattel houses, the owners of which could easily make millions by selling, but are content to live as they always have.

The parish is home to Queen's College, founded in 1683 by Colonel Henry Drax, a successful plantation owner. The school has had many names and incarnations since its inception, originally Drax's School, then The Free School, The Parochial Charity School and, finally in 1883, Queen's College. Originally, a girl's school, it is now co-ed and is recognized as one of the top schools in the Caribbean.

Inland, the parish is quite rural, with small villages dotting the landscape. Just a short drive from Holetown is The Portvale Sugar Factory and Museum, where sugar cane from all across the island is turned into sugar and molasses.

But people come to St James for the beaches and they are among the best and safest on the island.

Shopping

Main Street, Holetown (Rodney Nelson)

St James offers some of the best shopping on the island, from the Chattel House Village, offering gifts, crafts and souvenirs, to the West Coast Mall, with its collection of brand name stores and upscale boutiques, to the exclusive Diamonds International, an attractively appointed boutique at the Fairmont Royal Pavilion.

Holetown, the third-largest town in Barbados, is a good place to start your shopping excursion. Locally owned stores include **Island Living Clothing** on 2nd Street, where you can find clothing for infants, children and adults, all made from 100% cotton fabrics and featuring tropical designs. **Gaye Boutique** is another local store carrying exclusive designer beachwear, casual and evening wear.

The renovated **West Coast Mall** is home to shoe stores, photo stores, women's and men's clothing shops, and places selling everything from CDs to household furniture. Stores include **Pages Bookstore**, **Cave Shepherd** (the largest tax-free department store in Barbados), **Madison Boutique**, the **Super Centre Supermarket**, and the tax-free **Diamonds International**. Diamonds International is a family-run business with over 110 outlets throughout the Caribbean region, Mexico and the USA. They are a leading retailer of diamond jewelry, watches, designer jewelry and precious gemstones. Buying direct from the world's largest diamond cutters, they avoid the middlemen and pass the savings directly to their customers. Jewelers on staff will help you design a unique piece and craft it to your specifications. They also have an extensive selection of jewelry by Raima, La Nouvelle Bague, Errecibi, Crown Rings, Kings View, Jacob Jewelry and John Hardy, as well as watches by Cartier, Piaget, Audemars Piguet, Girard Perregaux, Gucci, Breitling. The store is the exclusive retailer for crystal, china and silverware on the West Coast. Brands such as Baccarat, Lalique, Daum, Bernardaud and Christofle are all available at the store. They have recently added a specialized pen boutique featuring limited edition pens made with artistic designs, unique materials, and world-class craftsmanship.

If you have any room left on your credit card, head to the **Chattel House Village**, located on the side of the highway. You'll find a brightly colored collection of chattel houses selling local crafts, gifts, artwork and souvenirs. Stores include **Best of Barbados Shop**, **Walkers World**, **Ganzee T-Shirts**, **The Gourmet Shop**, **Dingolay West** (selling handbags, sandals, jewelry and their own line of casual wear), and **Lazy Days** swimwear and surf shop.

A little farther south on the side of the highway is **Sunset Crest**, where a number of fruit stalls and stores offer souvenirs and gifts.

Sightseeing

If you are here in mid-February to early March, you can catch the **Holetown Festival**. Celebrating the arrival of the first English settlers in 1627, the festival is an exciting mix of modern and traditional music, dancing, parades, markets, sports, games, and food. There aren't many sites to visit in St James itself but the rest of the island is easily reached and you'll have no problem filling your time.

★★ The Parish Church

One of the original four churches on the island, located in Holetown near the island's first settlement, it sits on one of the oldest parcels of consecrated land in Barbados, known as God's Acre. The first church on the site was built within a year of the first landing in 1628. Built of wood, it was destroyed in 1675 by a

St James Parish Church

hurricane. Rebuilt of stone in the early 1690's, it survived storms and hurricanes for more than 200 years, but by 1874 wear and tear had taken its toll and it was partially demolished, to be replaced by a larger structure. The front and south entrances are over 300 years old and, apart from the sanctuary and north porch, added in the 1900's, the church is essentially the same as it was in 1874. The original baptismal font (1684) can still be seen under the belfry. The original bell in the southern porch, cast in 1669, has the inscription "God Bless King William, 1696." It predates the Liberty Bell in Philadelphia by 54 years.

There is a beautiful stained glass window depicting the *Ascension*, dedicated in 1924 to the memory of the fallen in World War I, and on the front pew is a plaque to the President of the USA and Mrs. Reagan, who worshipped here on Easter Sunday, April 11, 1982.

The church and its yard is the final resting place for many of the original settlers and other noted Barbadians.

 There is an old belief that church bells were rung to drive the devil out of the building. A gate in the north wall surrounding the churchyard, referred to as "The Devil's Gate," is opened about one hour before service. When the bell is rung it is believed the Devil leaves the church by this gate, which is closed as the service is about to begin, excluding him from the area.

Sir Frank Hutson Sugar Machinery Museum

The Sugar Machinery Museum

A couple of miles inland, this museum is in an old building beside the Portvale sugar factory, off highway 2A, north of Lawrence Johnson roundabout and the parish church of St. Thomas. Scattered outside are various pieces of sugar-making machinery; inside is more machinery and an exhibition about the story of sugar and its products. When I visited, it was off-season; no one was around so I wandered inside. Someone came over and asked for $4, but the whole place looked untended and uninteresting so I declined and left. I have seen glowing reviews and, apparently, the curator Douglas Corbyn provides an excellent commentary. Sir Frank Hutson amassed the collection, and the National Trust now administers the museum. During the cane-grinding season, you can visit the factory to see sugar being produced. Mon-Sat 9 am-5 pm. $7.50 when the factory is running Feb-May, $4 the rest of the time, children half-price. ☎ 246 432 0100.

Folkestone Marine Museum

This museum at the Folkestone Park and Marine Reserve is in an old building beside the Portvale sugar factory, off highway 2A, north of Lawrence Johnson roundabout and the parish church of St. Thomas. Unfortunately at this time it isn't much more interesting than the Sugar Machinery Museum. The museum is tiny, with some old shells and fish in jars, a shark's jaw, and a few tired exhibits. The aquarium was closed for repair when I was there. There are plans to renovate and expand the museum and this may well make it more interesting.

The Marine Reserve (See *Eco-Tourism* below) stretches for one mile (1. 6 km) along Folkestone Beach and there are picnic tables, vendors and water sports equipment available for rent right in front of the museum. ☎ 246 422 2871, ncc@caribsurf.com.

Adventures on Foot

Hiking

I've never tried it but it is supposedly possible to walk all the way from Holetown to Bridgetown at low tide. This would make for quite an impressive walk, but you'd need to find a way to get back at the end.

The **Barbados National Trust** organizes hikes from various locations throughout the island. Check with them to see if one is leaving from somewhere nearby. ☎ 246 426 2421.

Alternatively, set off inland and you will soon come to unspoiled areas where you can take a self-guided hike.

Golf

St James is home to four great golf courses. Unfortunately, they are all private. Guest passes are available but are extremely expensive.

★★★**The Royal Westmoreland** is a 27-hole course designed by Robert Trent Jones. The course lies on 500 acres of a former sugar plantation. Greens fees range from $75 to $190 depending on season, cart fee included. Club rental and lessons are available. The club is so exclusive that only guests and those staying at certain hotels, including Cobblers

Royal Westmoreland Golf Course

Cove, Coral Reef Club, Glitter Bay, and Royal Pavilion, have access. The blue of the Caribbean is visible from every hole. This is a beautiful course but, with the wind coming in off the Atlantic, driving can be quite difficult. If you're not staying at one of the hotels that have access, see if you can make friends with someone who is. You won't be disappointed!

Open daily, dawn to dusk. ☎ 246 422 4653, fax 246 419 7205.

★★★**Sandy Lane Golf Club** has three courses – The Country Club, and the Green Monkey, both designed by Tom Fazio, and The Old Nine. The Sandy Lane, built on a former sugar plantation, is the most prestigious course on the island. Tiger Woods chose the hotel as the place to get married, and apparently spent about $1.5 million to do it!

The Green Monkey is a 7,100-yard par-72 course and the Country Club is 7,060-yard, par-72 course that opened in 2001.

The Green Monkey is only open to guests of Sandy Lane and friends of Tiger Woods! The Country Club is pay-as-you-play but is very expensive. In 2006, the World Golf Championships/World Cup was played at the Country Club Course.

Open daily, dawn to dusk. ☎ 246 444 2500, golf@sandylane.com.

Adventures on Wheels

ATV Quads

Rent an ATV quad bike by the hour, half-day, or full-day. After a pre-ride safety and training course, don a helmet and head off into the country. You can ride off-road or on and, as they say in their ads, you get "free air-conditioning."

You must be over 21 and have a valid drivers license. ☎ 246 424 0165, atvquads4u@mail.com.

Adventures on Water

Beaches

St James is famous for its many sandy beaches and tranquil waters. It is very safe for swimming and offers great opportunities for snorkeling, scuba, and other water sports. I have listed three you might want to check out, but there are plenty more for you to discover.

Paynes Bay (barbadosawaits.com)

★**Fitts Village** is a fishing village that has several reefs just off-shore. It is very quiet and a great place to relax away from the crowds.

★**Paynes Bay** is just north of Fitts. You can reach the beach through a public entrance opposite the Coach House restaurant. The Coach House operates a beach stand selling drinks and snacks. Jet skiing and catamaran sailing are available on the beach.

★**Sandy Lane Beach**, south of Holetown, fronts the famous Sandy Lane Hotel (room rates easily run to $10,000 per week or more!). The beach is accessible through a lane running down the side of the hotel. It is a good spot for celebrity spotting and, if the sun gets too hot, you can shelter under the mahogany trees that line the beach.

Scuba Diving

The **Lord Combemere** is a 70-ft/ 23-m wreck sitting in 40 ft/13 m of water. Home to hatchet fish, lobsters and the occasional barracuda, the wreck is suitable for novice to intermediate divers. Moving away from the wreck to the reef, at about 60 ft you can find squirrelfish, black bars, and grunts, plus some stingrays and turtles.

Adventures on Horseback

★★Polo School

Sign up for a Polo Day Package at **Waterhall Polo Stables**. They have 108 stables, and over 100 trained horses, a full-size polo field, a club-house, a grandstand, and two professional polo instructors. You start the day with a morning coffee and instructional video, then you have a lesson

on a wooden horse. After a break for lunch, it's time for a lesson on a real horse. The lesson is recorded on video for analysis. Then, to end the day, you get to play a chukka (there are six chukkas, or periods, in a polo match, each lasting seven minutes). You'll return to your hotel tired but invigorated. ☎ 246 262 3282/246 432 9550, maryann@caribsurf.com.

Eco-Tourism

Folkestone Marine Reserve

The Marine Reserve stretches for a mile (1.6 km) from Coral Reef to Sandy Lane, and includes both Dottin's Reef and Vauxhall Reef. It's the primary observation area for the nearby Belairs Institute.

At Folkestone Park, there is an enclosed area where you can swim, snorkel with the fish, and sometimes (July to October) hawksbill turtles, or leatherbacks (February to June). There are a number of tours to Alleyne's Bay, a bit north, where you will find a larger number of turtles.

For $10, you can take a glass-bottomed boat to the reef and to a couple of wrecks farther down the coast. There is a diving platform about 300 ft (100 m) offshore, from where you can snorkel over the wrecks.

The beach at Folkestone is not one of the best, being usually crowded and quite noisy. Weekends are particularly busy. There is a lifeguard on duty and snorkeling equipment and sun beds are available for rent. There are lockers for rent, as well as toilets, and showers.

Church Point, St James, ☎ 246 422 2871, ncc@caribsurf.com.

Cultural Excursions

The Tides Gallery

The Tides Gallery

Not too many restaurants are also art galleries but The Tides is one. Displaying works of art from new and established artists on the island, the works are a mixture of Realist, Impressionist, and Abstract, changing every month. Prints are available from $50.

It's set right on the ocean so, if you love fine food and fine art, it's a great place to visit and a great place to eat. Open for lunch and dinner.

Balmore House, Holetown, ☎ 246 432 8356, fax 246 432 8358, thetidesrest@sunbeach.net.

Spectator Sports

★★★Polo

Head on over to the **Waterhall Polo Stables** and catch a game of polo. Tickets are only $2.50 and games are held every Wednesday and Saturday from October to May. There are local matches as well as visiting international teams but either way you are in for an exciting afternoon. Drinks flow freely and a barbecue dinner is served. If you've never been to a game before this is a must see. The Barbados Polo Club, Holders Hill, St. James, ☎ 246 437 5410.

Where to Stay

 St James is home to some of the best hotels and villas on the island, but there is more than just high-end luxury accommodation available. There are guesthouses and hotels to suit every taste and budget. So you don't have to be rich to enjoy the white sand beaches and, while you're out sunbathing or shopping, you never know which movie star or billionaire may be right there beside you. But don't worry. They won't bother you!

If you want the ultimate in luxury, consider renting a villa. The west coast of Barbados has some of the most luxurious villas anywhere, many sleeping 12 or more. So, although not cheap, if you have a group of friends or family together, they can be surprisingly affordable when compared to the cost of a luxury hotel. Most are fully staffed and your every need is taken care of. And if you fall in love with the place, it might be available for sale.

Barbados Holiday Home

Located in the Sunset Crest Development, this self-contained one-bedroom condo with en-suite shower sleeps three and includes air-conditioning, cable TV, security system, telephone, parking and private patio. Newly refurbished, the apartment comes at a very affordable price. Short-term rental rates range from $100 US per night. Long-term rates available on request.

Apt. 6 Alamanda Row, Sunset Crest, St James, ☎ 246 426 1957, www. barbadosholidayhome.com.

The West Coast

★Becky's by the Sea

A magnificent coral stone three-bedroom, two-bathroom villa just 50 yards (50 m) from Fitts Village beach, offering private accommodation with all the comforts of home. Rates from $250 per night.

Becky's by the Sea, Fitts Village, St James, ☎ 718 467 0635.

Best E Villas

Spacious air-conditioned two- and three-bedroom villas with kitchens, three minutes walk to Batt's Rock and Paradise beaches. Rates from $100 US per night.

Best E Villas, Green Ridge, Prospect, St James, ☎ 246 425 9751, errolbest@bestevillas.com, www.bestevillas.com.

Calypso Rentals Inc

Vacation rentals with kitchens, ranging from small cottages to exclusive beachfront villas. Rates from $80 US per night

Calypso Rentals Inc, St James, ☎ 246 422 6405, contactus@calypso-rentals.com, www.calypso-rentals.com.

★★Divi Heritage Beach Resort

The Divi Heritage is an intimate oceanfront 22-villa property for adult guests only. Perfect for romantic special occasions and quiet escapes, the resort is intentionally quiet, offering spacious suites and an intimate environment. Facilities include suites with ocean views, tennis courts and an activities coordinator.

Divi Heritage Beach Resort, Sunset Crest, St James, ☎ 800 367 3484, fax 246 432 1527, comments@diviresorts.com, www.diviheritage.com.

Island Villas

Island Villas are exclusive associates of Savills International and provide a selection of exceptional homes, villas, commercial property and land for sale in Barbados.

Island Villas Ltd, Trents Building, Holetown, St James, ☎ 246 432 4627, fax 246 432 4628, www.island-villas.com.

★★★Royal Westmoreland

This is a gated community of fabulous villas. Set in 500 private acres of tropical landscape, it is the ultimate retreat for affluent vacationers and homeowners in search of seclusion.

At the heart of the estate is one of the world's finest championship golf courses. Residents also enjoy exclusive use of the Sanctuary Spa, floodlit tennis gardens and the Tennis Academy, a clubhouse restaurant, "Little

Royals" children's facility, and access to a secluded section of pristine beach, just minutes from the estate.

There are four different styles of villa – **Resort Club**, **Royal**, **Premium**, and **Exclusive**. The villas can be bought or rented. Resort Club rates per night: high season $500; low season $300; peak season $1,000. Royal rates with pool: high season $1,143; low season $714; peak season $2,500. Royal rates without pool: high season $1,071; low season $643; peak season $2,300. Pre-

Royal Westmoreland

mium three-bedroom rates: high season $1,214; low season $857; peak season $2,750. Premium four-bedroom: high season $1,421; low season $1,036; peak season $3,200. Exclusive four-bedroom: high season $2,071; low season $1,250; peak season $4,500. Exclusive six-bedroom: high season $2,500; low season $1,357; peak season $5,000 per night.

Royal Westmoreland, St James, ☎ 246 422 4653, fax 246 419 7205, villarental@royal-westmoreland.com, www.royal-westmoreland.com, UK Booking Office ☎ 44 0 1524 782503.

★★★ Sandy Lane Hotel

As the chauffeured Bentley picks you up at the airport, glides along the country roads and drops you off at the end of a mahogany tree-lined driveway, you realize this is not your average holiday resort. Sandy Lane is

Sandy Lane Hotel

The West Coast

considered the premier address in the Caribbean, a home away from home for movie stars, rock stars and royalty. Perfect for a romantic getaway, it's a secluded retreat and an active sports destination, with some of the best golf in the entire Caribbean, or a family holiday.

The 112 luxury rooms and suites average 900 square feet and have widescreen plasma televisions, an interactive entertainment center, specially designed multi-spray showers, private bar, and private veranda.

Sandy Lane Hotel, St James, ☎ 246 444 2000, fax 246 444 2222, www.sandylane.com.

Sundance Apartments

Two luxury apartments, Sundance & Sunbeams, both with four bedrooms, located just 50 yards (50 m) from the beautiful beach, they are ideal for large families and groups. Sunbeams is wheelchair-accessible. Rates from $1,000 per week.

Sundance Apartments, Paynes Bay, St James, ☎ +44 1202 252805, www.sundancebarbados.co.uk.

★★★ The Fairmont Royal Pavilion

The Fairmont Royal Pavilion

The Fairmont Royal Pavilion is one of my favorite hotels on the island. Fairmont always manages to create hotels that are elegant but still friendly. The hotel is primarily a couples resort during the high season (November 1 to April 30). Children are welcome May 1 to October 31. Each of the 72 oceanfront rooms is decorated in a relaxed Caribbean style, with its own private patio or terrace. There is also a three-bedroom villa hidden in the lush gardens.

Sitting right on a beautiful beach, the hotel feels like a luxurious estate home, blending old-world charm with modern conveniences, you won't be disappointed if you stay here.

Rates from $440 summer and $845 winter, double occupancy.
The Fairmont Royal Pavilion, St James, ☎ 1 866 540 4485.

★★★ The Colony Club

The Colony Club is a 4½-star, 96-room retreat, sitting right on the beach, with four lagoon-style swimming pools meandering through seven acres of tropical gardens. Every room and suite has cable TV, air-conditioning, bath and shower, mini fridge and a private patio or balcony.

The resort has two restaurants and bars, beach and pool concierge service, exercise facility, two floodlit tennis courts, beauty salon and spa. There are complimentary water sports, including snorkeling, sailing, boogie boards, kayaking, windsurfing, and waterskiing, as well as a preferred tee time agreement with the spectacular Royal Westmoreland Golf and Country Club. If golf is your game, you want to play on this course! Rates from $305 in summer and $603 in winter, double occupancy.

Colony Club, Porters, St James, ☎ 246 422 2335, US 800 467 4519, UK 0800 587 3427, www.colonyclubhotel.com.

★★ The Lone Star Hotel

An exclusive boutique hotel, restaurant and bar with four air-conditioned suites, with shady terraces overlook the beach. All rooms are fully air-conditioned, equipped with phone, fax, Internet access, satellite TV, stereo/CD, wet bar, fridge and tea/coffee facilities, a large patio terrace, and direct access to the beach. Suites from $350-$725/night.

The Lone Star Hotel, Mount Standfast, St James, ☎ 246 419 0598, fax 246 419 0597, wowgroupltd@sunbeach.net, www.thelonestar.com.

★★★ The Sandpiper

One of the most exclusive small hotels in the West Indies, The Sandpiper is a member of the Small Luxury Hotels of the World and, together with their associate hotel, the Coral Reef Club, are the only family-owned and -managed luxury resorts on the island. The property has been re-landscaped and two new "Tree Top Suites" have been built.

The Garden rooms are air-conditioned, with king or twin beds, bathroom and patio or balcony and can accommodate two adults. One-bedroom suites have a separate living room containing a sofa bed, kitchen, bathroom and patio or balcony and can accommodate either three adults or two adults and two children under 12 years.

The two-bedroom suites have a separate living room containing a sofa bed, kitchen, two bathrooms and large patio or balcony and can accommodate up to six people.

The Treetop suites have their own private sundeck with plunge pool, a large wraparound terrace with covered dining for up to six people, a spacious living area, bedroom with either a four-poster bed or twin beds, plus

Preceding page: The Colony Club courtyard

a dressing room and bathroom. In the living room, there is a television, DVD player, CD player and a selection of DVDs and CDs.

The hotel has a restaurant, bar, lounge, and fitness center.

Winter rates per night: Garden Room from $680; one-bedroom suite from $950; two-bedroom suite from $1,670; Treetop Suites from $2,300.

Summer rates per night: Garden Room from $280; one bedroom suite from $385; two-bedroom suite from $830; Treetop Suites from $1,150.

The Sandpiper, Holetown, St James, ☎ 246 422 2251, fax 246 422 0900, coral@caribsurf.com.

★★★ The Tamarind Cove

Reopened in 2006 after extensive renovations, the 110 spacious guestrooms and suites each have a private balcony or patio, air-conditioning, bath and shower, cable television, and mini-fridge.

Fronting onto a 750-foot (250-m) crescent of white sand beach with three freshwater pools, extensive landscaped gardens and secluded courtyards, the hotel is a true tropical oasis. Two restaurants, a beauty salon, state-of-the-art fitness facility, business center with Internet access, function and event rooms, and a preferred agreement with the Royal Westmoreland Golf and Country club round out the luxury features of the Tamarind Cove.

Tamarind Cove, Paynes Bay, St James, ☎ 246 432 1332, US 800 467 4519, UK 0800 587 3427, www.tamarindcovehotel.com.

Villa Marie Guesthouse & Apartments

Guesthouse and apartments set in tropical gardens, 70 ft (23 m) from the beach. The guesthouse consists of seven units on two levels, all with en-suite bathrooms. The furnished apartments sleep four. Rates start at $65 per night.

Villa Marie Guesthouse & Apartments, Lashley Road, Fitts Village, St James, %% 246 417 5799, fax 246 417 5799, villamarie@sunbeach.net, www.barbados.org/villas/villamarie.

Westerlee Villas

Three properties on five acres of tropical gardens, with a swimming pool, just one mile from the beach and Holetown. The one- and two-bedroom cottages plus three-bedroom villa can be rented separately or together. Sleeps a total of 12+. Rates from $70 per night.

Westerlee Villas, Westmoreland, St James, ☎ 246 422 1087, carolkipling@ yahoo.com, www.westerleebarbados.com.

The West Coast

Where to Eat

Eating in Barbados is one of the great pleasures of the island, and some of the finest restaurants are on the West Coast. You can eat world-class gourmet meals or fast food, pizza and burgers, and somehow even a burger tastes better when you eat it by the side of the ocean.

★★Al Fresco at Treasure Beach

Al Fresco at Treasure Beach *(barbadosbarbados.com)*

Looking across the gardens and out to sea, Al Fresco serves award-winning cuisine, complemented by an extensive wine list, friendly service, and ever-changing daily specials. The menu is local and international and they are open for breakfast, lunch and dinner. After dinner, you can have coffee and liqueurs at a poolside table while enjoying the live entertainment provided on many nights.

Breakfast $13-$28; lunch $11-$35; dinner starters $8-$23, main courses $25-$48.

Al Fresco at Treasure Beach, Paynes Bay, St James, ☎ 246 432 1346, 246 432 1094, reservations@treasurebeachhotel.com, www.treasurebeachhotel.com.

★Angry Annies

You'll see this restaurant long before you get there! Painted in bright blues, reds and yellows. the outside reflects the cheerful atmosphere inside. The menu includes chicken, fresh fish, lobster, steak, lasagna, and more. They are well known for their curries and serve a wide variety every night.

Dinner: Starters $6-$11; main courses $16-$30.

Angry Annies, 1st Street, Holetown, St James, ☎ 246 432 2119.

★Blue Monkey Bar & Restaurant

A casual and affordable restaurant, right on the beach at Paynes Bay, serving a variety of homemade dishes from fish and chips to exotic curries and pasta, all prepared by Bajan Chef of the Year in 2002 and 2003, Wendell Phillips.

Lunch starters $6.50-$19, main courses $30-70. Junior menu for children.

Blue Monkey Bar & Restaurant, Paynes Bay, St. James, ☎ 246 432 7528.

★Café Indigo

A casual second-floor restaurant in Holetown, open for breakfast, lunch, and dinner, and serving a wide variety of dishes, from pizza to seafood to steak. A great place to take the kids!

Breakfast $3-$10, lunch $5-$30, dinner starters $5-$9, main courses $8-$20.

Café Indigo, Indigo Courtyard, Holetown, St. James, ☎ 246 432 0968.

★Calabaza

A Moroccan-themed restaurant overlooking the Caribbean, combining Eastern, Western and Caribbean cuisine. Open for dinner every day.

Two courses $65, three courses $77. 50.

Calabaza, Prospect, St. James, ☎ 246 424 4557.

Calabaza (barbadosbarbados.com)

★★Coral Reef Club

This is the restaurant at the hotel of the same name; the menu is a mix of Caribbean and international. There is entertainment most nights, a Bajan Buffet on Mondays, and a barbecue with floor show on Thursdays.

Lunch $6-$30, dinner starters $8-$15, main courses $22-$44.

Coral Reef Club, St. James Beach, St. James, ☎ 246 422 2372.

★★Daphne's

A sister restaurant to the famous Daphne's of Chelsea in London, this is a classic Italian-style restaurant reinvented for contemporary tastes. Beautiful décor and first-class service makes this beachside restaurant

Daphne's (barbadosbarbados.com)

great for a special dinner. Reputed to have the best cocktail bar in Barbados with cocktail hour from 5 to 7 pm featuring half-price drinks.

Starters $10-$20; main courses $20-$44.

Daphne's, Paynes Bay, St James, ☎ 246 432 2731.

★Groots Bar & Restaurant

Good classic dishes like cod, chips and mushy peas, curries, rotis, along with seafood and Chinese, reasonable prices and a fun atmosphere. Open Monday to Saturday. Closed in June.

Dinner starters $3-$16; main dishes $11-$26.

Groots Bar and Restaurant, Trents, St James, ☎ 246 432 7435.

★★★Il Tempio

Luciano Pavarotti says it's the best Italian food in Barbados!

Lunch starters $4-$21, main courses $16-$41, dinner starters $10-$21, main courses $22.50-$48.

Il Tempio, Fitts Village, St. James, ☎ 246 417 0057.

★★★Lone Star Restaurant

This was rated by *Restaurant* magazine as among the top 50 in the world for 2002, and by *Tatler* readers as one of the 101 best in the world for 1999, 2000, and 2003. Sitting right on the beach, with the waves lapping just a few feet away, it is a great destination for lunch or dinner, or the weekend "Traditional English Sunday Roast."

Lunch $10-$35; dinner, starters $10-$27, main courses $20-$40.

Lone Star Restaurant, Mt. Standfast, St James, ☎ 246 419 0599, wowgroupltd@sunbeach.net, www.thelonestar.com.

★★Olives Bar & Bistro

Winner of the Wine Spectator Award in 2001 and 2002, this cozy bistro serves up Caribbean and Mediterranean flavors using the best local ingredients. You can eat inside or outside in the courtyard. A steelpan band plays every Sunday from May to November. Upstairs is a lounge serving thin crust pizza and other light snacks. Open for dinner 6:30-10 pm. Bar open till late.

Olives Bar & Bistro, 2nd Street, Holetown, St James, ☎ 246 432 2112, fax 246 432 2938, olives@caribsurf.com.

★★★Palm Terrace

The elegance of Fairmont Royal Pavilion continues through to The Palm Terrace Restaurant. Moorish arches, palm trees and tropical plants contrast with white tablecloths and sparkling cutlery. The open-air restaurant sitting on the water's edge serves Caribbean-influenced contemporary cuisine. Live entertainment and the kind of service you would expect at a Fairmont Hotel complete the perfect intimate dining experience.

Palm Terrace

Palm Terrace, The Fairmont Royal Pavilion, St James, ☎ 246 422 5555.

★★Ragamuffins

The only West Coast restaurant in an authentic chattel house, serving lobster, West Indian curries, vegetarian dishes, and T-bone steak. Local cocktails and frosty beers are sold till late, the specials change daily, the atmosphere is fun and relaxed, and the value is great. Recommended by *Gourmet Magazine*, *Bon Appetit*, *Tatler*, and the *London Sunday Times*. Eat in, or outside in the tropical garden. The restaurant is small, so reservations are advised.

Starters $4-$12; main courses $12-$32.

Ragamuffins, 1st Street, Holetown, St James, ☎ 246 432 1295, raga@caribsurf.com.

★★The Sandpiper

An exclusive hotel with a great restaurant, low-key live entertainment most nights, a Bajan buffet on Wednesdays and a barbecue on Sundays.

Eclectic dishes using the freshest local ingredients. A member of Small Luxury Hotels of the World.

Lunch $8-$30. Dinner starters $8-$15; main courses $23-$40.

The Sandpiper, St James Beach, St James, ☎ 246 422 2251, fax 246 422 0900, sandpiper@caribsurf.com, www.sandpiperbarbados.com.

Sandy Lane

Two restaurants, **L'Acajou** and the more casual **Bajan Blue**. I haven't eaten there but they are sure to be good and sure to be expensive! A traditional afternoon tea is also served every day on the terrace.

Sandy Lane, Sandy Lane, St. James, ☎ 246 444 2000.

Sassafras

A blend of Caribbean and Pacific Rim flavors served in the relaxed atmosphere of a restored plantation house. Lunch starters $8-$11, main courses $10-$19, or two courses for $16, three courses for $20. Dinner starters $9-$12, main courses $12.50-$32.50, or two courses $26, three courses $30.

Sassafras, Derricks, St. James, ☎ 246 432 6386.

★★★ The Cliff

The Cliff (barbadosbarbados.com)

One of the West Coast's finest restaurants, The Cliff opened in January 1995 to rave reviews and. It was recently voted one of the top 50 restaurants in the world. Sitting on a cliff top, overlooking the Caribbean, bathed in candlelight and graced with fine art, the ambience is matched by the service, and only surpassed by the cuisine. For lovers of fine food this is the place to eat. Reservations required.

$92.50 for two-course meal; $112.50 for three-course meal.

The Cliff, Derricks, St James, ☎ 246 432 1922, fax 246 432 0980, www.
thecliffbarbados.com.

The Mews

See *Nightlife*.

The Mews, 2nd Street, Holetown, St. James, ☎ 246 432 1122.

★★★ The Tides

Tides is spread out over two floors, with a dining room, bar and art gallery on the main floor, and a second dining room on the second floor. Arrive early and enjoy the local art while sipping a cocktail, then head to one of the two dining rooms, get a table by the beach, and enjoy a great meal. With so many restaurants sitting right on the water's edge it is difficult to pick a favorite, but The Tides is definitely one of them. Serving seafood, and an

The Tides

array of contemporary meat and vegetarian dishes, and using only the freshest local ingredients, this is the perfect choice for lovers of fine food, fine art, fine decoration, and fine service.

Starters $11-$20; main courses $21-$44.

The Tides, Holetown, St James, ☎ 246 432 8356, www.tidesbarbados.com.

 For fast food there is a **Chefette** in Holetown, serving roti, pizza, chicken, sandwiches and salads.

Nightlife

Most of the nightlife in St James takes place at the hotels, where live bands and beach parties can be found most nights, but there are a number of other places where you can dance, drink, and eat the night away.

★Coach House

The Coach House at Paynes Bay is a 200-year-old bar and restaurant that has live entertainment every night, and sports from around the world via satellite TV. From Monday to Friday, there is a lunchtime buffet, and on Saturdays, there is an evening buffet.
Coach House, Paynes Bay, ☎ 246 432 1163.

★★ John Moore Bar

A rum shop on the waterfront mostly used by locals, but don't let that keep you away. Great rum punches, beer, and fresh fish dinners.
John Moore Bar, ☎ 246 422 2258.

Lexy – Piano Bar & Cabaret

I haven't visited this new bar but it is described as "a trendy spot where the concept of a piano bar is taken to a new level!"
Lexy – Piano Bar & Cabaret, 2nd Street, Holetown, St. James, ☎ 246 432 5399.

★★Ragamuffins

Check out this fun bar and restaurant, especially the Drag Show on Sundays, but make sure you book!
Ragamuffins, 1st Street, Holetown, St James, ☎ 246 432 1295, raga@caribsurf.com, www.ragamuffinsbarbados.com.

★Scarlet

Scarlet (barbadosbarbados.com)

An intimate space with dramatic lighting and an extensive variety of martinis, champagnes and cocktails, and a small tapas menu.
Scarlet, Paynes Bay, ☎ 246 432 3663.

★The Crocodile's Den

Described as the ultimate West Coast fun bar, the Crocodile Den is a sports and music bar. Games available include pool, darts, backgammon and other table games. Catch the latest sports action on the satellite TV, or just sit at the bar and listen to the live piano music.

Crocodile's Den, Paynes Bay, St James, ☎ 246 432 7625, fax 246 432 7626.

★★ The Mews

An upscale restaurant/ bar with a New Orleans feel, live music every Friday and a great atmosphere every night, especially after 10 pm.

The Mews, Second St, Holetown, ☎ 246 432 1122.

Also, check out:

Baku Beach Bar, Highway1 , Holetown, St. James, ☎ 246 432 2258.

Olives Restaurant Upper Lounge, 2nd Street, Holetown, St. James, ☎ 246 432 2112.

The Mews (barbadosbarbados.com)

Holetown Beach (barbadosawaits.com)

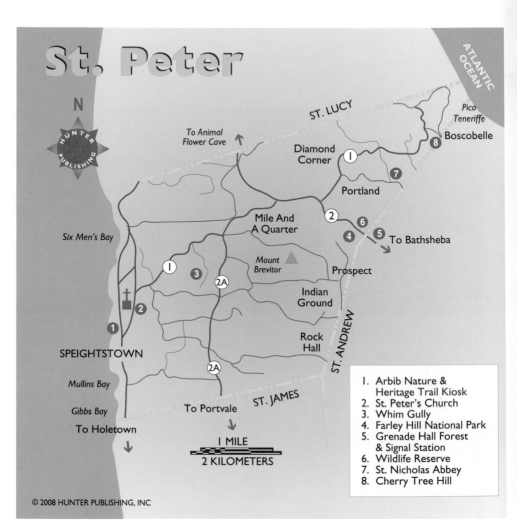

St. Peter

N

ATLANTIC OCEAN

ST. LUCY

To Animal Flower Cave

Diamond Corner ①

Pico Teneriffe

Boscobelle ⑧

⑦

Portland

Six Men's Bay

Mile And A Quarter

② ⑥

⑤ To Bathsheba

④

Mount Brevitor

Prospect

Indian Ground

① ③ ②A

SPEIGHTSTOWN

ST. ANDREW

Rock Hall

Mullins Bay

②A

Gibbs Bay

To Portvale

ST. JAMES

To Holetown

1 MILE

2 KILOMETERS

1. Arbib Nature & Heritage Trail Kiosk
2. St. Peter's Church
3. Whim Gully
4. Farley Hill National Park
5. Grenade Hall Forest & Signal Station
6. Wildlife Reserve
7. St. Nicholas Abbey
8. Cherry Tree Hill

© 2008 HUNTER PUBLISHING, INC

St Peter

Studiation beat eddication.
(Common sense is better than formal education.)

St Peter is in the northern part of the island. St Lucy is north of St Peter, St Andrew to the east, and St James to the south. It is the only parish other than St Lucy that has a coastline on both the east and west side of the island.

The west coast area is known as the Platinum Coast. It extends north from Holetown and consists of powdery white sand beaches, upscale hotels, the Port St Charles marina (the only marina in Barbados), and multimillion dollar homes. Other resorts, which either have been or are in various stages of completion, are Schooner Bay, Mount Brevitor, Suga Suga, and Black Bess.

Inland are rolling hills, many still covered by sugar cane, while to the east is the untamed, undeveloped Atlantic coast.

Speightstown is the main city in St Peter. Originally known as Little Bristol because of its strong trading connections with the city of Bristol in England, it was the first major port and commercial center in Barbados.

The city was a major trading center for sugar and slaves, and many historic buildings dating from colonial times can still be found here, especially on Queen Street, Orange Street, and Church Street.

Speightstown (barbadosawaits.com)

Over the last few years, as major new tourist areas have been developed, Speightstown has been revived and renewed. Although the area was quite run-down before, it did have a great island atmosphere that is now being lost to the new mega-developments. The new Port St Charles marina is a massive development that provides first-class service for visiting yachtsmen, but is a massive fenced complex designed to keep casual visitors away.

Shopping

Among the many other shops in Speightstown, there are three galleries: the **Gallery of Caribbean Art**, the **Shell Gallery**, selling shells of the world and related gifts, and **Mango's Art Gallery**. There is a **3 Diamonds International Jewelry Boutique** and a number of stores selling local and international merchandise. For something completely different, head over to the fishing complex and buy fish freshly caught from the ocean the same morning.

There is also a large supermarket in Speightstown that has everything you need if you are cooking for yourself.

Sightseeing

The Parish Church

Located in Speightstown, it is one of the six original parish churches. The first wooden church, built in 1629, was destroyed and then rebuilt in 1665. Then, in 1831, the church was leveled by a hurricane. The current church was built in 1837, Georgian in style, with pediments on the front and a square bell tower.

Destroyed by a fire in 1980, only the walls and tower were left standing. It was restored in 1983, and is now a beautiful example of Georgian church architecture.

St Peter Parish Church

★Farley Hill National Park

High on a hill in a mahogany forest overlooking the rugged Atlantic coast lie the ruins of a beautiful Georgian mansion. Sir Graham Briggs started work on Farley Hill in 1818 and over the next 50 years constantly made additions and improvements. It ultimately came to be regarded as the most impressive mansion in the country, but was destroyed by fire in 1965. In 1967 Queen Elizabeth II officially opened the grounds as the Farley Hill National Park.

With its spectacular setting, cool mahogany-tree shade, and fairytale ruins, Farley Hill Park is a favorite spot for weddings, picnics, and is home to the Barbados Jazz Festival and Gospelfest.

Farley Hill Park

★★★Barbados Wildlife Reserve, Grenade Hall & Signal Station

Across the road from Farley Hill Park is the Barbados Wildlife Reserve (see *Traveling with Children*). Barbados green monkeys roam freely back and forth. Admission to the reserve includes access to Grenade Hall Forest and the Signal Station.

★St Nicholas Abbey

St Nicholas Abbey

As you drive down the grand avenue of mahogany trees leading to St Nicholas Abbey, you feel as if you are driving into the past. The Abbey is one of only three genuine Jacobean mansions in the western hemisphere. The others are Drax Hall in the parish of St George and Bacon's Castle in Virginia. Despite its name, it was never an abbey and has never had anything to do with the church. Built in 1650-1660, by Colonel Benjamin Berringer, it has always been a sugar plantation house. The house has a

The West Coast

St Nicholas Abbey garden

rich history that reads like a Gothic romance novel. Sir John Yeamans, a business partner of the Colonel, had an affair with the Colonel's wife, Margaret. The Colonel challenged him to a duel and was killed. Sir John married Margaret and claimed the Abbey as his own. The Colonel's children sued and were ultimately granted ownership. Sir John and Margaret then left the island and moved to South Carolina.

The mansion passed to Berringer's son, then his granddaughter, Susanna, who married George Nicholas. Upon her marriage, the mansion automatically became the property of her husband, after whom it was named. Over the next few hundred years it was bought or inherited by a number of dif-

St Nicholas Abbey interior

ferent families, until in 1834 it passed by marriage to Charles Cave. From 1978 until his death in 2003, Lt. Colonel Stephen Cave OBE, the great-great-grandson of Charles Cave, owned it.

It has recently been sold and a new family is set to continue living the history of St Nicholas Abbey.

The house is open from Monday to Friday, 10 am-3:30 pm.

★Cherry Tree Hill

Driving up Cherry Tree Hill, you will be struck by an interesting fact – the trees that line the hill are in fact mahogany! It is believed that the hill was originally covered in cherry trees, but no one seems to know what happened to them. The trees that now cover the hill were brought to Barbados after the treaty of Paris in 1763.

Regardless of the trees, once you reach the top, which is approximately 850 feet (269 m), you will be treated to one of the most spectacular views in Barbados. The rolling hills of the Scotland District and the limitless Atlantic crashing against the east coast spread out before you. Make sure you bring your camera!

Cherry Tree Hill

Adventures on Foot

Hiking

 ★★The Arbib Nature & Heritage Trail. Starting at St Peter's Church (see above), explore the streets of Speightstown, then leave the town to discover sugar plantations, forests and beaches. Organized by the National Trust, well-informed guides take you on a three- to five-mile walk to discover the natural and cultural history of the town and surrounding areas. Winner of the Caribbean Ecotourism Award in 1999, it is an entertaining an informative way to spend a few hours.

Times are Wednesday, Thursday and Saturday, 9 am-2:30 pm. The interactive guided trail must be pre-booked by 3 pm the day before. Cost is $7.50. Reservations: ☎ 246 426 2421.

Adventures on Water

Beaches

 St Peter is home to many fine beaches and at Speightstown and Six Men's Bay to the north there are fishing complexes where you can watch the fishermen bring their catch to the market and buy freshly caught fish right on the beach.

★Six Mens' Bay. There is a fish fry every Friday and Saturday evening, where you can join the local residents and enjoy freshly caught local fish.

★Gibbs Beach. One of the most tranquil beaches on the island. Adjoining Mullins Beach, the water is calm and clear, perfect for snorkeling. Waterskiing is available and wave runners can be rented.

Six Mens' Bay

★★Mullins Bay. Mullins beach is one of the most popular beaches on the west coast. Swim in the blue waters of the Caribbean relax in the shade of a palm tree, or rent a jet ski. Have a rum punch at Mannies beach bar or a sunset dinner at the end of the day.

★Reads Bay. An unspoiled beach with a marked-off area for swimming to avoid jet skis, catamarans and other such risks.

★★Heywood's Beach. This wide, quiet beach just north of Speightstown is home to a number of rock-enclosed pools that arc perfect for wading or relaxing in, and are especially safe for young children. There are also shallow reefs that are excellent for snorkeling.

Scuba Diving

Just off Six Men's Bay in 60 feet of water lies the *Pamir*, a 165-foot wreck. There are a number of local dive operators who can take you out. (See *Land of Adventure*.)

Cultural Excursions

Gallery of Caribbean Art

An interesting gallery showcasing some of the best Barbadian and Caribbean art.

Open Monday-Friday 9:30 am-4:30 pm, Saturday 9:30 am-2 pm.

Northern Business Centre Speightstown, ☎ 246 419 0858, artcaribbean@ sunbeach.net.

Mango's Fine Art Gallery

Mango's Fine Art Gallery exhibits works from the internationally acclaimed artist, Michael Adams. Visitors to the gallery can enjoy the vibrant colors, inspired by the beauty of nature, that fill his works.

Mango's Fine Art Gallery, West End, #2 Queen Street, Speightstown.

Where to Stay

 In St Peter, you can find luxury hotels, budget apartments and everything in-between. The following is a sampling.

★★★ Almond Beach Village

A former sugar plantation set on 32 acres with over a mile (1.6 km) of white sand beach. Almond is an all-inclusive resort with 395 guest-rooms. Rooms have balconies or patios with dining sets, two-poster beds, mahogany-stained furniture, cushioned arm-chairs, tile floors,

Almond Beach Village (africansounds.com)

tropical-print fabrics, and ceiling fans, in addition to air-conditioning.

There are 10 freshwater swimming pools and two freshwater Jacuzzis. Numerous water and land sports are available, including Hobie Cat sailing, snorkeling, windsurfing, reel fishing, aqua cycles, kayaks, fishing, squash, tennis and par 3 nine-hole golf.

There are several fine-dining restaurants ranging from elegant to informal, a full-service nursery, a kids club for children three to 12, and a spa for adults.

Rates from $430 to $630, all-inclusive.

Almond Resorts, St Peter, ☎ 246-422-4900, www.almondresorts.com.

Bajan Services

Bajan Services is a company specializing in villa, apartment, condo, and beachfront home rentals and sales.

The West Coast

Contact Bajan Services, Newton House, Battaleys, St Peter, ☎ 246 422 2618, fax 246 422 5366. For sales, sales@bajanservices.com. For rentals, villas@bajanservices.com, www.bajanservices.com.

Caspian Beach Apartments

Five minutes walk from Speightstown, the apartments offer affordable beachfront accommodation with spectacular views of the Caribbean. One- and two-bedroom apartments have double bedrooms with en-suite shower rooms, living areas equipped with sofa beds, kitchens with fridge, stove, kettle, toaster, coffee maker, and private balcony.

Rates from $100 per night.

Caspian Beach Apartments, Sand Street, Speightstown, St Peter, ☎ 246 422 2520, 246 422 2025, contactus@barbadosholidayrentals.com, www. barbadosholidayrentals.com.

★★★Cobblers Cove

Cobblers Cove (islandinns.com)

A member of the prestigious Relais & Chateaux group, Cobblers Cove has the elegance of an English country house set in the secluded tropical surroundings of the west coast of Barbados. The 40 suites have air-conditioned bedrooms, wet bar with drink-stocked fridge, tea and coffee making facilities, robes and toiletries. Most have connecting doors to the adjacent room with sofa beds. Waterskiing, Sunfish sailing, windsurfing, snorkeling, the use of the gym, and day and night tennis are included.

No children from January 7th to March 27th (dates may vary). Rates from $310 per night.

Cobblers Cove, Speightstown, St Peter, ☎ 246 422 2291, fax 246 422 1460, US/Canada 1 800 890 6060, reservations@cobblerscove.com, www. cobblerscove.com.

★Gibbs Garden

Across the road from Gibbs Beach, Gibbs Garden is a spacious three-bed-room, four-bathroom cottage with a swimming pool, and surrounded by its own completely enclosed, landscaped garden. It has two sitting rooms, a dining room, and patio overlooking the garden and swimming pool. It sleeps up to six people.

Rates are $400 per night in summer and $650 per night in winter.

Gibbs Garden, St Peter, US/Canada ☎ 866 978 5239, UK 0800 097 1753, villas@bajanservices.com.

Karekath Apartments

Karekath Apartments are five fully furnished and equipped apartments with kitchens. The apartments are secluded, offering guests the opportunity to relax in a private beach garden, or on the upstairs gazebo. Karekath Apartments contain all the amenities, including a fully equipped kitchen, dishwasher, microwave ovens, air-conditioning, am/fm cassette radios, cable color television, VCR/DVDs, personal safe, hair dryer, etc. There are also washer and dryer facilities. Each apartment comfortably sleeps six.

Karekath Apartments, Speightstown, ☎ 246 425-1498, fax 246 424-8427, stay@karekathapartments.com.

*Kings Beach Village

The village consists of 32 one- and two-bedroom luxury townhouses and bungalows set around a central swimming pool and bar, in a tropical garden. Choose from one- , two- , and three-bedroom villas, each with en-suite bathroom, fully equipped kitchen and private terrace. The units are sold as timeshares but can also be rented.

Kings Beach Village, St Peter, ☎ 246 422 1690, fax 246 422 1691, info@kingsbeachvillage.com, www.kingsbeachvillage.com.

*Legend Garden Condos

Set in a lush tropical garden, the Legend is a 250-year-old plantation house at Mullins Bay, sitting just a few hundred feet from the beach. Eight condos can each accommodate from one to four people. All rooms are air-conditioned with single, queen- or king-size beds, private bathrooms with tubs and/or showers, TV, and a fully equipped veranda kitchen.

Rates: Apr 11-Dec 11, $75-$100 per night; Dec 12-Jan 8, $105-$130; Jan 9-Apr 15, $95-$120.

The Legend Garden Condos, Mullins Bay, St Peter, ☎ 246 422-8369, fax 246 422-2056, legendcondos@sunbeach.net.

**Little Good Harbour

Just minutes north of Port St Charles, in the fishing community known as Shermans, is Little Good Harbour, a cluster of luxury one- , two- , and

Little Good Harbour (lanzarote-villas.com)

three-bedroom traditional-style chattel cottages and three-bedroom, three-bath garden units. All have living and dining rooms, fully equipped kitchens, en-suite bathrooms and garden patios. Little Good Harbour offers all the privacy of a personal villa but with the amenities and security of a luxury hotel. Rates start at $265 per night.

Little Good Harbour, Shermans, St Peter, ☎ 246 439 3000, fax 246 439 2020, info@littlegoodharbour-barbados.com, www.littlegoodharbourbarbados.com.

★New Haven Mansion

Newhaven Mansion is a privately owned converted mansion standing in three acres of lush tropical gardens. The property features Latin balconies and arches, and consists of six two- or three-bedroom superior apartments, which are air-conditioned and fully equipped. Daily maid service is provided.

The property has its own freshwater swimming pool and private access to Gibbs Beach, 300 feet away (100 m).

Rates for winter (Dec 14-April 16), three-bedroom $290-$320 per night, two-bedroom $250, one-bedroom $160-$180. Summer (April 17-Dec 13), three-bedroom $160-$185, two-bedroom $135, one-bedroom $85-$95.

New Haven Mansion, Stephen L. Nelson, ☎ 407-549-3705, UK 44 121 354 2420, www.barbadosholidayhomes.com.

★★★Seacruise Villa

A luxury five-bedroom villa with a great view of the Northwest Coast, and only two minutes walk to Fryers Well beach. There is a private spa/dipping pool and an outdoor swimming pool. Daily maid service, chef, car and airport transfer are all included. It can be rented as a two-, three-, four-, or five-bedroom villa, with the rental price pro-rated.

Summer rates (April 15-Dec 15): two-bedroom villa from $2,500 per week; three-bedroom from $3,400; four-bedroom from $4,300; five-bedroom from $5,000. Winter rates (Dec 16-April 15): two-bedroom villa from

$3,500 per week; three-bedroom from $4,400; four-bedroom from $6,200; five-bedroom from $7,700.

Sea Cruise Villa, Fryers Well, St Peter, ☎ 246 437 9342, hughr@caribsurf.com, www.seacruisevilla.com.

★Sugar Cane Club Hotel

A small hilltop resort set in beautiful tropical gardens overlooking the Caribbean Sea. Sugar Cane consists of 22 fully appointed studio

Pool at Seacruise Villa

apartments with kitchenette, private bathroom, token-operated air-conditioning, ceiling fans, hairdryers, color televisions with satellite broadcast, direct dial telephone, radios, and patios or balconies. The resort has a restaurant, bar, sauna, swimming pools, shuffleboard court, dartboard, pool and table tennis tables and parking lot. Daily maid service, currency exchange, Internet and fax facilities. Free transport to the beach every hour. Rates from $78 per night.

Sugar Cane Club Hotel, Maynards, St Peter, ☎ 246 422 5026.

Sunset Sands

Four spacious air-conditioned suites with sea-view patios. Each suite has a fully equipped kitchen, bathroom with tub and shower, TV, phone, and daily maid service. Great for couples and families.

Sunset Sands Beach Apartments, Sand Street, Speightstown, St Peter, ☎ 246 438 1096, fax 246 438 1881, sunsetsands@caribsurf.com, www.sunsetsands.com.

Tight Lines

A newly constructed apartment with two double bedrooms, five minutes drive from Gibbs Beach. Sitting 400 feet (133 m) above sea level, it is cooled by the constant breeze from the east. One bedroom has a double bed, the second has twin beds; there are also two fold-up single beds and a cot available. There is a well-equipped kitchen, bathroom with walk-in shower, a lounge/dining area, a covered patio, and enclosed garden.

Rates: June 1st to Nov 30th $45 per night, Dec 1st to May 31st $50 per night.

The West Coast

Tight Lines, #1 Bakers Ave, Bakers, St James, ☎ 246 422 4622, bblackman@caribsurf.com.

Where to Eat

East Moon

 Reasonably priced set dinners are available for groups of two or more. Choose from a variety of sweet and sour dishes, seafood, Szechuan specialties and vegetarian dishes. The appetizers include spring roll, steamed wonton, prawn crackers and breaded jumbo shrimp.

Lunch specials start at $8, dinners with starters cost $17-$25.

East Moon, Road View, St Peter, ☎ 246 422 4739.

★The Fish Pot

The Fish Pot (far-flung.co.uk)

The Fish Pot restaurant is part of a converted fort at Little Good Harbour. Sitting directly on the beach at Sherman's fishing village, the open terrace dining area looks out over the Caribbean.

The menu features fresh fish and seafood with classic Caribbean cuisine. There is also a selection of soups, salads and other light fare. If laid-back, with style and excellent service is your goal, then this is the place to go.

Open for breakfast, lunch and dinner daily. Lunch starters $11-$21, main coursess $34-$84. Dinner starters $12-$18, main courses $38-$80.

The Fish Pot, Little Good Harbour, Shermans, St Peter, ☎ 246 439 3000, fax 246 439 2020, info@littlegoodharbourbarbados.com.

★★La Mer Restaurant

Set in a beautiful lagoon, surrounded by luxury yachts, La Mer serves up fresh fish and tender cuts of meat seared on a wood or lava rock grill, vegetarian dishes from the wok station, or select your own lobster from the lobster pot. After a romantic dinner, retire to the Onyx Bar for a Cognac or nightcap.

Dinner Monday to Saturday from 6:30 pm; Sunday Brunch from 12 noon. Reservations required. Main courses $24-$50. Sunday brunch $60.

La Mer Restaurant, Port St Charles, St Peter, ☎ 246 419 2000, lamer@ caribsurf.com.

★★Mango's By The Sea

An award-winning restaurant amid bamboo trees and hanging palm leaves. Candlelit tables set on a terrace overlooking the Caribbean; friendly service and fresh local ingredients make dinner a romantic taste sensation. There is live entertainment on some nights, and right next door is Mango's art gallery, which features the silk-screen prints of artist Michael Adams. A complimentary shuttle from all hotels and villas between Holetown and Speightstown is offered.

Open every evening from 6 pm. Starters $8-$16, main courses $25-$45.

Mango's By The Sea, West End, #2 Queen Street, Speightstown, St Peter, ☎ 246 422 0704, mangos@sunbeach.net.

★★Mannie's Suga Suga

Mannie's Suga Suga is a beach bar, serving international and Bajan favorites by day and Asian fusion/Caribbean at night. Mannie's provides great food and drinks at very affordable prices. Breakfast, lunch, dinner and snacks served all day and late into the night.

Not to be missed is the Sunday Brunch. While listening to the sounds of the steel pan, enjoy a selection of fresh salads and garden vegetables, rice, macaroni pie, steamed vegetables, stew, grilled fish, baked chicken, fresh roast beef – all prepared to perfection. And, for dessert, choose from coconut macaroon or chocolate chip cookies, fresh seasonal fruit, thick chocolate cake, cherry cheesecake (all homemade by the pastry chef).

On Monday there is a dinner and cabaret show featuring great music, fantastic costumes, fabulous dancing and plenty of laughs. After the show, the DJ stays on to play.

During the day put up a flag and your choice of food or drinks will be delivered to you. There are also water sports, including kayaks, jet skis, banana boats, rubber tubes towed by a speedboat, para sailing, catamarans, glass bottom boats, waterskis, or you can snorkel or swim with the turtles. A great way to spend the day for the entire family.

Mannie's Suga Suga, Mullins Beach, St Peter, ☎ 246 419 4511, fax 246 422 0021, coucoustick@msn.com.

The West Coast

★★The Terrace Restaurant

Located in Cobblers Cove, the Terrace is renowned for its French cuisine and romantic setting, on a terrace overlooking the Caribbean.

Breakfast from $17, lunch $8-$37, dinner starters $10-$23, main courses $28-$48, five-course dinner $75.

The Terrace Restaurant, Cobblers Cove, St Peter, ☎ 246 422 2291, www.cobblerscove.com.

The Terrace (far-flung.co.uk)

Nightlife

Most of the nightlife in Barbados is centered in Bridgetown and the St Lawrence Gap, 20 minutes to a half-hour drive away. Outside of these areas, many hotels and restaurants provide entertainment.

★★Fisherman's Pub

For a touch of the real Barbados, featuring steel pan, limbo, calypso, and authentic Bajan culinary delights, including, cou cou and flying fish, the national dish. Hours 11 am-1 am Monday-Tuesday, Thursday, Saturday; 11am-3am Wednesday, Friday; noon-midnight Sunday.

Fisherman's Pub, Queen's Street, ☎ 246 422 2703.

★★Mannie's Suga Suga

Monday night dinner and cabaret show featuring great music, fantastic costumes, fabulous dancing and plenty of laughs. After the show, the DJ stays on to play. ☎ 246 419 4511.

The East Coast
St John

Tek time en' laziness.
(By taking your time, you can achieve a lot.)

St John is on the East Coast of Barbados, and is bordered by St Joseph to the north, St George to the southwest and St Philip to the southeast.

It is undeveloped but very scenic, with lush vegetation and stunning views of the Atlantic.

Shopping

The only shopping in St John's is the occasional roadside or beach vendor selling souvenirs and T-Shirts.

Sightseeing

★★ The Parish Church

Built in 1836 after a hurricane destroyed the original church dating from 1660, St John's Parish Church is a classic Gothic building, perched on a cliff overlooking the Atlantic Ocean. The chancel was added in 1876. The interior includes a beautifully crafted

St John's Parish Church

St John's Parish Church stained glass

spiral staircase and a pulpit constructed from six different kinds of wood: ebony, locust, Barbados mahogany, manchineel, oak and pine. The floor is paved with ancient memorial tablets from earlier churches built on the same site.

The centuries-old graveyard is home to tombs and family vaults, the most interesting of which is the tomb of Ferdinand Paleologus, a descendent of Constantine VIII (the Christian Emperer of Constantinople) who was murdered in 1453. Paleologus emigrated to Barbados and died here in 1678.

★Codrington College

Sitting high on a hill overlooking the Atlantic Ocean, at the end of a long driveway lined with cabbage palm trees, is Codrington College. Built in 1743, after Christopher Codrington bequeathed the estate and a considerable sum of money at his death in 1710, it is the

Codrington College

oldest Anglican theological college in the Western Hemisphere.

Take a self-guided tour through the grounds, visit the magnificent lily pond and wander to the edge of the property for a spectacular view of the East Coast and the Atlantic.

★★Hackleton's Cliff

Hackleton's Cliff stretches from St John's through to St Joseph. Created by the break-up of the coral limestone crust of the island, it rises straight up from the ocean almost 1,000 feet (305 m). According to legend, it is named after a man who committed suicide by riding his horse off the cliff.

The cliff top is overgrown, but there are points where you get great views along the east coast from Ragged Point Lighthouse in the south to Pico Tenerife in the north.

Prevailing winds along the east coast

Adventures on Foot

Hiking

There are magnificent scenic walks along the east coast. Walking from one small fishing village to another, for example, can make for a stimulating and interesting hike. From Martin's Bay to Consett Bay is about three miles (five km). Bathsheba to Martin's Bay is about the same. Or, for the really adventurous, you can hike about 16 miles (26 km), all the way from Pico Tenerife in the north to Ragged Point in the south.

Adventures on Water

Beaches

St John's has a number of very attractive beaches, most of which are great to visit but unsafe for swimming. The Atlantic swells flow all the way from Africa, with nothing to interrupt their prog-

The East Coast

ress until they reach the east coast of Barbados. They do however offer some great surfing.

Bath Beach (barbados.org)

★★**Bath** is one of the safest and most popular beaches on the East Coast of the island. There is a large offshore reef, which protects the beach, and there is a lifeguard on duty. A red flag is displayed when the sea is too dangerous for swimming.

To the north is a small waterfall and the remains of the railway line that originally ran from Bridgetown to Bathsheba.

During the week, the beach is usually quite deserted but it gets busier on the weekends, when the locals like to use it. There are showers and washrooms, a playground for the kids and places to buy food and drinks, along with beach vendors selling fishcakes. After swimming, treat yourself to lunch on the grass under the shade of the casuarina trees.

★**Consett Bay**. Consett Bay is not easy to reach, since the road is steep and overgrown. It's best attempted in a 4X4. Once you get there, however, you will find a pretty fishing village where, from the jetty jutting out into the water, you can watch the fishermen return with their catches.

★**Martins Bay**. A little farther north you come to another unspoiled fishing village, Martins Bay. If you like lobster, this is the place for you. Once a stop on the Bridgetown-to-Bathsheba rail line, it is now a peaceful village clinging to its old lifestyle.

Where to Stay

★★★Villa Nova

Villa Nova is in the middle of nowhere – no crowds, no traffic, no noise, and no children under 12.

Built in 1834 as a grand plantation house and set in 15 walled acres of tropical forest and lush gardens, it reopened in 2001 after a multi-million-dollar refurbishment. The 28 suites designed by Nina Campbell are beautifully furnished and have spacious bathrooms with walk-in showers, ceiling fans, wicker furniture and elegant verandas. Towering mahogany trees, royal palms, bearded figs, mango trees, and one of only six cannonball trees on the island surround the black-tiled swimming pool.

Handpicked for their experience, friendliness, and attention to the needs of the guests, the staff ensures that guests feel both pampered and relaxed.

Doubles from $650 in winter, $450 in summer; suites from $800 in winter, $600 in summer. Continental or à la carte breakfast is included.

Villa Nova, St John, ☎ 246 433 1524, fax 246 433 6363, info@ villanovabarbados.com, www.villanovabarbados.com.

 There are no restaurants or cafés and no nightlife in St John.

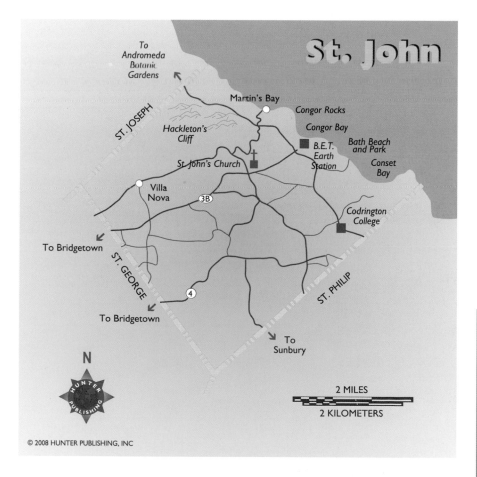

© 2008 HUNTER PUBLISHING, INC

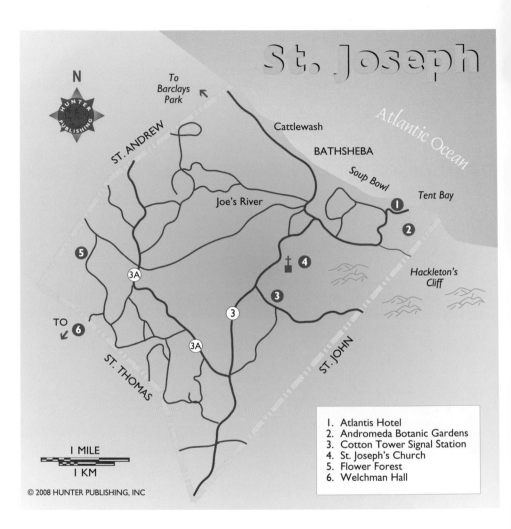

N

HUNTER PUBLISHING

St. Joseph

To
Barclays
Park

ST. ANDREW

Cattlewash

BATHSHEBA

Atlantic Ocean

Soup Bowl

Joe's River

① Atlantis Hotel

②

Tent Bay

⑤

3A

④ ✝

Hackleton's
Cliff

③

TO ⑥

③

3A

ST. JOHN

ST. THOMAS

1 MILE

1 KM

© 2008 HUNTER PUBLISHING, INC

1. Atlantis Hotel
2. Andromeda Botanic Gardens
3. Cotton Tower Signal Station
4. St. Joseph's Church
5. Flower Forest
6. Welchman Hall

St Joseph

The sea en' got nuh back door.
(The sea is not a safe place.)

St Joseph is on the eastern side of the island, bordered by St Andrew to the north, St Thomas to the west, and St John to the south. Part of St Joseph is known as the Scotland District, due to its physical similarity. The main town is Bathsheba, with about 5,000 inhabitants. Like most of the East Coast, it is undeveloped but is home to a number of local and international surf competitions.

Shopping

Shopping is limited to a few stalls along the beach, mostly selling souvenirs, local jewelry, and T-shirts.

Sightseeing

★★ The Parish Church

Standing at the top of Horse Hill, the original church, built before 1641, was destroyed by a hurricane in 1831. Rebuilt in 1839, it offers panoramic views of the Scotland District and the Atlantic coast.

Cotton Tower

Not far from the parish church is the Cotton Tower, the second of two remaining signal stations (Gun Hill is the other)

St Joseph's Parish Church

built by the British army in the 19th century, as part of the island defenses. The Barbados National Trust maintains it.

Barclay's Park

Overlooking the Cattlewash area is 50-acre Barclay's Park. The park, opened by HM Queen Elizabeth II in 1966, is popular for picnics and family gatherings. It is also the venue for the Crop Over Festival's Party Monarch calypso competition.

★★Hackleton's Cliff

Hackleton's Cliff rises 1,000 ft (305 m) above the Atlantic Ocean and offers spectacular views of the east coast (see *St John*).

★★★Bathsheba

Bathsheba boulders

Drive east along Highway 3 until you think you are about to drive into the Atlantic – then, suddenly, you are there. A sleepy fishing village, a spectacular beach, huge coral boulders, and crashing waves tell you you have reached one of the most scenic and unspoiled places in Barbados

Bathsheba, the wife of King David, was mostly famous for taking milk baths in order to keep her skin beautiful and soft. Legend has it that Bathsheba got its name from the white waters of the Atlantic surf, which resembles Bathsheba's bath, both in its appearance and in its health-giving properties.

Try soaking in the **Bathsheba Pools**. These are carved out of the coral reef and splashed by the surf. They are several feet deep and offer a welcome respite from the sun's heat. And, unless you are an expert surfer, they are the only safe place to go into the water. The undertows and riptides here make it dangerous even to walk in the ocean as the incoming waves can drag you out to sea with their strong undertow. But sit in one of the pools, a rum punch in your hand, the astonishing power of nature provided by the Atlantic, the idyllic beauty of the village with the hills behind, and you can imagine just what heaven must be like!

If you can drag yourself away from the beach, there are a number of restaurants, rum shops and hotels where you can have lunch or dinner while overlooking the sea.

Street art, Paris Hill

Bathsheba's peace is broken several times a year when local and international surfing championships come to town. If you happen to arrive during one of these competitions, head to the **Bajan Surf Bungalow**, order a Banks beer, sit back, and watch some of the best surfers from around the world compete for prizes of up to $10,000.

Adventures on Foot

Hiking

Explore the sea life in tide pools, climb along the wind-buffeted rock formations, or just walk along the miles of shell-filled beaches swept by the magnificent Atlantic Ocean.

There are many scenic coastal walks (see *St John*).

Adventures on Water

Beaches

St Joseph has great beaches for sunbathing and picnics, although most are dangerous for swimming. But tidal pools, exposed at low tide, are interesting to explore or to bathe in. The area is popular with professional surfers and many competitions are held at the "Soup Bowl" in Bathsheba.

Cattlewash derived its name from the cattle that used to wade into the sea there. It is known as one of the best health resort areas in Barbados. Popular with locals, its constant sea breeze and warm tidal pools make it a great spot to relax.

As with most beaches on this coast, there are strong currents and swimming is not recommended.

Just south of Cattlewash, is **Tent Bay**, home to a small fish market. Fishing boats depart early in the morning and return in the evening. Stop for lunch, or Sunday brunch, in the Atlantis Hotel, an East Coast landmark for over 100 years.

Bathsheba Beach. (Rodney Nelson)

Surfing

The famous Barbados **Soup Bowl**, at Bathsheba, is the premier destination for surfers. The Soup Bowl is fast, with powerful rights, long walls and hollow tubes. It has the most consistent surf on the island, with breaks from two to 20 feet; the best breaks are between September and January, with smaller breaks between July and August.

Eco-Tourism

★★Flower Forest

The Flower Forest

A half-mile (one-km) path winds through the 50 acres of the flower forest, which is located on Highway 2, in the Scotland District. Offering spectacular scenery and a sweeping view of the rugged East Coast, with brilliantly colored flowers breaking up the green backdrop, the forest is an oasis of calm and serenity. The

Facing page: The Soup Bowl

In the Flower Forest

occasional calls of the birds and monkeys chattering in the trees are the only sounds that break the silence. Built on a former sugar plantation, the flower forest is home to more than 100 varieties of tropical flora, and is a must-see for anyone with an interest in plants, flowers or gardening.

You can cover the forest in about 45 minutes if you rush, but you are encouraged to take as much time as you like. Leave the path and get closer to nature, or sit and relax on one of the benches placed throughout the forest.

There is a snack bar selling hot dogs, flying fish and other snacks, as well as a gift shop.

Wheelchair facilities and access are provided, but the trails are uneven and it may be difficult. Walking sticks and umbrellas are also available.

The Flower Forest is open seven days a week, from 9 am to 5 pm. There are several organized tours available. The entrance fee is $7 per person.

Flower Forest of Barbados, Richmond, St Joseph, ☎ 246 433 8152, fax 246 433 8365.

★★Andromeda Botanic Gardens

Overlooking the small fishing village of Trent Bay are the beautiful Andromeda Gardens. The Gardens were started by Mrs. Iris Bannochie in 1954, on land that had belonged to her family for more than 200 years. She lived with her husband John in

Andromeda Botanic Gardens

Facing page: Path through Andromeda Botanic Gardens

the house in the middle of the garden. The garden are named for the legendary Greek goddess Andromeda.

Individual gardens are home to collections of tropical plants, including orchids, hibiscus, cactus, bougainvillea and begonias. Many rare plants and hybrids have been obtained from other botanists and personal expeditions to other islands

★ Joe's River Tropical Rainforest

Located on the outskirts of Bathsheba, with the extraordinary Hackleton's Cliff on one side and the powerful Atlantic Ocean on the other, the site is a nature-lover's paradise.

The 85 acres of woodland and rainforest are home to giant ficus, cabbage palm trees, mahogany trees, white woods, and bearded fig trees. There are picnic areas and nature trails throughout the forest, and even some wooden houses where you can stay overnight.

Spectator Sports

Surfing

Bathsheba is the site for many surf competitions, both local and international, with August to November being the peak times. The national surfing championships take place in October and the internationally famous Independence Pro Surfing Championships are in November.

Where to Stay

★ Atlantis Hotel

The Atlantis is an old-fashioned hotel with simple rooms, no radio, TV, or telephone. There are only 10 rooms for rent; the others have permanent guests, including Barbadian author, George Lamming. The hotel attracts an eclectic clientele, including artists, surfers, and academics. Its location makes it perfect for nature lovers and people who want to get away from the hustle and bustle of the world. It has easy access to many of the island's areas of natural beauty and is just minutes from the Bathsheba "Soup Bowl," home of many surfing competitions. All the public areas have been renovated, and works of local artists are hung on the walls.

Winter rates for a single are $85 B&B or $100 MAP (Modified American Plan, which includes two meals a day); for a double/twin $110 B&B or

$140 MAP. Summer rates for a single, $55 B&B $70 MAP; double/twin $70 B&B, $100 MAP.
The Atlantis Hotel, Tent Bay, Bathsheba, St Joseph, ☎ 246 433 9445, 246 433 7180, www.atlantisbarbados.com.

Bali-Hai Country House

This spot is high above Bathsheba and surrounded by open countryside, flower-filled gardens, and an orchard with bananas, mangoes, and limes. Take a walk to the end of the garden and you can hike into the surrounding hills.

There are two spacious fully equipped, two-bedroom apartments with kitchens, both on the ground floor. Each unit sleeps four; a folding bed can also be supplied for an extra child under 11-years-old. Both units are on the ground floor, are disabled-accessible, have a shady veranda and joint use of the pool. Smoking is not permitted. A personal cook can be arranged for $245 per week. Daily maid service is included.

Rates in summer $250, in winter $300 per night.
Bali-Hai Country House, Bonwell Road, Horse Hill, St Joseph, ☎ 246 433 2066, info@balihai-countryhouse.com, www.balihai-countryhouse.com.

★★ The New Edgewater Hotel

Originally built in the 1700s, it was first known as Tenby House, then Tent Bay House, Edgewater Hotel, Edgewater Inn, and now the New Edgewater Hotel. Recently renovated and upgraded, all rooms now have air-conditioning, TV, phone, and fridge. However, if you listen carefully on a quiet night you can sometimes hear the ghostly sounds of Mrs. Carter playing the piano (she owned the hotel in the 1940's).

Pool at New Edgewater Hotel

The reception area is new and the pool has been refurbished with a pool bar and deck. The hotel's restaurant is a local favorite and offers Bajan cuisine with a view of the Atlantic.

Rates in winter from $105, in summer from $85 per night. All-inclusive packages also available, including seven nights accommodation, airport transfer, car rental, breakfast, lunch, and dinner, plus island tours. Rates for these packages range from $750 per person for an ocean-view room in summer to $850 for a superior ocean-view or rainforest-view room to $1,125 for a deluxe/honeymoon oceanside suite in winter.

New Edgewater Hotel, Bathsheba, St Joseph, ☎ 246 433 9900, fax 246 433 9902, resedgewater@caribsurf.com, www.newedgewater.com.

★Round House Inn

Built in 1832, the relaxed and informal, Round House Inn & Bar commands breathtaking views of the Atlantic. Owned and operated by Mr. and Mrs. Robert Manley, the hotel offers comfortable accommodations, fine dining and live entertainment. All rooms overlook the ocean

Entrance to the Round House Inn

and have shower, toilet, roof deck or access to a roof deck.

Single-bed room $60, double-bed room $75, king-size bed room $85, king-size bed and two decks $100.

Round House Inn, Bathsheba, St Joseph, ☎ 246 433 9678, fax 246 433 9079.

Where to Eat

★Atlantis

The Atlantis is something of an institution in Barbados, and everyone from Prime Ministers to road workers comes for Sunday brunch. Recently renovated, it has stayed true to its heritage. The food is said to be as simple as ABC – All Bajan Cuisine – and the buffet offers the widest array of Bajan food on the island. Open for breakfast lunch and dinner. Three-course lunch $18; three-course dinner $23.

The Atlantis Hotel, Tent Bay, Bathsheba, St Joseph, ☎ 246 433 9445, fax 246 433 9495.

Atlantis Hotel dining room

★Bonito Beach Bar & Restaurant

Bonito Beach Bar and Restaurant is a cheerful family restaurant on the beach in Bathsheba. The seafood is fresh from the ocean and the produce is grown locally. The specialty is a Caribbean buffet featuring local favorites that include fresh seafood, fruits and vegetables. Popular choices are homemade cheesecake and fresh fruit punch that can be made with or without rum. Bonito also has a second-floor dining room with a view of the Atlantic. Open daily 10 am-6 pm. Average cost $23.

Bonito Beach Bar & Restaurant, Bathsheba, St Joseph, ☎ 246 433 9034.

★Cliffside Restaurant & Bar

Serving breakfast, lunch, dinner, and Sunday brunch, the Cliffside Restaurant in the New Edgewater Hotel sits above the "Soup Bowl" in Bathsheba. Serving Bajan food in a dining room overlooking the ocean, the Cliffside is a great place for a casual meal. Starters $4-$12.50, main courses $10-$17.50.

Cliffside Restaurant & Bar, New Edgewater Hotel, Bathsheba, St Joseph, ☎ 246 433 9900, fax 246 433 9902, resedgewater@caribsurf.com, www. newedgewater.com.

★★★Naniki

One of the most unusual restaurants in Barbados, Naniki, part of the Lush Life Nature Resort, is set in the rolling hills of St Joseph. The natural beauty of the landscape that lies just beyond its glass walls creates the ambience of the restaurant. The décor is exceptional, greenheart panels and beams, appamaat (wood from the pink poui tree) furnishings, and stone-like tiles predominate. Straw mats, clay pottery, colorful plates, wood sculptures, paintings

Naniki

and fresh flowers from the on-site anthurium farm contribute to the natural beauty of the restaurant. An outdoor porch allows you to enjoy the views of the surrounding hills while enjoying a refreshing breeze along with your meal.

The next phase of Lush Life will be a Health Spa bearing the name Madinina, a word meaning "beautiful flower," which is what the Carib Indians called the island of Martinique. Ten cottages, grounds landscaped with fruit trees, ornamental plants, vegetable and herb gardens and nature trails will complete the Agro-Eco-Tourism Resort.

The menu includes a selection of vegetarian dishes. Lambie (conch), sea egg and crab back add an exotic slant to the tasty grilled or seared fish fillets. Grilled or baked meats cooked to perfection and served with different salad combinations and staples from the Caribbean region such as yam, sweet potato and breadfruit, together with the famous Bajan corn meal cou cou, are beautifully presented. For lunch, seared flying fish, grilled dorado, stewed lambi (conch), curried chicken, and jerk chicken or pork are accompanied by cou cou, peas and rice, or salad. At dinner, grilled snapper, local black-belly lamb, seared shrimp, and pork loin are specialties. On Sundays, they serve "A Taste of the Caribbean" buffet with all the fixin's. Live jazz performances are presented, and a jazz festival is planned. Average entrée price is $20.

Naniki, Suriname, St Joseph, ☎ 246 433 1300.

★ The Round House Inn Restaurant & Bar

The Round House Inn

Built in 1832 and sitting on top of a ledge overlooking the Atlantic, it is next to the "Soup Bowl" so you can eat while watching the surf competitions taking place below. The atmosphere is informal, the service friendly, and on a hot day the breezes blowing off the Atlantic will keep you cool. At night, a romantic meal under the moon is a special treat. The bar stocks over 70 brands of rum and provides some of the best live entertainment on the island. Open for breakfast, lunch and dinner.

Starters $5-$13, main courses $16-$26.

Round House Inn Restaurant & Bar, Bathsheba, St Joseph, ☎ 246 433 9678, fax 246 433 9079.

Nightlife

There are no nightclubs in St Joseph, but the **Round House Restaurant & Bar** has live entertainment. If you want nightlife, you are only half an hour from St Lawrence Gap, where there is as much nightlife as anyone could want.

Otherwise, sitting and sipping a rum punch or a Bank's beer is about the most exciting thing there is to do. But doing that as you overlook the ocean isn't so bad!

St Andrew

Don' rush de brush and trow 'way de paint.
(Haste makes waste.)

St Andrew lies in the north-eastern part of the island, surrounded by St Peter to the north, St James to the west, St Thomas to the south, and St Joseph to the southeast. Its rolling green hills resemble the hills of Scotland and parts of the parish are known as the Scotland District. It is home to the highest point on the island, Mount Hillaby. It is unspoiled and undeveloped, with long stretches of beach, and the Turner's Hall Woods nature reserve.

Shopping

There are no shopping areas in St Andrew, but if you visit Chalky Mount Potteries, you can find unique pieces that you can buy direct from the kilns.

Sightseeing

From the potters at Chalky Mount to the ancient beauty of Turner's Hall Wood, the historical Morgan Lewis Mill to the rugged beauty of the countryside and the white sand and awesome power of the Atlantic beaches, St Andrew is a sightseers delight.

★ The Parish Church

The historic parish church is located on Hwy 2 near Belleplaine.

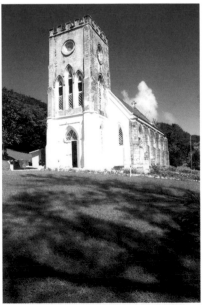

St Andrew's Parish Church

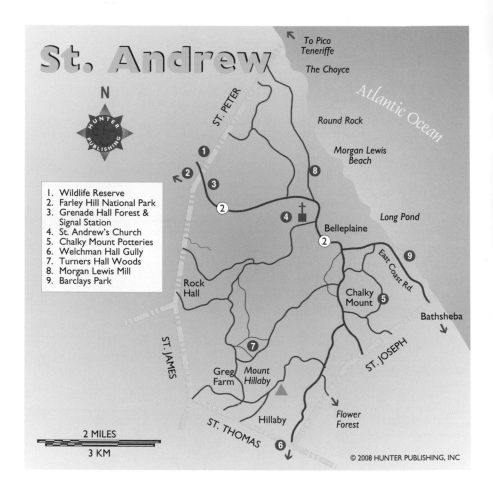

St. Andrew

1. Wildlife Reserve
2. Farley Hill National Park
3. Grenade Hall Forest &
   Signal Station
4. St. Andrew's Church
5. Chalky Mount Potteries
6. Welchman Hall Gully
7. Turners Hall Woods
8. Morgan Lewis Mill
9. Barclays Park

2 MILES
3 KM

© 2008 HUNTER PUBLISHING, INC

★Chalky Mount Potteries

High in the hills, overlooking the east coast is a small village where for 300 years the residents have made pottery. The skill, passed on from father to son, continues to this day. Stop in at the Chalky Mount Cooperative, which features the work of several potters or stroll the streets, admire the views, and stop in at the potters houses.

★Morgan Lewis Mill

There are only two intact sugar mills in the entire Caribbean; one is in Antigua, the other is here in St Andrew. The Morgan Lewis Mill dates from 1727 and was in continuous use until 1945.

For more than 200 years, wind-driven mills helped produce the sugar that was a major contributor to the island's wealth. The Dutch-influenced mill underwent major restoration by the Barbados National Trust, and has a fully intact wheelhouse and sails.

Inside the mill is a display documenting the history of sugar-making, and an exhibit of equipment used in the sugar-making process.

The mill, one of the "Seven Wonders of Barbados," is located on a hill, which provides spectacular views of the east coast.

Open Monday to Friday, 9 am to 5 pm. ☎ 246 422-7429 Entry: $10 for adults (children half-price).

★★Mount Hillaby

Rising to a height of 1,115 ft (343 m), Mount Hillaby is the highest point of the island. Take your camera and

Morgan Lewis Mill (Rodney Nelson)

get some spectacular shots of the north, east, and west coasts of the island.

Long Pond

Fed by four rivers, Long Pond River, Constitution River, Joe's River, and Bruce Vale River, and sitting on a remote area of the east coast, Long Pond is a favorite with bird watchers and a great location for fishing and crabbing.

Adventures on Foot

Hiking

The sparse population and undeveloped nature of the Scotland District and East Coast offer plenty of opportunities for interesting hikes and spectacular views. A popular place for walking and hiking is **Turner's Hall Woods** (See *Eco-Tourism*).

The East Coast

Adventures on Water

Beaches

Long stretches of beach contribute to the rugged beauty of St Andrew. Huge waves and strong currents make them very dangerous for swimming but, for beautiful views and relaxing hours, they are unbeatable.

Especially worth a visit are **Lake's Beach**, **Morgan Lewis Beach**, and **Walker's Beach**.

Adventures on Horseback

Jahworks Stud & Riding Stable

Jahworks Stud and Riding Stables specializes in mountain and beach trails, lessons, horsemanship, dressage and show jumping. They also have a unique therapy program for "differently abled" persons. ☎ 246 422 9905.

Eco-Tourism

★ Turner's Hall Woods

When the first English settlers arrived in Barbados in 1627, the island was covered by a dense tropical forest. But, by 1650, most of the forest was cleared for agricultural development, particularly sugar cane. This led to Barbados becoming the richest place in the English-speaking world. The 50 acres, (20 hectares) of Turner's Hall Woods are one of the last remaining areas of tropical forest on the island.

More than 32 different species of trees including sand box, silk cotton, fustic, cabbage palm, trumpet tree, bullet, white cedar, locust and macaw palm, plus 30 species of shrubs, grow at Turner's Hall.

The woods, located on the Turner Hall Plantation south of Morgan Lewis Mill, are a great place for hiking and walking.

Cultural Excursions

★ Spring Vale Eco Heritage Museum

The Springvale Eco-Heritage Museum is located on a 200-acre (80-hectare) former sugar plantation. The owner conducts tours through his home and organic garden, while explaining what domestic life was like in Barbados during the early 20th century. Discover how food was stored and prepared, clothes were laundered, and herbs were used for medicinal purposes. There is also a nature trail and café.

Hours 10 am-4 pm Mon-Sat. Sunday by appointment.

Highway 2, St Andrew, ☎ 246 438 7011, newden@sunbeach.net

Where to Stay & Eat

 There are no hotels or guesthouses in St Andrew. The café at the Spring Vale Eco Heritage Museum is the only place to eat in St Andrew.

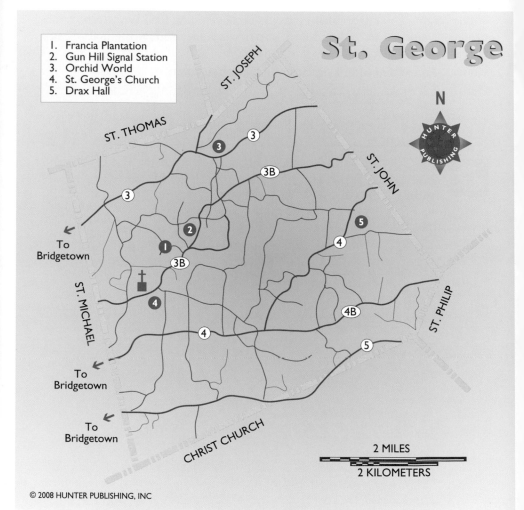

St. George

1. Francia Plantation
2. Gun Hill Signal Station
3. Orchid World
4. St. George's Church
5. Drax Hall

N

ST. JOSEPH

ST. THOMAS

ST. JOHN

ST. MICHAEL

ST. PHILIP

To Bridgetown

To Bridgetown

To Bridgetown

CHRIST CHURCH

2 MILES
2 KILOMETERS

© 2008 HUNTER PUBLISHING, INC

The Central Parishes

St George

Wha' hurt turkey don' hurt duck.
(What is a problem for one person may not be for another.)

St George sits in the center of the island, and, along with St Thomas, is one of only two land-locked parishes. St John is to the northeast, St Philip to the east, Christ Church to the south, and St Michael to the southwest.

Shopping

Brighton Farmer's Market

For something a little different, get up early on a Saturday morning and make your way to the Brighton Farmer's Market at the 17th-century Brighton Plantation. Offering a great selection of locally grown fruits and vegetables, this open-air market starts at about 6.30am when farmers from across the island arrive with their produce. Prices are as much as 75% lower than in the supermarkets and, once you have made your selections, you can stop for a breakfast of coffee and croissants. For interesting souvenirs of the island, there are also craft stalls and local artists showing their work. ☎ 246 429 2639.

Sightseeing

★★ The Parish Church

A hurricane destroyed the original church on this site in 1780. The present church, built in 1784, is the oldest ecclesiastical building on the

St George Parish Church

island. One of the largest Georgian-style churches in Barbados, it houses sculptures by Sir Richard Westmacott, the creator of Lord Nelson's statue, and an altar painting, *Rise to Power*, by Benjamin West, the first American President of the Royal Academy.

Drax Hall

Drax Hall is the oldest of the three remaining Jacobean mansions in the Western Hemisphere. It was here that sugar was first cultivated commercially in Barbados in 1642. Built by the Drax brothers, James and William, it was one of the earliest and biggest sugar properties in Barbados. It features classic Jacobean architecture, with steep gable roofs, stone corner finials, casement gable windows and a magnificent Jacobean staircase with a richly carved hall archway of mastic wood.

Owned, though not lived in, by the Drax family, Drax Hall unfortunately is not open to the public.

★Francia Plantation House

Francia Plantation House sits on a hillside overlooking St George valley. Built in the early part of the 20th century, it is owned and occupied by descendants of the original owner. Still a working plantation, the house is furnished with period pieces and antiques, and houses a collection of antique maps dating back as far 1522. After visiting the house, you can stroll through the tropical gardens and orchards.

Francia Plantation House

☎ 246 429 0474, fax 246 435 1491.

Gun Hill Signal Station

The Lion at Gun Hill Signal Station

Just five minutes drive from St George parish church, Gun Hill Signal Station is one of two remaining signal stations, built in 1818. Used to warn of approaching ships and slave rebellions, it stands at a height of 700 ft (233 m).

The Barbados National Trust restored and landscaped Gun Hill in 1983. It now houses a collection of military memorabilia. Captain Henry Wilkinson carved the landmark coral stone lion, just below the signal station, in 1868, with the assistance of four military laborers. It stands seven feet/2.1 m tall. Open Monday-Friday, 10 am-4 pm.
☎ 246-429-2871.

Adventures on Foot

Hiking

The Barbados National Trust organizes Sunday walks at 6 am and 3:30 pm. The hikes are listed in the newspaper, or you can obtain a schedule for $2.50 from the National Trust

Barbados National Trust, ☎ 246 426-2421, fax 246 429-9055.

Eco-Tourism

★Orchid World

Between Gun Hill and St John's Church, on Highway 3B in St George, Orchid World houses one of the finest collections of orchids in the Caribbean.

Orchid World (barbadosawaits.com)

Blossoms at Orchid World

Occupying six acres at a height of 800 ft (265 m), its meandering paths take you past a waterfall, a coral grotto, and five different orchid houses. Surrounded by sugarcane, there are many spots offering views of the countryside and ocean beyond. If you visit at the right time, you may spot the stunning schomburgia, a plant that briefly blooms just once a year.

Beside native Barbadian flowers there are orchids imported from Thailand, Singapore, Hawaii and the USA.

Where to Stay

Danville Apartments

Danville offers two self-contained two-bedroom apartments set in the countryside away from the hustle and bustle of the island. The apartments are bright and nicely furnished, including two bedrooms, a bathroom, a fully equipped kitchen, dining and living room areas with television and telephone. There is also an outdoor laundry room with a washing machine.

Danville is the perfect getaway spot. You'll need a car to get to the rest of the island but, if you want peace and quiet, you can't do much better.

Facing page: Orchid World

Rates: $50 per night, $300 per week, $900 per month. Pick-up from the airport $20.

Rock Hall, St Judes, St George, ☎ 246 233 3003, info@danvilleapts.com, www.danvilleapts.com.

Where to Eat

The only eating spot in St George is the **Chefette Restaurant**, ☎ 246 430 3431. It offers good quality fast food at reasonable prices. However, Christ Church is just minutes away, with its numerous restaurants and bars.

Nightlife

You don't come to St George for nightlife, but the nightspots of Christ Church are just a short trip away.

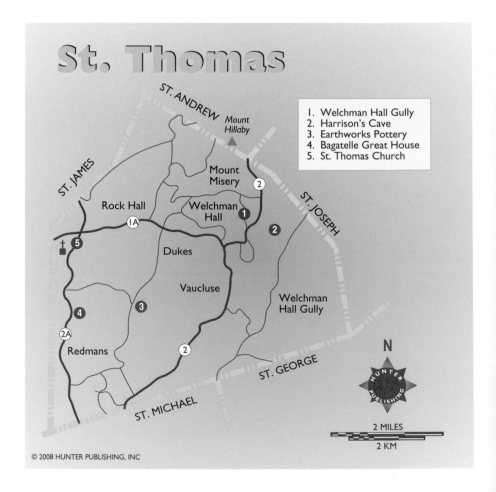

St Thomas

Don' rush de brush and trow 'way de paint.
(Haste makes waste.)

St Thomas is one of two parishes that are not on the coast, the other being St George. St Thomas is bordered by St Andrew to the northeast, St Joseph to the east, St George to the southeast, St Michael to the southwest, and St James to the west.

Shopping

The best shopping destinations are **Earthworks Pottery** and **HP Batiks** for unique gifts and artworks. (See *Cultural Attractions* below.)

Sightseeing

What St Thomas lacks in beaches it more than makes up for in the beauty of the countryside. Harrison's Caves and Welchman Hall Gully are two particularly beautiful natural areas. At Earthworks Pottery, you can watch the potters at work and buy some unique pieces to take home with you, while at Fisherpond Plantation House you can tour the house then

St Thomas Parish Church

stroll through the lush gardens.

For the more athletic, you can tour the parish on foot, by mountain bike, and on horseback.

★ The Parish Church

The church, built in 1836, is the fourth one on this site. The three previous churches were destroyed by hurricanes in 1675, 1780, and 1831. Located on Highway 2A, it is has fewer Gothic features than usual for churches built in that period but it is a fine example of 19th century architecture.

Adventures on Foot

Hiking

 The **Highland Adventure Centre** offers tours for all ages and fitness levels. The two-hour tour takes you through little villages, stopping to admire the local flora and fauna along the way, including the green monkeys that inhabit the local woods. Then return to Highland, put your feet up and have a cool drink while you discuss the day's hike with your fellow travelers.

Highland Adventure Centre, Cane Field, St Thomas, ☎ 246 431 8928, fax 246 438 8070, neilhighland@hotmail.com.

Adventures on Wheels

Mountain Bike Tours

 Set off from the **Highland Adventure Centre** (see above) on a spectacular 7½-mile (12-km) tour. Travel through the heart of Barbados, along secondary and tertiary paved roads, through heavily wooded areas, and small remote villages. Stop for a complimentary refueling stop at a local rum shop, then continue on through the scenic countryside toward Bathsheba. The tour finishes at Barclays Park Bar where you'll receive a free drink and transportation back to Highland.

This 1½-hour tour is one of the most exhilarating bike rides on the island.

Don't forget to bring your camera.

Adventures on Horseback

Horseback Tours

 The Highland Adventure Centre (see above) also offers a 1¼-hour horseback ride. Suitable for everyone, from first-timers to experienced riders. The horses, all thoroughbreds, are well trained and easy to ride. This scenic tour takes you past plantation houses, quaint villages, and provides views of three different coastlines. Bring your camera.

Eco-Tourism

★★★Harrison's Cave

Harrison's Cave is one of the island's most famous attractions.

It was first written about in 1795, and then virtually forgotten for nearly two centuries until Barbadian Tony Mason and Danish speleologist Ole Sorensen "rediscovered" them in 1976.

This unique phenomenon of nature features underground caves with stalactites hanging from the roof, stalagmites rising from the ground, and streams of crystal-clear water dropping from rushing waterfalls and forming lakes of

Stalagmites in Harrison's Cave (Neil Evans)

pure, cold, bright green water. The Great Hall, an enormous cavern 100 ft (34 m) high, and the Twin Falls where the cave's two rivers join are both quite amazing.

A tour guide drives you in an electrically operated tram through the caves, stopping at the lowest level where you leave the tram and walk along by the

In Harrison's Cave (Neil Evans)

spectacular waterfall.

Designed to fit in with the natural limestone bedrock, the Visitor's Centre provides a refreshment area and handicraft shops, along with an exhibit of Amerindian artifacts excavated from various sites around the island.

Harrison's Cave is open every day of the week. The first tour starts at 9 am and the last is at 4 pm. ☎ 246 438 6640.

★Welchman Hall Gully

Welchman Hall Gully

About a half a mile (one km) north of Harrison's Caves is Welchman Hall Gully. This mile-long (1.6-km) densely wooded gulley was originally part of the Harrison's Cave network until the roof collapsed, leaving this natural trench in its place. Planted with exotic shrubs and trees since 1750, the site gives a glimpse of what the island looked like in the 16th century. The Barbados National Trust took over Welchman Hall Gulley in 1962.

 The first grapefruit was created in Welchman Hall Gully as a result of cross-pollination between the pommel, a fruit originally from Indonesia, and the sweet orange. The grapefruit was named because it grows in grape-like clusters.

Cultural Excursions

★★Fisherpond Plantation House

Fisherpond Plantation House is a restored 350-year-old home filled with antiques and memorabilia. Surrounded by lush gardens, it has been the location for many a wedding and party. Owner, John Chandler, is happy to give personal tours through the house. Groups of six or more may book for lunch or dinner and enjoy the exclusivity of this spectacular home. A planter's buffet lunch is

Fisherpond Plantation House

served on Sundays. Reservations are essential.

Fisherpond Plantation House, ☎ 246 433 1754, rainchandler@hotmail.com.

★★Earthworks Pottery

Established in 1983 by master potter, Goldie Spieler, Earthworks is now run by her son David and a staff of 24. Sitting at the top of Shop Hill, Earthworks Pottery makes beautiful one-of-a-kind hand-finished tableware, vases, bowls and art works.

Red clay ceramic pieces fired to stoneware temperatures make the pottery ideal for homes or restaurants. If you have something you want made from clay, from custom tiles to a bathroom sink, they'll happily make it for you. Everything is hand-finished and hand-decorated with underglaze colors. The products are lead-free, food-safe, and dishwasher- and microwave-safe.

You can tour the pottery during work hours and watch as the potters make unique pieces.

Potter at Earthworks Pottery

Leaving the pottery, head next door and watch batiks being made by hand at the adjacent **Batik Studio**.

Next to the Batik Studio is the **Potter's House at On The Wall**, where the best of Barbados' art is available. Then stop at the **Tree House Café** and enjoy art works by Marguerite St John, along with the spectacular view and delicious snacks and drinks on the veranda overlooking the valley. Open Monday-Friday 9-5, Saturday 9-1. Closed Sundays and public holidays.

Earthworks Pottery, Edghill Heights #2, St Thomas, ☎ 246 425 0223, fax 246 425 3224, eworks@caribsurf.com.

Spectator Sports

★★★Polo

Polo has grown in popularity in Barbados over recent years, and the island now has four polo fields where international matches are played. Apart from the Barbados Polo Club, three new polo fields have opened at Waterhall, Lion Castle and Clifton, all of which offer great views as well as spectacular sport

For a really different experience, head over to one of the fields and spend an afternoon enjoying the sport of kings while sipping on a glass of champagne, followed by a traditional Bajan buffet.

The polo season runs from November to May and matches are played on Saturday and Sunday afternoons in January, February and March.

The Barbados Polo Club, Holders Hill, St. James. Contact: Vicki Gonzalez, ☎ 230-1308.

Lion Castle, St. Thomas. Contact: Kent Cole, ☎ 429-7139.

Clifton, St. Thomas. Contact: Bruce Bayley, ☎ 433-8800, bbayley@ insurecgi.com.

Waterhall, St. James. Contact: Jamie Dickson, ☎ 262-3282, jrdickson@ aol.com.

Where to Stay

Dreams Guest Apartments

 Eight modern apartments, including studio, one-bedroom, two-bedroom, or three-bedroom, all fully furnished with television, phone, stove, microwave, toaster, coffeemaker, etc. There is a large swimming pool and deck. Rates include maid service and use of laundry facilities.

Studio winter $70, summer $50; one-bedroom winter $80, summer $60; two-bedroom winter $90, summer $70; three-bedroom winter $100, summer $80 – all double occupancy.

Dream Guest Apartments, ☎ 246 421 8422.

High Holdings Guesthouse

High Holdings

A small, budget-friendly guesthouse set on a ridge in a tropical garden with views extending to the Caribbean. There is a sundeck, heated pool, lounge bar and dining room. Bedrooms have double beds, air conditioning and ceiling fans. Bathrooms have tubs and showers. Rates are on a bed and breakfast basis.

Bed & breakfast (per person per night) $50; dinner $25; lunch $10.

High Holdings, Old Sharon, St Thomas, ☎ 246 425 2580, 246 425 2579, info@highholdings.com, www.highholdings.com.

Where to Eat

★★Fisherpond Great House

A 350-year-old plantation house restored to its original splendor. A popular spot for weddings and corporate entertaining. Groups of six or more can book lunch or dinner and have the house exclusively to themselves.

The 2006 *Zagat* survey ranked Fisherpond Great House as No. 1 for best Barbadian food. A planter's buffet lunch, for which they are renowned, is served every Sunday. Reservations essential.

Fisherpond Great House, ☎ 246 433 1754.

★Lord Willoughby's Tavern

A casual and relaxed pub, open 24 hours a day, serving breakfast, lunch and dinner, and featuring a variety of live music, along with darts, pool, and slots. Popular with both locals and visitors, it offers affordable food, served in a friendly and funky atmosphere.

Popular dishes include fish and chips, burgers, and chicken and mushroom pie.

Price range under $15 per person.

Lord Willoughby's Tavern, Bagatelle, St Thomas, ☎ 246 421 6767.

Nightlife

St Thomas is undeveloped as a tourist area and has extremely limited nightlife. However, **Lord Willoughby's Tavern** is very popular, and is open 24 hours a day, offering live music, darts, slots, and pool. See above.

Bagatelle Great House & Wine Bar

Part of the same complex as Lord Willoughby's, Bagatelle has a large wine list, a tapas menu and live music. Popular with a slightly older crowd and a great place to go for a quiet evening.

Bagatelle Great House

Bagatelle Great House & Wine Bar, Bagatelle, ☎ 246 421 6767.

The Central Parishes

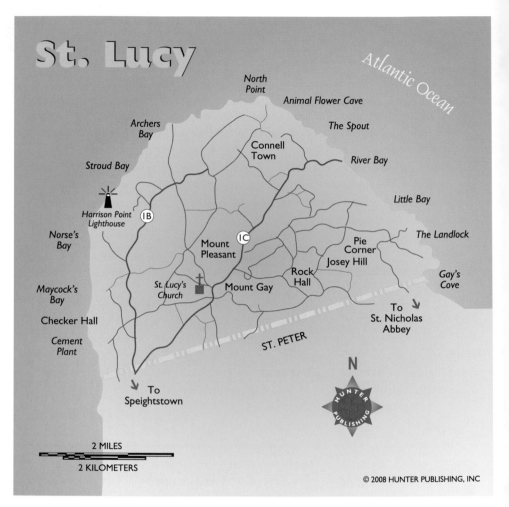

The North
St Lucy

If greedy wait, hot wud (would) cool.
(Patience will be rewarded.)

St Lucy is the northernmost parish in Barbados, surrounded on three sides by the Atlantic Ocean. Windswept, lightly populated and undeveloped, its rugged coast has few beaches and they are difficult to access. At its northwestern tip is Harrison Point, home to one of only three lighthouses still in operation. To the south is the parish of St Peter, while to the north, west, and east is the Atlantic.

The landscape ranges from lush and green in the south to desolate and windswept in the north. The west coast of St Lucy has sandy coves, where you can sometimes see turtles swimming offshore. As you move farther north in the parish, massive waves pound against the rocks with all the fury of the Atlantic Ocean.

Shopping

St Lucy is a remote, undeveloped area. Shopping is only available at gift shops at the various attractions in the parish.

Sightseeing

Rugged cliffs, pounding surf, windswept and remote, St Lucy is a photographers paradise.

★★ The Parish Church

In the Trents/Nessfield area, at the end of the Duncan Hill Highway at the Church Hill roundabout is the historic parish church. This is the fourth one built on this site. The first, built of wood in 1629, was one of the six original parish churches in Barbados. Rebuilt in 1741, the present church features a running gallery on three sides, and is essentially Georgian, with the characteristic tower.

St Lucy Parish Church

★ Animal Flower Cave

This cave at the far north of the parish is worth a visit. A guide takes you down a flight of rough steps into the cave, which opens out onto the restless Atlantic. There are few animal flowers (sea anemones) left, but the guide will point out the ones there are. There is a bar, serving snacks and, of course, rum at the top, along with a souvenir shop.

 Caution: The steps down to the cave are steep and the cave itself is rocky and slippery.

Animal Flower Cave

Cove Bay

★ Cove Bay

From The Animal Flower Cave, drive southeast to Cove Bay. Although not easy to get to (you must drive across a field that is home to sheep, goats and other wildlife), the destination is worth it. It is a great spot to stop for a picnic, relax on the beach while being cooled by the constant trade winds, or just enjoy the scenic beauty of the unspoiled island coast.

Facing page: View from Animal Flower Cave

★Harrison's Point Lighthouse

Then head west to Harrison's Point Lighthouse, built in 1925 on the northwestern tip of the island. It provides some good photo opportunities, especially late in the afternoon when the sun is low in the western sky.

Adventures on Foot

Hiking

There are no guided hikes in St Lucy, but the area is so scenic, you can park your car almost anywhere and find a great route to hike inland or along the coast.

Adventures on Wheels

St Lucy is the most undeveloped part of the island and to get around you must either take a tour or rent a car. Road signs, as everywhere in Barbados, are inconsistent or non-existent, but the island is so small you'll always find what you're looking for eventually. If you pull over to the side of the road and get out a map, someone will almost certainly stop and give you directions. Take a picnic, as there aren't any restaurants or hotels here. There are many scenic areas where you can stop and enjoy the views undisturbed by traffic or other visitors.

Adventures on Water

Surfing

For surfers there are two great locations in St Lucy, **Maycocks Bay** and **Duppies**. Both are on the northwest coast. Duppies is for expert surfers only, while Maycocks is more forgiving, but not for beginners.

Beaches

★★**Little Bay**. A little north of Cove Bay (see *Sightseeing* above) is Little Bay. Carved out of the rock is a natural swimming pool, where you can swim in complete safety while the power of the Atlantic sends waves smashing onto the shore only a few feet away.

During the week, Little Bay is usually deserted. It's a great spot for families but, for a truly romantic experience, bring a bottle of champagne, some fresh fruit, and the man or woman of your dreams. Sit in the warm

water, watch the pounding waves as they send magnificent spumes of water high in the air, and enjoy the serenity as the sun slowly turns the sky a thousand shades of purple while the afternoon turns into night.

Alternatively, climb to the top of the cliffs for a dramatic view of the coastline.

★River Bay. A little farther north is River Bay, so called because a freshwater river runs into the sea here. Crowded on the weekends and holidays, but much quieter, if not deserted, during the week, it is a popular local picnic area. Washrooms, change rooms, and showers are available. At low tide, it is a good swimming area. However, there are dangerous currents if you venture too far out.

 You must take extreme caution when swimming here. DO NOT let children swim alone!

There are picnic tables set in the shade of the trees where you can watch the wild Atlantic while enjoying an al fresco lunch.

Cultural Excursions

Besides the parish church, you can also visit St Swithins Church, St Clements Church, and the Bathsheba Chapel.

Where to Stay

 St Lucy is undeveloped and there are no hotels in the parish. There is a **guesthouse** run by Mr. Rudolf Griffith. There are two rooms available at a cost of $30 per night including breakfast. Evening meals can be provided for $10. ☎ 246 439 9685, fax 246 439 7217, griff@hotmail.com.

★★★Beach View Villa

A new three-bed, 3½-bath air-conditioned villa set on a ridge overlooking the West Coast. Two minutes walk from the beach and five minutes drive to the shops and restaurants in Speightstown. There is a private dip pool and courtesy access to a larger outdoor pool. The villa comes with daily maid service, Internet access, video, CD, VCR, and satellite TV. A cook is optional.

Apr 15-Dec 15 $2,499 per week, Dec 16-Dec 22 $3,200, Dec 23-Jan 05 $7,000, Jan 06-Apr 14 $3,200.

Beach View Villa, Fryers Wells, St. Lucy, ☎ 246 429 2244, stmarva@ caribsurf.com.

★★★ Sea Cruise Villa

A luxury five-bedroom townhouse villa in Fryers Wells, it sits on a bluff with views to the west, over Half Moon Fort Bay and the Caribbean beyond. The villa can be rented exclusively as two, three, four or five bedrooms. The rental rate includes tax, the daily staff (chef, maid/laundress and pool attendant), a vehicle and transport to and from the airport.

Facilities include private outdoor swimming pool, private dip pool/spa on patio, fully air-conditioned, ceiling fans, balcony, deck, patio.

Winter: two bedrooms $3,500per week, three bedrooms $4,400, four bedrooms $6,200, five bedrooms $7,700. Summer: two bedrooms $2,500, three bedrooms $3,400, four bedrooms $4,300, five bedrooms $5,000. Christmas/New Year $12,000 per week.

Sea Cruise Villa, Fryers Well, ☎ 246 437 9342, fax 246 422 5901, hughr@ caribsurf.com.

★★★ Sea Symphony Villa

A six-bedroom house with full staff, and free pick-up and return to the airport. A vehicle is available for guest use.

Rates: two-bedroom $3,000 per week summer, $4,000 winter; six-bedroom $6,400 per week summer, $9,700 winter.

Sea Symphony Villa, Fryers Well, ☎ 246 437 9342, fax 246 422 5901, hughr@caribsurf.com.

Where to Eat

 There is a snack bar at the Animal Flower Cave, but very little else.

Index